EUROPEAN COMPETITION POLICY

EUROPEAN ASPECTS

A Collection of Studies relating to European Integration

Law Series
No. 12

European Competition Policy

Essays of the Leiden Working Group on Cartel Problems

edited by

THE EUROPA INSTITUTE OF THE UNIVERSITY
OF LEIDEN

with a foreword by

H. H. MAAS
Professor of the Law of International Organisations,
University of Leiden

A. W. SIJTHOFF - LEIDEN - 1973

ISBN 90 286 0363 8

Library of Congress Catalog Card Number: 73-84431

Printed in the Netherlands

FOREWORD

Those who, in the Netherlands, have lived together for better and for worse during twelve and a half years have a cause to celebrate a jubilee, called "a copper wedding". In imitation of this Dutch custom, the members of the Working Group on Cartel Problems, founded by the Europa Instituut of the University of Leiden in december 1958, on the occasion of their 100th meeting decided to prepare the publication of a number of papers, as a memoir for what may be called "the copper jubilee of the Working Group".

This Working Group has about twenty members and consists of both lawyers and economists: legal advisers to corporations, civil servants in the Dutch administration and with the Commission of the European Communities, sollicitors, professors and lecturers in several Dutch universities. In all their diversity they have one thing in common: a great interest in cartel problems and a deep knowledge of competition policy, especially in the European Communities. About ten times a year they meet to discuss the latest developments in European competition policy: especially legislative acts, decisions of the Commission and judgements of the Court of Justice of the European Communities.

The present volume of essays edited by the secretary of the Working Group, Mr. Thomas van Rijn, is symbolic of the form of cooperation in the Working Group. Each author discusses a subject in which he has acquired almost unique expertise.

Although written separately their studies present collectively a critical survey of the most important features of European competition policy to day. I want to express the gratitude of the Europa Instituut to the contributors to this book who, with their collective efforts have given proof of the usefulness of regular cooperation between scholars and practitioners as embodied in the Leiden Working Group on Cartel Problems. May this Group serve as a model elsewhere.

Leiden, May, 1973 H. H. Maas

TABLE OF CONTENTS

LIST OF ABBREVIATIONS

Adv-Gen.	Advocate-General of the Court of Justice of the European Communities
Amer. J. Comp. L.	American Journal of Comparative Law
Amer. J. Int. L.	American Journal of International Law
Ann. franç. dr. int.	Annuaire français de droit international
Arch. VR.	Archiv des Völkerrechts
Art. (s)	Article(s)
AWD	Aussenwirtschaftsdienst des Betriebs-Beraters
BFH	Bundesfinanzhof
BGH	Bundesgerichtshof
BIE	Bijblad bij de Industriële Eigendom
Brit. YB. Int. L.	British Yearbook of International Law
BVerfG	Bundesverfassungsgericht
Cah. dr. européen	Cahiers de droit européen
Ch.	Chapter
C.M.L.R.	Common Market Law Reports
CCH	Commerce Clearing House: Common Market Law Reporter
C.M.L. Rev.	Common Market Law Review
Colum. L. Rev.	Columbia University Law Review
EC	European Communities
EEC=EWG=CEE	European Economic Community
ECSC=EGKS=CECA	European Coal and Steel Community
Euratom=EAG=Euratom	European Atomic Energy Community
Europa-Arch.	Europa-Archiv
EuR	Europarecht
Gen. Rep.(s)	General Report(s) of the High Authority (ECSC) or Commission of the European Communities
GRUR (Int).	Gewerblicher Rechtsschutz und Urheberrecht (Internationaler Teil)
Harv. L. Rev.	Harvard Law Review
HR	Hoge Raad

Int. Comp. L. Qu.	The International and Comparative Law Quarterly
Int. Organ.	International Organization
J. Common Mkt. Stud.	Journal of Common Market Studies
Michigan L. Rev.	Michigan Law Review
Minn. L. Rev.	Minnesota Law Review
Modern L. Rev.	Modern Law Review
n.	footnote
N.J.W.	Neue Juristische Wochenschrift
Neth. Int. L. Rev.	Netherlands International Law Review
No.	Number
N.Y.U.L. Rev.	New York University Law Review
O.J.	Official Journal of the European Communities
Pas. Lux. Juris.	Pasicrisie Luxembourgeoise: Jurisprudence
Recueil	Recueil de la Jurisprudence/Reports of Judgements of the Court of Justice of the European Communities
Rec. d. Cours	Recueil des Cours de l'Académie de droit international
Rec. Dalloz: Chron. Juris.	Recueil Dalloz: Chronique jurisprudence
Rev. crit. dr. int. privé	Revue critique de droit international privé
Rev. Marché Commun	Revue du Marché Commun
Rev. trim. dr. europ.	Revue trimestrielle de droit européen
Riv. dir. int.	Rivista di diritto internazionale
S.E.W.	Sociaal Economische Wetgeving
Stat.(s)	Statute(s)
U.N.	United Nations
Va. L. Rev.	Virginia Law Review
Vol.(s)	Volume(s)
WuW	Wirtschaft und Wettbewerb
Yale L. J.	Yale Law Journal
Z. ausl. int. Priv. R.	Zeitschrift für ausländisches internationales Privatrecht

LIST OF CONTRIBUTORS

A. D. Ham
Dr. Jur.; Head of the Department of International Competition Affairs, Ministry of Economic Affairs

W. L. Snijders
Professor of Competition Law, University of Tilburg; Senior Advisor of the Directorate Prices and Competition, Ministry of Economic Affairs

W. Alexander
LL. D.; Advocate at the Bar of the Hague; Associate with Barents, Gasille & Mout

H. W. de Jong
D. Sc. (Econ.); Associate Professor of Economics, University of Amsterdam

A. van Oven
Professor of Company Law, University of Leiden

M. R. Mok
Professor of Economic Law, University of Groningen; Senior Advisor in the Ministry of Justice

J. G. van de Wielen
Dr. Jur.; Officer at the Department of Prices and Competition, Ministry of Economic Affairs

H. W. Wertheimer
Dr. Jur.; Economic and Legal Advisor

B. H. ter Kuile
Dr. Jur.; Advocate at the Bar of the Hague; Associate with De Brauw & Helbach

P. VerLoren van Themaat
Professor of Social and Economic Law, University of Utrecht

Chapter 1

RULES CONTROLLING RESTRICTIONS ON COMPETITION IN THE UNITED KINGDOM AND IN THE COMMON MARKET

by *Mr. A. D. Ham*

I. *Introduction*

It was in 1953 that The Economist wrote: "competition is still a dirty word in these islands"[1] and in 1964 the same weekly observed: "that apart perhaps from the Netherlands, there is neither in the United Kingdom nor in the other countries of the E.E.C. a deep commitment to competition".[2] Whether these statements are true or not, the fact is that, since the latter date quite a few things have changed, at least from the viewpoint of the place competition policy takes in the whole of national and supra-national policy. In the United Kingdom the Resale Prices Act 1964 came into force, the Restrictive Trade Practices Act 1968 amended the Restrictive Trade Practices Act 1956 and the Monopolies and Mergers Act 1965 extended the scope of the then existing monopolies legislation. In the Common Market after the first implementing regulation pursuant to Articles 85 and 86 of the Rome Treaty (Regulation No. 17 of February 6th, 1962)[3] the Council of Ministers and the Commission issued regulations and communications tending to bring into operation gradually and effectively the Articles 85 and 86 of the E.E.C. Treaty.[4] Apart from general regulations also regulations pertaining to particular sectors of industry such as transport and agriculture came into force.

The decisions by the Commission based on the Articles 85 and 86 started in 1964 with a negative clearance Decision (Grosfillex-Fillistorf[5]) and cover since then a considerable number of issues as to the scope and extent of the E.E.C. rules on competition.

1. Cited by E. Hennipman "De taak van de mededingingspolitiek" "De Economist", 1966, 409.
2. Ibid.
3. J.O., 204/62.
4. The E.E.C.-Treaty is not alone in having rules on competition, directly applicable to enterprises in the Member Countries. Also apply to them Articles 65 and 66 of the E.C.S.C.-Treaty of April 18, 1952, the Treaty establishing the European Coal and Steel Community. A short introduction to these rules is given on page 39.
5. O.J., 915/64.

Already in 1962 László Gombos, Ll.D wrote[6] that "should Britain enter the Common Market, Articles 85 en 86 would, in due course, become substantive law in this country and their full impact would be felt, alongside our own Monopolies and Restrictive Trade Practices Legislation".

Now that the United Kingdom is indeed a full member of the European Communities as of January 1st, 1973, there may be some use in trying to work out a comparison of European competition law and United Kingdom law on monopolies and restrictive trade practices, as both legislations, taken in a large sense, stand now.

II. *Generalities*

Before actually coming to this comparison it seems indicated to make briefly some observations upon the basic objects of both sets of provisions.

The United Kingdom legislation is intended "to prevent the development of rigid structures in economy which may hinder adaption to changing conditions and to preserve the conditions of free competition which stimulate efficiency". The main principle underlying the legislation is the belief that competition is in general desirable. Broadly speaking (collective resale price maintenance is an exeption) no restrictive practice is condemned outright from a legal point of view although there is a presumption – in the case of both the Restrictive Trade Practices Act 1956 and the Resale Prices Act 1964 – that the practices concerned are, in general, contrary to the public interest. They can be justified only against strict criteria laid down in the respective Acts to be examined by an impartial tribunal.[7, 8]

Apart from that, the legislation on monopolies and mergers provides "a means by which the Government and the public can be informed about their operations and gives the Government powers to check resulting abuses".[9] The objective of this latter part of legislation is to increase industrial efficiency and international competitiveness. A basic assumption however is that there is no one right structure which would be equally applicable for all industries.

6. 59 The Law Society's Gazette, 1962, 249.

7. In their first judgment given on November 3, 1958 L.R. R.P. 6, the Court pointed out that they were not required to say whether an agreement was a good or a bad thing; this question of policy was settled by Parliament in section 21 of the Act (the so-called "gateways"), (see here under p. 9). The task of the Court was the ordinary task of a Court of Law to take the words of the Act according to their proper construction and see if, upon the facts proved the case fell within them.

8. Guide to legislation on restrictive business practice O.E.C.D. 1971. United Kingdom, s. 0., 7 and 9; s. 2, 1.

9. Ibid.

The approach is empirical and pragmatic recognising the diversity of industrial situations.[10, 11]

In so far as competition policy is operated by the Government which is the case with monopolies and mergers—this policy is not regarded in isolation but as one of a number of possible instruments of economic policy which the Government may apply in dealing with problems of a sector of industries. Among these instruments one may mention tariff or fiscal measures, regional or other subsidies or a restructuring policy.[12]

In the European Economic Community competition policy has a far more marked place. This in first instance can be explained by the nature of the competition policy in relation to the economic aims of this Community. Article 2 of the Treaty establishing The European Economic Community states that "it shall be the task of the Community by establishing a common market and progressively approximating the economic policies of member-States to promote throughout the Community a harmonious development of economic activities". To establish such a common market with the features of a domestic market it does not suffice to abolish customs duties, quotas and measures with equivalent effect, which measures on a governmental level are likely to prevent and/or to restrict inter-State trade. To reach the situation that the so-called four freedoms—i.e. the free movement of goods, of services, of persons and of capital—are fully realised it is also needed, that care is taken that no new barriers are erected nor existing ones maintained by admitting enterprises either by means of an agreement or by exploitation of market power to endanger the movement of free trade between member-States—e.g. by preventing the entry of foreign products or services into home market or by artificially distorting competition in another way.[13]

In a somewhat broader context competition policy in the Community aims also at pertaining to optimal production and distribution. As Article 3(f) of the Treaty puts it: the activities of the Communities shall include "the

10. *Mergers, a guide to Board of Trade practice*, (HMSO 1969), 1.

11. Voices are now being heard that changes to a more distinctive monopolies- and merger policy should be made. So E. Dell (The Times, February 23, 1972) Minister of State, (1968-1969) responsible for competition at the Board of Trade: "Parliament should depart from neutrality in its view of monopolies and mergers and enact a general presumption in favour of competition".

12. The creation of the Industrial Reorganisation Corporation, now abolished, in 1968 served to encourage and support structural reorganisation including mergers where this is thought valuable, and represented the positive complementary role of industrial restructuring policy.

13. cf. P. VerLoren van Themaat, "the Anti-Trust policy of the European Economic Community" in: *Comparative Aspects of Anti-Trust Law in the United States, the United Kingdom and the European Economic Community*", International and Comparative Law Quarterly, Supplementary Publication, nr. 6 (1963).

institution of a system ensuring that competition in the common market is not distorted".

The process of integration–which exposes enterprises to competition of new competitors–and of the increase of technological progress–which require the enterprises to adjustments – entails also another aspect of European competition policy i.e. to help firms to adapt. In the field of restrictive agreements a way in which firms can adapt themselves is by cooperating with other firms. Competition policy in Europe has been aware of the fact that cooperation in certain situations–by way of specialisation agreements, joint research and development etc.–may prove to be helpful under certain conditions when enterprises want to adapt.

As to monopolies and mergers the policy of the Commission is that, while acknowledging that mergers may bring about an adjustment to the new scale of the market and hence in these cases can be considered as beneficial from the viewpoint of a better allocation of factors of production, mergers however in those markets the structure of which is already such that additional mergers between firms would compromise workable competition are to be seen as a threat to effective competition. For that reason Article 86 is construed by the Commission to mean that a merger which eliminates effective competition constitutes a case of improper practices and will consequently be prohibited.[14]

III. *Nature and scope of the United Kingdom legislation*

This section and the following one will deal first with the nature and scope of the United Kingdom legislation on restrictive trade practices and then with the nature and scope of the rules of competition, and their implementation, in the legislation of the European Economic Community. An attempt will be made to conclude these sections with an evaluation of the differences which exist. Both sections will focus on the two principal areas of interest for competition policy i.e. restrictive agreements and monopolies c.q. mergers.[15, 16]

14. Cf. Second programme of economic policy on medium term. Ch. II. point 11, O.J., 1969, L 129.

15. For the text of the law and for explanatory notes on the legislation of the United Kingdom see: the "Guide to legislation on restrictive business practices" O.E.C.D. Vol. III.

16. The legislation concerning resale price maintenance: the Resale Prices Act 1964 will not be dealt with in this article.

1. *Restrictive agreements*

The control of restrictive trade practices is exercised in the United Kingdom under the Monopolies and Restrictive Practices (Inquiry and Control) Act 1948,[17] the Restrictive Trade Practices Act 1956,[18] the Resale Prices Act[19] and the Restrictive Trade Practices Act 1968.[20]

Under section 15 of the Monopolies and Restrictive Practices (Inquiry and Control) Act 1948 the Monopolies Commission, on a reference on collective discrimination made to it by the Board of Trade, found in its report (1955[21]) that the practices referred to it "in some degree restrict competition." The majority of the Commission recommended that the practices–exclusive agency, collective boycotts, aggregated rebates and other discriminatory trade practices–should be prohibited, although provision might be made for exempting certain agreements after individual scrutiny. A minority however was not convinced that all the practices referred to the Commission are generally injurious to the public and recommended that agreements to discriminate should be registered and that an official should be required to bring them one by one before a tribunal to decide whether each was contrary to the public interest.[22] When in 1956 a bill was introduced, the Restrictive Trade Practices Bill, the proposals of the minority appeared to have been followed. The Restrictive Trade Practices Act 1956 was amended in 1968 i.e. Part I of the Act which concerns the registration and judicial investigation of restrictive trading agreements.

1.1. One of the key points in these Acts is the registration of agreements. Once an agreement is registered, it generally comes subsequently under examination that is of a judicial nature.

The agreements are to be registered in a public register with the Registrar, an office held by a former senior civil servant appointed by the Crown "during her Majesty's pleasure".

The subsequent judicial examination is done by the Restrictive Practices Court, which is a superior Court of Record[23] presided by a High Court Judge.

17. 11 and 12 Geo 6, Ch. 66.
18. 4 and 5 Eliz. 2, Ch. 68.
19. 1964, Ch. 58.
20. 1968, Ch. 66.
21. H.M.S.O. 1955.
22. See in more detail on the origins of the Restrictive Trade Practices Act 1956: V, Korah, "*Monopolies and Restrictive practices*", (1968).
23. "This is a break with the traditional courts of record which tend to be courts of general jurisdiction", I.A. MacDonald, "The Restrictive Practices Court: A Lawyer's view", 17 Oxford Economic Papers, 1965, No. 3.

It is therefore important to know whether an agreement[24] is registrable.

Subject to exceptions and exclusions to be dealt with later on, part I of the Act applies to any agreement "to which the parties are or include two or more persons carrying on business within the United Kingdom in the production or supply of goods or in the application to goods of any process of manufacture and under which restrictions are accepted by two or more parties (whether carrying on business within the United Kingdom or not) in respect of

(abbreviated) – the prices to be charged
– the terms or conditions
– the quantities or descriptions
– the processes of manufacture
– the persons or classes of persons acquiring or supplying the goods".

About the nature and range of arrangements covered it may be pointed out that

– the 1956 Act prohibits in its section 24 agreements for the collective enforcement of resale prices by the withholding of supplies or discrimination;
– the Acts are not concerned with restrictions on the supply of services;
– "Goods" includes ships and aircraft minerals, substances and animals (including fish) (section 36);
– to be registrable the agreement must have been entered into by two or more persons. Section 26, subsection 2, provides that for the purposes of any provision of this Part (i.e. Part I) of this Act referring to two or more–or not more than two–persons, two or more persons being interconnected bodies corporate or individuals carrying on business in partnership with each other, shall be treated as one person.

Two or more companies which are members of a group comprising a company and its subsidiairies are treated as one person.

– As far as "carrying on business within the United Kingdom" is concerned, section 36, subsection 3, states that a person is not to be treated as carrying on such a business by reason only of the fact that he is represented for the purposes of that business by an agent within the United Kingdom. Furthermore section 8, subsection 8, provides that Part I of the Act does not apply to agreements relating exclusively to exports from the United Kingdom.[25] If however agreements of this description contain restrictions which would be registrable if they related to the United Kingdom market, particulars of the agreement must be sent to the Department of Trade and Industry. Details of export agreements are not published.

24. This word includes any agreement or arrangement whether oral or in writing and whether or not it is intended to be enforceable by legal proceedings.

25. See hereunder as to monopolies legislation on this point, p. 10 *et seq.*

– Up till the amendment by the Restrictive Trade Practices Act 1968 it was equivocal if the term "restrictions in respect of the prices to be charged" did cover agreements by which parties inform each other about the prices to be charged. Since the enactment of the 1968 Act there is an explicit provision (section 5) which enables the Board of Trade (now the Department of Trade and Industry) to call up for registration by Order information agreements. The definition of information agreements is so worded as to cover all categories of information agreements, not only price-information agreements. In 1969 an Order under section 5 was laid before Parliament in draft; the Restrictive Trade Practices (Information Agreements) Order 1969. It came into operation February 1st 1970 and called for the registration of certain types of information agreements relating to prices and conditions of sale.

1.2. In both Acts different categories of agreements are exempted from registration. Apart from the exemption already mentioned above concerning export agreements, the main exemptions are: agreements authorised by Statute (section 8, subsection 1, 1956 Act). Also certain exclusive agency contracts are exempted.[26] Furthermore section 8, subsection 4 exempts from registration agreements relating to patented goods and processes provided that the only restrictions listed in section 6(1) that are accepted are in respect of

– the invention to which the patent relates or
– articles in respect of which the design is or is proposed to be registered and to which it is applied, as the case may be.

By the 1968 Act the exemption from registration of agreements to comply with standards approved by the British Standards Institution was extended to agreements to comply with other standards for the time being approved by the Department of Trade and Industry.

Two kinds of exemption by administrative procedure may be mentioned separately.

First the agreements considered to be of national importance. Section 1 of the 1968 Act introduces an administrative procedure with regard to this category of agreements. To be eligible for exemption an agreement must be calculated to promote the carrying out of an industrial or commercial project or scheme of substantial importance to the national economy and the object of the agreement must be the promotion of efficiency or the creation or improvement of productive capacity. Exemption is to be granted by order of

26. If the supplier-party to an exclusive agency contract falls within the scope of application of the monopolies legislation this kind of agreement may be referred to the Monopolies Commission; cf. Report on the supply of petrol in the United Kingdom 1965.

the Department of Trade and Industry but the Department of Trade and Industry may not make an order unless the agreement is submitted to them in draft. The restrictions accepted under the agreement must be reasonably necessary to achieve the object or the scheme. Any exemption granted must be for a specified period. Where an agreement ceases to be exempt it becomes registrable unless it is abandoned or all the restrictions are removed from it.

The second administrative procedure by which exemption may be given is the exemption from registration of agreements made in support of the prices and incomes policy. A power to exempt agreements and trade associations recommendations made at the Government's request is given to the Department of Trade and Industry and to the Ministers in charge of other departments which have also responsibilities in connection with the prices and incomes policy. The exemption is only for a specified period, which cannot exceed two years.

Finally in some other Acts exemptions from registration are conferred. The Agriculture (Miscellaneous Provisions) Act 1968 gives exemption to agreements made by Statutory Agricultural Marketing Boards if these are approved by the Minister for Agriculture. Certain agreements are also exempted under the Plant Varieties and Seeds Act 1964, the Agricultural and Forestry Associations Act 1962, the Gas Act 1965, the Cereals Marketing Act 1965 and the Agriculture Act 1967, and the Iron and Steel Act 1967 (by which the principal companies concerned were brought under public ownership).

1.3. Agreements subject to registration are to be registered with the Registrar of Restrictive Trading Agreements who is charged in the first place with the duty of preparing, compiling and maintaining a register and secondly of taking proceedings[27] before the Restrictive Practices Court (here after referred to as "the Court").

The register for which the Registrar is responsible is open to public inspection. In those cases where in the opinion of the Department of Trade and Industry publication of an agreement would be contrary to the public interest or where information as to particulars would substantially damage the legitimate business interests of any person, agreements of these kinds may be entered in a special section of the register which is not open to public inspection (section 11, subsection 3, 1956 Act). This provision has been applied very strictly.

The Registrar is given certain rather wide powers to obtain information and documents. It is a criminal offence–the only penal provision in the

27. It is the Treasury Solicitor who acts for the Registrar and is responsible for briefing the barristers who appear for him.

1956 Act—to furnish false documents or recklessly to make false statements or wilfully to alter, suppress or destroy documents.

The Registrar may also be empowered by the Board of Trade to remove from the register insignificant agreements i.e. agreements not of such significance, as to call for investigation by the Court. Besides his duty of maintaining the register the Registrar may refer a registered agreement to the Court for the purpose of obtaining a declaration whether or not any restrictions falling within the scope of the Act are contrary to the public interest (section 20, 1956 Act).

Where any such restrictions are found by the Court to be contrary to the public interest the agreement shall be void in respect of those restrictions i.e. these cannot be enforced by civil action nor damages can be asked in case of non observance.

The Court normally requires an undertaking that the parties will not give effect to such an agreement or make any other to like effect to which part I of the Act (Registration and Judicial Investigation of Restrictive Trading Agreements) applies.

1.4. The Restrictive Practices Court consists of five judges together with not more than ten other members who are to be persons "appearing to the Lord Chancellor to be qualified by virtue of his knowledge or of experience in industry, commerce or public affairs". The Court is presided over by a High Court Judge.[28]

The Court is bound to find the restrictions referred to it contrary to the public interest unless it is satisfied of one or more of the circumstances set out in paragraphs (1.1) of section 21 of the 1956 Act and of section 10 of the 1968 Act (the so-called "gateways") and is further satisfied, in any such case that the restriction is not unreasonable having regard to the balance between those circumstances and any detriment to the public or to persons not parties to the agreement which results from the operation of the restriction. This latter balancing operation provision is often called the "tailpiece".

This system places upon the parties to an agreement the onus of establishing that each restriction in it is beneficial to the public or otherwise desirable according to the criteria of section 21 and in addition that the benefits are not outweighed by detriments.

The gateways permit a restriction to be defended roughly speaking on the following grounds: protecting consumers against injury, counteracting restrictive measures taken by others enabling the negotiation of fair terms with a preponderant supplier or customer, preventing a serious and persistent adverse effect on employment, preventing a reduction in the volume or

28. A High Court judge is appointed by the Crown on the advice of the Lord Chancellor from among barristers of at least ten years' standing (Judicature Act 1925).

earnings of export business, or no material impact on competition.[29]

The respondents have also to prove that the restriction is not unreasonable having regard to the balance between these circumstances and any detriment to the public.

It may be mentioned here, that the Court in applying these criteria will use the civil law proof that it will make the "balance of probabilities".

When after the Registrar has referred the agreement to the Court, the respondents do not defend their case, then the Court declares the agreement contrary to the public interest.

2. *Monopolies*

2.1. It was with the Monopolies and Restrictive Practices (Inquiry and Control) Act 1948[30] that in the United Kingdom the first specific legislation on restrictive business practices came into force. It provided for the establishment of a kind of administrative tribunal, the Monopolies and Restrictive Practices Commission, which was empowered to investigate and report upon matters referred to it by the Board of Trade. The definition of these matters included the conditions prevailing in relation to the supply of any goods whereby at least one-third of the United Kingdom market was supplied by or to one person or body corporate, or by or to two or more persons acting together, whether by agreement or not, in a manner which restricted competition.

The words "whether by agreement or not" meant that also restrictive trade practices agreements should fall under the scope of the law. This situation was modified when the Restrictive Trade Practices Act 1956 came into force. Part III of this Act (called: amendments of Monopolies and Restrictive Practices Acts, 1948 and 1953[31] etc.) reduced the scope of matters which might be referred to the Commission by excluding all agreements subject to the provisions of part I of the 1956 Act,[32] which include practically all agreements designed to restrict competition in the home market. The Restrictive Trade Practices Act 1956 therefore reduced the scope of activities of the Commission i.e. of investigations and reports, but the Monopolies and Mergers Act 1965[32a] considerably extended that scope. At this moment, that

29. See for full text app. A.

30. 11 and 12 Geo 6.Ch. 66.

31. The Monopolies and Restrictive Practices Act 1953 modified the 1948 Act by providing for a permanent Chairman and for allowing the Commission to be enlarged to a maximum of 25 members and to work in groups. These new provisions were, however, repealed by the Restrictive Trade Practices Act 1956 (section 28).

32. *Supra*, p. 5 *et seq.*

32a. The attempt, in early 1962 by Imperial Chemical Industries to take over control of Courtauld's Ltd. gave rise to much concern. The fact that the Government

is after the enactment of the Monopolies and Mergers Act 1965, the Monopolies Commission[33] is empowered upon reference by the Department of Trade and Industry to investigate:

– monopoly conditions in the supply, processing or export of goods or in the provision of services if at least one-third of all the goods or all the services are supplied or provided in the United Kingdom or any substantial part thereof by or to one person (a single firm or a holding company with its subsidiaries) (section 3 of the 1948 Act, and section 2 of the 1965 Act);

– oligopoly conditions in the supply, processing or export of goods or in the provision of services if at least one-third of all the goods or all the services are supplied or provided in the United Kingdom or any substantial part thereof by two or more persons, who whether by agreement or not, conduct their respective affairs so as to prevent or restrict competition in connection with the production, supply, processing or export of goods or services (section 3 of the 1948 Act and section 2 of the 1965 Act);

– mergers, either completed or prospective, where the result of the mergers is to create or increase a monopoly (as described above) in the supply of any goods or services in the United Kingdom or a substantial part of it, or where the value of the assets taken over or to be taken over exceeds £ 5 m;

– newspaper mergers, where a newspaper proprietor whose newspapers, together with the paper to be taken over have an average circulation per day or publication amounting to 500.000 or more copies. In these particular cases, before the Department of Trade and Industry may give consent, the matter has to be referred to the Monopolies Commission (section 8 of the Monopolies and Mergers Act 1965);

– restrictive agreements relating solely to export and restrictive agreements relating solely to services since these categories of agreements do not fall within the scope of Part I of the Restrictive Trade Practices Act 1956.

Although, as can be seen, the Act gives power to consider unlike the restrictive practices legislation, export restrictions, few explicit references on export restrictions, however, have been submitted to the Monopolies Commission, whereas the Monopolies Commission itself has been of the opinion that a domestic reference did not include inquiry into exports.[34]

---

had no powers in this respect, induced the Conservative Party to establish a committee under the chairmanship of Lord Poole to prepare a report. This report "*Monopoly and the Public Interest*" (1963) together with the Governments White Paper on the question in 1964 finally led to the Act of 1965.

33. This name was chosen in the Restrictive Trade Practices Act 1956 (section 28).
34. C.K. Rowley, "*The British Monopolies Commission*", (London, 1966), 75.

2.2. The Monopolies Commission cannot investigate on its own initiative but only upon reference by the Department of Trade and Industry. A reference by the Department defines the subject that is the goods or services concerned, the particular merger to be considered or the agreement to be investigated. The references of the Board of Trade or since 1969 the Department of Trade and Industry do not mention the detailed motives for the reference which means that in stating the matters to be investigated by the Commission the Department in fact defines already the relevant market without giving further details as to the criteria on the basis of which these definitions were made. The reports of the Monopolies Commission however may give considerations on the relevant market (e.g. report Ross Group/Allied Fisheries 1966).

The Commission may be asked to confine its investigation to findings of fact or, in addition, to report whether the matters investigated operate or are expected to operate against the public interest. If so, the Commission may recommend what action they think should be taken. In the case of a merger reference[35] the Commission will report, whether the merger or the proposed merger operates or may be expected to operate against the public interest and where it finds the criteria are satisfied, make recommendations as to the action be taken.

The Department of Trade and Industry may also require as far as monopoly and oligopoly conditions are concerned the Commission to submit to them a report on the general effect on the public interest of practices of a specified class, being practices other than those covered by the Restrictive Trade Practices Act 1956, which in the opinion of the Department are commonly adopted as a result of, or for the purposes of preserving conditions to which the principal act (the 1948 Act) applies or of any specified practices which appear to the Department to have the effect of preventing, restricting or distorting competition in connection with the production or supply of goods, the supply of services or the export of goods from the United Kingdom (section 5, 1965 Act).

Four such general references have been made: on collective discrimination (1955) on common pricing (1956) on recommended prices (1967) and on restrictions accepted by members of professions (1967).

For the investigation of monopolies or oligopolies having been referred to the Monopolies Commission section 14 of the 1948 Act mentions the following points to be taken into account: all relevant matters including economical production and distribution, efficient organization of industry,

35. Which may be done at any time up to six months after it has taken place, or from the date the Department learned of it. Where a merger has not been completed the Department has power to prohibit by statutory instrument any further steps to carry the merger through pending the report of the Commission. The time period allotted to the Commission cannot be more than six months. This period may be extended with another three months if necessary.

encouragement of new enterprise, effective distribution of labour, materials and capacity, technical improvements and market expansion.[36] As can be seen these criteria are of an extensive general nature, which may partly be explained by the tentative character of this first Act, tentative in the sense it did not take a definite position as to the phenomenon of market power.

As to merger references the Commission is simply required to take into account all matters which appear in the particular circumstances to be relevant and to take account of any formal published directions by the Department of Trade and Industry in this respect. No such directions have been published so far.[37]

Both under the monopolies part and under the merger part of the legislation the Department of Trade and Industry has extensive powers to remedy undesirable effects. Once a practice adopted by a monopoly or oligopoly has been found by the Monopolies Commission to be against the public interest – but only under that condition–the Department is empowered to

- declare unlawful, or require termination of agreements entered into by the monopoly
- declare unlawful refusal to deal and tie-ins
- declare unlawful discriminatory practices
- require publication or notification of prices
- regulate prices charged for goods or services

(section 10, 1948 Act, section 3, 1965 Act).

In practice these powers have rarely been applied.[38]

Usually the Department secures voluntary compliance by the enterprises concerned to carry out the recommendations of the Monopolies Commission or it obtains from them undertakings that they will act in accordance with the recommendations. So on the recommendation on monopoly conditions in the supply of colour film (1966) Kodak was induced to moderate its profits and pass on some of this benefit to consumers in the form of lower prices. In the case of household detergents (1966) a reduction of promotional expenditure was secured.

In merger cases if the Commission finds that the merger operates or may be expected to operate against the public interest, the following measures may be taken:

- the prohibition or restriction of the merger
- the divestiture

36. See for full text of section 14: app. B.

37. See for more detail on this point and on other points regarding mergers: "Mergers" a guide to Board of Trade practice" (London, H.M.S.O., 1969).

38. Of the some 30 investigations by the Monopolies Commission under this heading only three Orders have been made: on dental goods (1951), on imported hardwood and softwood timber (1960) an on petrol(1966).

– the order to temporarily restrain (stand still-orders) until the investigation is completed (section 3 and 6 1965 Act).

In one case sofar an Order has been made i.e. the one prohibiting the Rank Organisation from taking steps which might tend to a merger between Rank and the De la Rue Company or from acquiring any of De la Rue's stocks or assets (1969). In the other cases voluntary compliance as to the execution of the Monopolies Commission's recommendations has been secured.

What happens when undertakings are infringed, is, that the Department of Trade and Industry will refer to the Commission the question whether and to what extent the parties concerned have complied with the–earlier– recommendation of the Commission (section 12 of the 1948 Act, section 6 (5) 1965 Act). After a second reference an Order may be made.[39] If an Order is not complied with, section 11 of the 1948 Act provides that compliance shall be enforceable by civil proceedings by the Crown for an injunction or for any other appropriate relief.

IV. *The rules of competition of the European Economic Community*

The nature and scope of the rules of competition and their implementation in the European Economic Community are first of all contained in the Articles 85 to 90 of the Treaty itself and furthermore in a number of implementing regulations either issued by the Council of Ministers or issued within the framework set by the Council, by the Commission of the European Communities. In this section as in section 3 two areas of interest for competition policy will be dealt with i.e. the restrictive agreements and monopolies c.q. mergers.[40]

1. *Restrictive agreements*

Article 85 embodies the rules concerning restrictive agreements in a wide sense, or to use the phrase of the Restrictive Trade Practices Act: independent from the question "whether or not the agreement or arrangement is intended to be enforceable by legal proceeding".

39. Such a case was present in the Monopolies and Restrictive Practices Order (Imported Hardwood and Softwood Timber) Order 1960 (S.I. 1960/1211) following the report of the Commission (1958) on second reference on imported timber: Report whether to what extent the recommendation of the Commission has been complied with.

40. According to Article 87 of the Treaty the Council of Ministers can only act on a proposal submitted to it by the Commission.

It prohibits in its paragraph 1 restrictions of competition which are likely to affect trade between member-States. A non-exhaustive list of types of agreement prohibited is given in this paragraph. Agreements prohibited by Article 85, para. 1 are automatically void. A decision may be sought to get an exemption from the prohibition of para. 1. The conditions for giving such an exemption are contained in Article 85, par. 3.[41]

Article 85, para. 1, is a self executing prohibition, directly addressed to enterprises.[42] As Article 85, para. 3, provides that under certain conditions the prohibition contained in paragraph 1 may be declared inapplicable to certain agreements, decisions or concerted practices–or to groups of them– this declaration requires action by a competent authority.

Pursuant to Article 87 of the Treaty the Council of Ministers has issued Regulation No. 17[43] to implement Articles 85 and 86[44] Regulation No. 17, by which only the Commission can issue such a declaration.[45] Combined with the far-reaching powers given to the Commission to make investigations and the power to impose fines and penalty payment to be dealt with below,[46] these powers conferred to the Commission show that, at least as far as restrictive trade agreements are concerned, the new possibilities created by the Treaty for a supra-national approach have been fairly realised even in the prefederal stage of the Community so as to ensure the safeguard for in-distorted competition throughout the Common Market.

Before going into a more detailed analysis of the implementing regulations, it should be mentioned here that the provision of Article 85 applies to goods and services and to all branches of industry but for the limitations which can be seen in the following annotations:

– Article 42 provides that the Articles 85 and 86 apply to agricultural production and trade in agricultural products as mentioned in Annex II to the

41. See for full text of Articles 85 (and 86): app. C.

42. Judgment of the Court of Justice of April 6, 1962, Case no. 13/61 (De Geus en Uitdenbogerd v.Bosch), *Recueil*, VIII, 103; [1962], CMLR, 27.

43. First Regulation implementing Articles 85 and 86 of the Treaty (O.J., 204/62).

44. As the provisions of Regulation No. 17 are applicable to both Articles 85 and 86, the analysis in this section, dealing with restrictive agreements is also valid with regard to dominant positions (Article 86) that is: apart from the notification procedure in Regulation No. 17 which only refers to Article 85.

45. Section 9(1). Section 9(3) provides that the national authorities remain competent to apply Article 85, para. 1, and Article 86 as long as the Commission has not initiated a procedure to grant a negative clearance, to oblige enterprises to put an end to infringements or to apply Article 85, para. 3. In practice these powers have been applied by the national administrative authorities very rarely. The Court of Justice declared in its judgment of March 18, 1970 (Bilger v. Jehle, case No. 43/69, *Recueil*, XVI, 137) that the "national authorities" include national judicial authorities. See for the effect of this judgment on the provisional validity for agreements: the contribution of Van der Wielen, infra, 140-159.

46. p. 19-20.

Treaty only to the extent determined by the Council. By Regulation No. 26[47] the Council of Ministers made Articles 85 and 86 applicable to this sector of the economy under certain provisions;

– Transport enterprises in the rail, road and inland sectors are subject to special rules by virtue of Regulation No. 1017/68[48] of the Council. This regulation is based both on Articles 75–which forms part of the transport chapter of the Treaty (Articles 74 to 84)–and 87;

– Article 90, para. 2 of the Treaty provides that any undertaking entrusted with the management of services of general economic interest or having the character of a fiscal monopoly will be subject to the rules of the Treaty, in particular the rules of competition in so far as the application of such rules does not obstruct the de jure or de facto fulfillment of the specific tasks entrusted to such undertakings. The development of trade must not be affected to such an extent as would be contrary to the interests of the Community;[49]

– Article 223 of the Treaty exempts producers and traders in arms, ammunition and war material from the application of the rules of competition under certain conditions mentioned in this Article;

– Article 232, para. 1, finally makes an exception for the application of the E.E.C.-rules of competition to those restrictions on competition which are dealt with in the Treaty establishing the European Coal and Steel Community of April 18, 1951. This latter Treaty has special provisions on this subject i.c. the Articles 65 and 66.

Now turning to the regulations implementing Article 85 and Article 86 as distinct from the particular fields just mentioned above, it first should be observed that of these regulations only Regulation No. 17 applies also to Article 86 and secondly that Regulation No. 17 does not attempt to make explicit Articles 85 and 86, but merely provides for a procedure by which the application of these Articles is rendered possible.

Rather than commenting upon each implementing regulation in particular, an effort will be made to range the contents of them in a number of categories of subjects by which as is hoped the field will be so covered as to be useful for the purpose of this contribution.

Three main subjects may be distinguished

1.1. negative clearance (Article 2, Regulation No. 17)

1.2. application of Article 85, para. 3 (Article 6, Regulation No. 17)

1.3. complaints (Article 3, Regulation No. 17)

47. O.J. 993/62, amended by Regulation No. 49 of June 29, 1962. O.J. 1571/62.
48. O.J. 1968, L 175/1.
49. Cf. VerLoren van Themaat, *infra*, 240-251.

1.1. negative clearance. The purpose of a negative clearance is to get a statement of the Commission that there are no grounds for it to intervene under Article 85, para. 1, or Article 86, with respect to a certain agreement, decision or practice. This statement may be given on the basis of the facts in the possession of the Commission. In principle such a statement is not binding upon the national courts when violation of Article 85 or Article 86 is alleged in a civil suit. It may however, have a certain value in forming the judge's opinion.

Up till the end of 1971 some ten negative clearances were given. The Commission issued several general statements on non-applicability of Article 85, para. 1, to certain restrictions e.g. on restrictions of minor importance[50] and on patent-licences.[51] These statements may be seen as a kind of "block" negative clearance.

1.2.1. application of Article 85, para. 3. Apart from the exemptions expressly stated in different regulations, as a general rule it may be said that to have applied by the Commission Article 85, para. 3, parties to an agreement (or to a decision of associations) have to notify to the Commission the agreement to which they are parties.

The system of notification laid down in Regulation No. 17 can best be described by making a distinction between "new" agreements i.e. agreements concluded after March 13, 1962 (the date of the coming into force of Regulation No. 17) and "old" agreements i.e. those agreements already in existence before March 13, 1962.[52]

The principal provision for "new" agreements is Article 4, Regulation No. 17: agreements–by which term the words in Article 85, para. 1, agreements, decisions and practices will henceforth be indicated–coming under the scope of Article 85, para. 1, have to be notified if the enterprises concerned want Article 85, para. 3 to be applied.

Article 6 of Regulation No. 17 provides that in normal cases the decision of the Commission to apply Article 85, para. 3, has no effect prior to the date of notification even if the conditions of Article 85, para. 3, were fulfilled before that date. Article 15 of Regulation No. 17 gives a safeguard against the imposition of fines once notification has taken place. The safeguard is valid for the time after the notification and till the time of the decision, unless the Commission has informed the parties concerned after a preliminary examination that application of Article 85, para. 3, is not justified.

For some categories of agreements defined in Article 4, para. 2, Regula-

50. *Infra*, 18; cf. Wertheimer, *infra*, 172.

51. *Infra*, 23; cf. Wertheimer, *infra*, 166.

52. "New" agreements for U.K. enterprises will be those concluded after December 31, 1972 and "old" agreements will be those already in existence before January 1, 1973.

tion No. 17,[53] notification is not obligatory, which means that a decision to apply Article 85, para. 3, may be applied with retro-active effect for as long a time as the conditions of that paragraph have been fulfilled. The guarantee against fines (Article 15, Regulation No. 17) can, however, only be obtained by notification. The rules for the notification of "old" agreements do not differ considerably from the rules for "new" agreements. The differences are that

a. a time-limit has been fixed for the notification of the old agreements;

b. fines for infringement of Article 85, para. 1, even prior to notification cannot be imposed if those time-limits have been observed;

c. a special provision (Article 7, Regulation No. 17) renders possible adaption of agreements which did not satisfy the requirements of Article 85, para. 3, if these agreements were notified before the time-limit mentioned.

As to old agreements for which there is no obligation to notify, Article 7, Regulation No. 17, provides for a notification if the enterprises concerned want to make use of this facility, for which the time-limit was fixed at a later date than the date mentioned under *b* and *c*.

1.2.2. By virtue of Article 4, para. 2 of Regulation No. 17 are exempted from notification agreements

a. to which the parties are enterprises of only one member-State and relating neither to imports nor to exports between member-States;

b. between two enterprises with the sole effect of fixing resale prices or of imposing restraint in the inherent rights of an acquirer or user of industrial property rights;

c. the sole object of which is the development or uniform application of standards and types or joint research to improve techniques.

1.2.3. By virtue of Regulation No. 67/67[54] the Commission, empowered to this end by the Council (Regulation No. 19/65),[55] applied Article 85, para. 3 to certain specified classes of exclusive agency contracts. This means that for agreements which satisfy the conditions set out in Regulation No. 67/67 an obligation to notify no longer exists.

1.2.4. Another Notice of the Commission was made[56] in which the Commission with regard to certain forms of cooperation between enterprises—such as agreements having as their sole object joint market research, joint provisions of credit guarantees, joint placing of research development contracts—stated that as a general rule it should not be necessary for the legal situation to be clarified to have a decision of the Commission in an individual

53. *Infra*, 1.2.2.
54. O.J. 849/67; [1967] CMLR, D1 *et seq.*; cf. Wertheimer, *infra*, 169.
55. O.J. 533/65; cf. Wertheimer, *infra*, 168.
56. O.J. 1968, C 75/3 and C 84/14; cf. Wertheimer, *infra*, 170.

case. This also means that notification will no longer be necessary for agreements of these types.

1.2.5. In the Official Journal of June 2, 1970.[57] the Commission made a statement in which it was set out that those agreements which do not affect to an appreciable degree competition and trade between member-States, are not covered by Article 85, para. 1. Hence there is no need to notify such agreements.

1.2.6. Regulation No. 2821/71 of the Council[58] empowers the Commission to grant category-exemption in application of Article 85, para. 3, to certain groups of agreements on standards, research and development and specialisation. An implementing regulation by the Commission with regard to specialisation agreements was published.[59] It states that specialisation agreements when they satisfy the conditions laid down in that regulation are exempt from notification.

Once the decision is made by the parties to the agreement that notification appears to be necessary the main lines of the procedure to be followed by the Commission is that inquiries and investigations are carried through. In the case that the Commission reaches the conclusion that Article 85, para. 1 may be declared inapplicable, a decision–subject to what is said on the liaison with the competent authorities of the member-States[60] –to that effect is taken usually for a certain period. The decision may be given under certain conditions and may be revoked, among other things when as to an essential element in the decision the factual situation changed. If, on the contrary, the Commission rules that the conditions of Article 85, para. 3 appear not to have been fulfilled, the Commission takes a decision to that effect and makes use of Article 3, Regulation No. 17 which empowers the Commission to require by decision the enterprises concerned to bring to an end the infringement of Article 85, para. 1 (this being the consequence of the conclusion that the conditions of Article 85, para. 3 are not fulfilled).

The third possibility is that the notified agreement does not after all, enter into the scope of Article 85, para. 1. In that case no formal decision is taken unless parties may want a negative clearance.[61]

The Commission may impose fines upon enterprises (Article 15 of Regulation No. 17) where, intentionally or negligently, they–in short–do not collaborate with investigations[62] or where they infringe Article 85, para. 1.

57. O.J. 1970, C 64/1; cf. Wertheimer, *infra*, 172.

58. O.J., 1971, L.284/46; [1972], CMLR, D 4-7; cf. Wertheimer, *infra*, 174.

59. Regulation No. 2779/72 O.J., 1972, L 292/23.

60. *Infra*, 20.

61. *Supra*, 17.

62. Fines may also be imposed for not collaborating with investigations having no relation to a notification.

Penalty payments are also provided for (Article 16, Regulation No. 17).

No formal decision can be taken by the Commission without having consulted the Advisory Committee on Restrictive Practices and Monopolies. This committee is composed of national civil servants competent in this field. The consultation takes the form of submitting to the Committee a draft-decision.

The decisions are published. The publication will have regard to the legitimate interest of enterprises in the protection of their business secrets. (Article 21, Regulation No. 17). It should be mentioned that the notified agreements are not made public. Only when the Commission intends to give a negative clearance or a decision by which Article 85, para. 3 will be applied, it will publish a summary of the agreements. The same proviso as to the protection of business secrets is then valid (Article 19, Regulation No. 17).

1.3. complaints. Any natural or legal person who shows a legitimate interest may apply to the Commission that in its opinion there exists an infringement, by parties to an agreement, of Article 85. para. 1, or Article 86. A request to the same effect may be made by member-States. If the Commission finds that this allegation is justified it may by means of a decision oblige the enterprises concerned to put an end to the infringement (Article 3 of Regulation No. 17). The Commission may also apply Article 3 upon its own initiative.

From the decisions of the Commission appeal is open to the Court of Justice of the European Communities.[63] Article 17 of Regulation No. 17 provides furthermore that the Court of Justice shall have full jurisdiction within the meaning of Article 172 of the Treaty[64] to review decisions whereby the Commission has fixed a fine or penalty payment; it may cancel, reduce or increase the fine or penalty payment.

The Articles 85 and 86 being directly applicable the national courts may also in principle decide in civil proceedings about the applicability of Article 85 (1) or Article 86.

2. *Monopolies*

As was said earlier Regulation No. 17 is equally implementing Article 86. Apart from the notification aspects the provisions of Regulation No. 17 are also applicable when action is considered on the basis of Article 86, which Article prohibits, sofar as the trade between member-States may be affected thereby, improper practices of a dominant position in the Common Market or

63. See for the extent of the appeal: *infra*, 30.

64. Article 172 reads: "The regulations enacted by the Council pursuant to the provisions of this Treaty may confer upon the Court of Justice full jurisdiction as to the merits in regard to the penalties provided for in these regulations".

any substantial part thereof. A non-exhaustive list of practices deemed to be improper practices is added to Article 86.[65]

On the basis of Article 87 of the Treaty the Council of Ministers may on proposal of the Commission issue regulations or directives to put into effect, among other things, the principles set out in Article 86. No official proposal has yet been made.

There exists no specific merger legislation in the E.E.C. The European Parliament passed a resolution–June 7, 1971–in which it stated that a pre-merger notification should be introduced for mergers by which a certain market-share or a certain size is reached. No further quantitative or qualitative indications were given however.

V. *Areas of convergence and of difference in both sets of provisions.*

The following observations will be confined to those points which are thought to be the main ones. They may be considered under four heads
1. scope of applicability
2. registration
3. criteria
4. procedure

1.1. As may be seen from the foregoing sections there are differences in the applicability of the legislation with regard to the protection, provided by the legislations, against restrictions of competition in the field of services.

Article 85 applies equally to services–apart from a possible definition, on the basis of Article 87, section 2 (c) of the extent to which the provisions of Article 85 are to be applied in the various economic sectors (of which the Regulation No. 1017/68 on transports is an example)–while agreements relating to services are not covered by Part 1 of the Restrictive Trade Practices Act 1956, and therefore are not registrable. This, however, does not mean that the United Kingdom legislation completely ignores agreements relating to services. One of the amendments to the Monopolies and Restrictive Practices (Inquiry and Control) Act 1948 by the 1965 Act is that the principal Act as to the potential references to the Monopolies Commission was extended in relation to services (section 2 of the 1965 Act).[66] However, only those agreements can be considered to which the one-third criterion applies i.e. that at least one-third of the services is supplied within the United

65. See for full text of Article 86: app. C.

66. Four references on the supply of services were made since 1965: overseas motor insurance (1965), estate agents (1966), haircutting services (1967) and fire insurance (1968), and a general reference on restrictive practices in the supply of professional services was made in 1967.

Kingdom or any substantial part thereof,[67] by two or more persons who conduct their respective affairs so as to prevent or restrict competition in relation to those services. Or, alternatively those agreements the result of which is that, in the United Kingdom or any substantial part thereof, services are not supplied at all. It has been a political decision to decide that the supply of services should be brought within the monopolies legislation, though in Decmber 1969 for another group up till then equally non registrable, the information agreements, it was decided to bring these agreements within the restrictive practices legislation. It is not perfectly clear for which reasons, other than political, the restrictive practices legislation was not extended to the supply of services, as the impact on competition of restrictive agreements in the field of services will in general not be considerably different from the impact of restrictive practices in the field of supply of goods.

1.2. Another area in which a difference can be noted is the applicability of the rules of competition in the E.E.C. Treaty to public sector enterprises, at least in principle (Article 90 and Article 37 as far as national trading monopolies are concerned) and the non-applicability to the public sector of both the monopolies and restrictive practices legislation.[68] (Section 2 of the 1948 Act and section 8 of the 1956 Act).

Apart from differences caused in this respect by different attitudes in the E.E.C. and in the United Kingdom as to the role competition policy should play in the whole of economic and industrial policy, there still is room, it seems, to raise the question whether by excluding e.g. public monopolies from the application of the monopolies legislation the control of Parliament may be sufficiently effective to counteract possible restrictive practices of these monopolies.

On the other hand to be fair it should be mentioned that in the E.E.C. Article 90 did not find any application up till now, that is the Commission did not address any directives in this respect to member-States.[69] In its first

67. The supply of services is to be understood as "the undertaking and performance by way of business of engagement for any other matter than the supply of goods and includes both the rendering of services to order and the provision of services by making them available to potential users. It does not include the rendering of services under a contract of service".

68. See C.K. Rowley, *op cit.*, note 34, 67, footnote 2 where the author mentions the fact, "that this exemption incensed many members to the Conservative Party during discussion of the Bill in the House of Commons". "Nevertheless", the author continues to say, "the exemption has not been remedied during the long period in which the Conservatives were in power".

69. A negative decision has been given in the GEMA-case. According to the Commission the GEMA–an association managing musical copyright in Germany–was not

report on competition policy[70] the Commission indicated that investigations are being conducted, in particular on the relation between the State and public enterprises. Article 37–the adjustment of national trading monopolies so as to realise that no discrimination exists between national enterprises of member-States–however, has been implemented to such a degree that most of the national monopolies started to adjust their policies.[71]

1.3. A third point on which both the legislations have a somewhat different set of provisions has to do with patents. Under United Kingdom Law this only is relevant for the restrictive practices legislation, the monopolies legislation rendering possible, as was mentioned above, reference with regard to "the prevalence of conditions" relating to patents and trademarks.

The fact that under E.E.C.-legislation Article 4, para. 2b, Regulation No. 17 exempts only certain kinds of licensing agreements from the compulsory notification,–i.e. those restrictions imposed upon the licensee which have a direct bearing on the exercise of industrial property rights–indicates already that from the moment the holder of an industrial property right in a licensing agreement exceeds the limits of the exercise of this right itself, his agreement may fall under the provisions of Article 85, para. 1.

It is true, that in a notice of December 21, 1962[72] the Commission mentioned a number of clauses in licensing agreements, which in its opinion did not fall under the provisions of article 85, para. 1 but most of the clauses mentioned are to be considered as covered by the exercise of the industrial property right itself and for that reason could not fall within the scope of Article 85, para. 1. But with regard to other rather common restrictions in licensing agreements such as an exclusive right to produce or sell the product patented, the Commission made it clear[73] that in general this exclusive right is not excluded from the application of Article 85, para. 1. Whether other restrictions, such as cross-licensing, will also be considered as falling under the provisions of Article 85, para. 1, was not yet decided but it seems doubtful that to such agreements Article 85, para. 1 would not be applicable.[74]

---

to be considered as an enterprise performing services of public utility, as meant by Article 90. Decision of June 2, 1971, O.J., 1971, L 134/15.

70. Annex to the 5th General Report on the Activities of the Communities (Brussel-Luxemburg, 1972), 158.

71. *Id.* at 160-165.

72. O.J., p. 2921/62.

73. Cases Burroughs–Delplanque and Burroughs–Geha, decisions of the Commission of December 22, 1971, O.J. 1972, L 13/50 and L 13/53; [1972] CMLR, D 67 *et seq.* and D 72 *et seq.*; cf. Wertheimer, *infra*, 179-180.

74. See generally Wertheimer, *infra*, 160-227.

Under United Kingdom legislation, however, the relevant provisions give rise to presume that a much wider field of agreements relating to industrial property rights is not covered by the restrictive practices legislation, which in fact means that these agreements are exempt from registration. Section 8, subsection 4 of the 1956 Act provides, as far as patents and licences are concerned, that no registration is needed with regard to a licence granted by the propietor of a patent nor with regard to an agreement for a licence, "under which no such restrictions as are described in section 6, subsection 1 of the Act are accepted, except in respect of the invention to which the patent or application for a patent relates or articles made by the use of that invention". The restrictions described in section 6(1) of the Act, it may be recalled, are those in respect of

a. the prices to be charged
b. the terms or conditions
c. the quantities or descriptions
d. the processes of manufacture
e. the persons or classes of persons acquiring or supplying the goods

Under these provisions of section 8(4) combined with section 6(1) it appears that as long as the restriction relates exclusively to the things mentioned in section 8 (4) quite a variety of agreements on patent licences are not registrable, notably such agreements as e.g. exclusive licences, cross-licensing and licences subject to price restrictions.[75,75a]

1.4. On the subject of exclusive agency contracts there also each of the legislations follows a different pattern. In the Common Market quite a substantial policy has been elaborated defining and determining which kinds of vertical exclusive agency contracts between only two persons may be authorised under Article 85, para. 3 and which other kinds of these agreements fall within the scope of Article 85, para. 1. Roughly speaking this policy comes down to the conclusion that while recognising the utility of such agreements to contribute to the constitution of one integrated market–producers thereby being able to develop their exports to other member-States introducing in this way more competition in the markets of these member-States–on the other hand some specific kinds of such agreements were to be considered to be

75. R. Graupner, "*The Rules of Competition in the European Economic Community*" (The Hague, 1965), is of another opinion (p. 60) and finds the exemptions of section 8(4) rather narrow.

75a. The Patent Act of 1949 contains in its sections 37, 40 and 57 however, important provisions against the abuse of patent rights. cf. G. Bernini and G.W. Tooley, "Patents and Antitrust Laws"in: *Comparative Aspects of Anti-Trust Law in the U.S., U.K. and the E.E.C.*, International and Comparative Law Quarterly, Supplementary Publication nr. 6 (1963), 133 and 143.

contrary to the aims of one integrated market. In particular exclusive agency contracts entailing a complete protection for the agent against competition from outside the territory allotted to him belonged to that category of agreements which could not be authorised.[76, 76a]

To know whether under United Kingdom a certain vertical exclusive agency contract is registrable or not a detailed and complicated analysis of different sections of the 1956 Act is necessary.[77] The result of this analysis is that the great majority of "sole agency" agreements between two enterprises, neither of which is a trade association, are exempted from registration. To this category belong e.g. agreements by which an agent is protected against competition by agents from other territories (absolute territorial protection) or agreements by which the agent undertakes not to sell competing products or agreements by which manufacturers of competing products appoint each other as exclusive agents for these products.

Although, at least theoretically, the lenient legal attitude in the United Kingdom towards these agreements may impair in certain cases access to markets in which these agreements operate, it is not to be expected that a change in this attitude will be imminent. In their report on refusal to supply which was published in July 1970 the question of exclusive agency contracts was considered to a certain extent by the Monopolies Commission. The Commission concluded that no mischief had been uncovered by their inquiry which would justify their recommending further substantial legislation as a remedy.

1.5. Finally with regard to pure export agreements which section 8(8) of the 1956 Act exempts from registration–mixed export agreements being those agreements containing also restrictions for the home market–the legal position of the United Kingdom is in general equal to the one take by most other member-States.

In so far as agreements within the Common Market are only designed to regulate exports outside the territory of the Common Market and which are not likely to affect trade between member-States, these agreements are equally not covered by Article 85.[78]

76. See on this subject in more detail the contribution of Professor Snijders, *infra,* 52-83.

76a. For the purposes of this section the word "agent" is taken to mean "independent distributor".

77. The sections involved are: 8(3). 6(1). 7(2) and 8(9).

78. For a case in which it was not clear at the outset whether the restrictions related only to export outside the Common Market, see decision of the Commission of November 6, 1968. O.J. 1968, L. 276/25 (Rieckermann-AEG/Elotherm); [1968] CMLR, D 78 *et seq.*

1.6. Both legislations converge materially on the line taken with regard to agreements being not of such significance, as to call for investigation.

In the United Kingdom the Department of Trade and Industry may give a direction to the Registrar discharging him from taking proceedings in the Court in respect of such an agreement (section 9 (2) of the 1968 Act). Before 1968 the Registrar might be empowered by the then competent Board of Trade to remove from the register these agreements, (section 12 of the 1956 Act). The new system was chosen because of the inconveniences inherent in the old one: the agreement was no longer available for inspection and it might have had to be registered again if registrable modifications were made.

In the Common Market the Commission issued a Notice in May 1970[79] announcing which agreements on account of their minor importance did not fall under the prohibition of Article 85, para. 1. The minor importance was indicated by giving a quantitative definition of the limit under which it could not be said that the agreements had an appreciable effect upon competition. The underlying idea was to contribute in this way to cooperation of small and medium-sized enterprises.

The British system may appear to have the slight disadvantage that the enterprises concerned are in ignorance about the fact whether or not their agreement may enter into the category of being of no substantial economic significance. But as the fulfilment of the obligation to register entails a complete protection of the validity of the agreement in question, not much harm seems to be done.

2. This leads to the second subject to be discussed: the convergence between the effect of the British system of registration and that of the European Community's system of notification.

In both systems agreements the parties to which having met the conditions of registration or notification are valid as long as the competent authority has not rendered its decision. The reverse situation that is to say that agreements, which are registrable or required to be notified are void when these agreements are not duly registered or notified, is also true for both systems. Other than under United Kingdom law, the conclusion for the Common Market that agreements, existing at the date of the coming into force of Regulation No. 17, are valid as long as there is no decision by the competent authority, cannot be drawn from this Regulation itself, but is part of the contribution the Court of Justice of the European Communities made by its judgements to the development of European competition law.

79. O.J., 1970, C.64/1; [1970] CMLR, D 15 *et seq.*

In its judgments of July 9, 1969[80] and of March 18, 1970[81] the Court stated

a. that agreements existing at the date of the coming into operation of Regulation No. 17 and duly notified have full legal force as long as the Commission has not decided on the basis of Article 85 para. 3 on the basis of the provisions of Regulation No. 17 (this reference to "the provisions of Regulation No. 17" is meant to be an illusion to the power of the Commission to inform parties to an agreement after a preliminary examination, that application of Article 85, para. 3 is not justified (Article 15 (6));

b. that agreements existing at the date of the coming into operation of Regulation No. 17, but exempted from notification and not notified have full legal force up till the time that the Commission takes a decision that Article 85, para. 3 will not be applied or that the conditions for applying Article 7 of Regulation No. 17 are not met.[82, 83]

The Court justified these statements among other things by pointing out that another solution would too much impair legal security.[84]

On the other hand the Court in its judgment of April 6, 1962[85] stated that agreements falling under the provisions and existing at the date of the coming into force of Regulation No. 17 which are required to be notified and have not been notified are automatically void, this taking effect on the date of the coming into force of Regulation No. 17.

In the United Kingdom the law itself–section 20(3) of the 1956 Act–declares that when restrictions are found by the Court to be contrary to the public interest the agreement shall be void in respect of these restrictions. There is no retroactive effect to the findings of the Court and not the agreements itself but only the restrictions in it, which are found to be contrary to the public interest, will be void.[86] Whether the rest of the agreement remains

80. Case No. 10/69. (Portelange v. Smith Corona Marchant International), *Recueil* XV, 309-318.

81. Case No. 43/69 (Bilger v. Jehle), Recueil, XVI 127-139.

82. Article 7 of Regulation No. 17 lays down transitional provisions for agreements, existing at the time of the coming into force of Regulation No. 17 and which do not meet the conditions for application of Art. 85, para. 3. Although these conditions may not have been met in the past, the Commission nevertheless is empowered, subject to certain conditions, to determine the period to which the prohibition shall apply.

83. See for the question of the provisional validity the contribution of Van der Wielen, *infra*, 140-159.

84. These judgments have met much criticism, the main one being that the Court by so deciding deprives from Art. 85, para. 1 its prohibitive character. See Baardman "*Tien jaren Europees kartelrecht*", (Zwolle 1972), 17.

85. *Recueil* VIII, 111

86. Cf. the judgment of the Court of Justice of the European Communities, Cases 56 + 58/64 (Grundig/Consten v. Commission) *Recueil*, XII, 498; [1966] CMLR, 474 - 475, where the Court mutatis mutandis, holds the same opinion.

valid depends upon the part the restrictions represent in the agreement.

To safeguard that the judgment of the Court has its effect, the law provides that the Court may, upon the application of the Registrar, make such orders as appears to the Court to be proper for restraining all or any of the persons party to the agreement from

a. giving effect to or enforcing or purporting to enforce, the agreement in respect of the restrictions, found to be contrary to the public interest;

b. making any other agreement (whether with the same parties or with other parties) to the like effect (section 20(3)). This seems an effective weapon to enforce the decision of the Court. No such explicit possibility exists under the E.E.C. Regulation No. 17. One may suppose, however, that Article 3 of this Regulation–providing for the power to put an end to an infringement–does not exclude such a judgment.[87] Furthermore the Commission may impose by decision a penalty payment in order to compel the enterprises concerned to put an end to an infringement of Article 85 in accordance with a decision taken pursuant to Article 3 of Regulation No. 17 (Article 16(1) of Regulation No. 17).

Apart from the effect the findings of the Restrictive Practices Court have upon the validity of an agreement as laid down in section 20(3), the 1968 Act (section 7) contains a provision by which an agreement may also be automatically void.[88] The 1956 Act provided in section 10 an obligation to furnish particulars of a registrable agreement. It did not, however, contain a penalty for failure to comply. This situation was remedied by section 7 of the 1968 Act, where a sanction for failure to furnish particulars was introduced. If such particulars have not been duly furnished within the proper time, the agreement is void in respect of the relevant restrictions and it is unlawful to give effect to or to enforce or purport to enforce any such restriction. The Registrar concluded in his report cited above: "This is the position by virtue of the operation of the Act itself and does not depend upon the institution of any legal proceedings".

3. A few words may be added on a third point where a difference between both legislations is present: the criteria to be applied when examining if and to what extent an agreement will be found not to be contrary to the public interest respectively will get an authorisation on the basis of Article 85, para. 3.

87. Of the decisions of the Commission by which infringements on Art. 85, para. 1 were found, only the decision in the case Grundig/Consten of September 23, 1964 (O.J. 2545/64) holds a decision more or less comparable to the order which might be given under Section 20(3) of the British Act.

88. Cf. Report of the Registrar of Restrictive Trading Agreements July 1, 1966 to June 30, 1969, excerpt of it being reproduced by XV The Anti-Trust Bulletin 1970, 563.

The purpose of the latter Article was defined by the Court of Justice in its judgment of July 13, 1966: [89] "Article 85 aims at implementing the means of Community action indicated in Article 3, especially 'the establishment of a system ensuring that competition . . . is not distorted' so as to attain 'the establishment of a common market' which constitutes one of the fundamental objectives set out in Article 2".

"Article 85 as a whole should thus be respositioned in the context of the provisions of the preamble to the Treaty which clarify it and especially those relating to the elimination of barriers and fair-competition necessary for the realisation of the market unity".

In other words the application of Article 85, para. 3, leaves only room for such considerations in relation to the conditions mentioned in that paragraph, as are in conformity with the aims the Treaty wants Article 85 to reach, that is a system of undistorted competition. This means that by considering the application of Article 85, para. 3, the Commission disposes of a "yardstick" by which to judge in each particular case the arguments put forward by the parties in favour of their agreement. These arguments have to be judged as the Court of Justice said in another judgment[90] of July 13, 1966 "in the light of Article 85" which, the Court concluded, would mean that for instance the proof that an agreement contributes to improving production and distribution should not be based on advantages which appear to the parties to the agreement indispensable, but on advantages to be ascertained and only those which compensate the disadvantages by the restriction in the agreement.

No such unequivocal commitment to competition is present in the United Kingdom law. Section 21 of the 1956 Act reflects the position in the United Kingdom that competition policy is amongst a number of other policies together tending to create a coherent economic policy.

It is left to the Restrictive Practices Court within the framework of this general attitude to review and judge the restrictions referred to it. It has been given a range of gateways by which an agreement containing registered restrictions may "survive" the presumption that it is contrary to the public interest, some of them explicitly mentioning specific aspects of economic policy: gateway (e): localised unemployment and gateway (f): export earnings.

It may be recalled[91] that the Court by considering the arguments put forward by the parties applies the civil law proof i.e. makes use of a balance of probabilities. Which on its turn means that the Court in weighing the effect on the existing restriction against the effect of the removal of the restriction,

89. Case No. 32-65. (Government of the Italian Republic v. Commission), *Recueil* XII, 589; [1969] CMLR, 60-61.

90. Grundig/Consten v. Commission, note 86 at p. 522.

91. See *supra*, 11.

will more than once have to refer to developments which contain a certain amount of uncertainty.

Furthermore given the diversity of the gateways it seems unavoidable that the decisions of the Court will mainly be based on the characteristics of each case in particular, or, to put it less strictly, that a pragmatic approach will be prevalent.[92] It is in this respect interesting to note that professor Hunter made the suggestion[93] to replace the wording of the "tailpiece"—"to be further satisfied that the restriction is not unreasonable, having regard to the balance between its beneficial characteristics and any detriment to the public or persons not parties to the agreement, resulting or likely to result from the operation of the restriction"—by a formula which reads: "to be further satisfied that the beneficial circumstances of any restriction are clearly and unambiguously substantial enough "to overcome a basic presumption in favour of free competition", hereby introducing "a sufficiently positive instruction on how to operate a public policy rule at this most critical phase of judicial considerations".

4. Some final remarks on the different systems of procedure will conclude this chapter. It is not intended to deal at length with the question whether preference should be given to an administrative procedure or to a judicial procedure.

In five[94] of the actual member-States administrative authorities are responsible for the application and execution of competition policy. It is usually thought that the advantages attached to this system outweigh the possible advantages of a judicial system as in matters of enforcement of competition policy it is considered that a purely juridical approach would not do credit to necessary assessment of economic points.

In particular, under the rules of competition of the Common Market, Article 85, para. 3, calls for a considerably thorough economic inquiry and evalution of the issues at stake.[95] (It should be added that appeal from the

92. Cf. A. Hunter, "*Competition and the Law*" (London 1966), 156: "It now becomes most difficult to forecast the result of restrictions coming before the Court. Who could have, for example, predicted the circumstances which gave success to the Black Bolt and Nut Agreement, the Standard Metal Windows agreement or the Glazed Floor and Wall agreement. The upholding of the Net Book agreement—for various non-legal reasons—could have been forecast but it was sustained on a combination of grounds which do not hold out much precedent for other restrictions". It may be remarked aside, that apart from a possible effect of precedent, the often produced argument that a judicial review has the advantage of giving a certain amount of certainty to industry, appears to be undermined.

93. *Id.* at 159/160 and 277.

94. Belgium, France, Germany, Luxembourg and the Netherlands.

95 CF. statement of Von der Groeben, April 16, 1963, the then member of the Commission responsible for competition policy, cited in "*Summary of Conferences in*

Commission's decisions can be lodged, unrestricted in those cases where sanctions were imposed by the Commission, restricted–i.e. to see whether the law has been properly applied or whether the action of the Commission was "ultra-vires"–in other cases.)

The first "tribunal" under British legislation was of an administrative nature: the Monopolies and Restrictive Practices Commission set up in 1948. Its primary function was to institute inquiries into industries where monopolies were thought to exist. The decision whether or not to take action against monopoly conditions was taken by the Minister concerned.[96] The picture changed when in 1956 the Restrictive Trade Practices Court was established, the Monopolies Commission remaining equally in function. It was thought that a court of law would provide the necessary speed, certainty and impartiality which virtues some critics of the Monopolies Commission considered to be not a completely safeguard in the investigations of the Monopolies Commission. "The Commission was disliked by Industry, which felt it was combining the functions of detective, prosecutor and judge".[97]

The system of judical examination evolved by the 1956 Act has had considerable success. In his report on restrictive trade agreements covering the period July 1, 1966 to June 30, 1969[98] the Registrar announced that "by the 30th June 1969 1240 of the agreements on the register had been brought to an end by the parties and 960 had been varied so as to remove all the restrictions with which the 1956 Act is concerned. 35 agreements has been referred to the Court and the proceedings are not completed but it is likely that few will be contested".

The Registrar is of the opinion that this is "an indication that the Act, in conjunction with the cases determined under it, is achieving its larger purpose of preventing the making of agreements which restrict or discourage competition rather than terminating them after they have been made and operated for some period".

Probably this success the origin of which was already earlier apparent, has contributed to the extension of the Court's jurisdiction to resale price maintenance, the Resale Prices Act 1964.

Despite this positive conclusion as to the activity of the Court, some

---

Europe", (April 1963), app., part 2. Hearings before the Subcommittee on anti-trust and monopoly of the Committee on the Judiciary. United States Senate 88th Congress, purs. to S. Res. 56, Washington, 97-586 O, 265.

96. Cf. G.C. Allen, *Monopoly and Restrictive Practices* (London 1968), 91: "The passing of the Act brought a striking change in policy as well as procedure. The law had now ceased to be neutral in respect of certain restrictive practices and had become definitely hostile".

97. I.A. MacDonald. *op.cit.*, note 23, 354.

98. In XV "The Anti-Trust Bulletin", 1970, 573.

persistent doubt, to use the language of the 1956 Act, has been voiced on the suitability of a court of law to deal with questions of restrictive practices. The question is usually indicated as the question of justiciability:[99] whether restrictive practices are inherently suitable to the judicial solution as preconised in the framework of the Act, that is necessarily implying–when doing the balancing operation–predictions about economic conditions and behaviour. It is argued that decisions in these matters are rather political than judicial and that a court of law should not have been charged with this task. That such a doubt appears to be justified is shown by the Court's decision in the Yarn Spinners' case[100] where the Court came to the conclusion that as far as the gateway(e) provision was concerned, the termination of the agreement would lead to persistent adverse local unemployment but that on balance this was preferable to a misallocation of the country's productive resources. "Although subsequent interpretation of the 1956 Act has minimised the effect of the Yarn Spinners' Case, it is nevertheless important. For it emphasizes the extent to which the Restrictive Practices Court has been given power to make far-reaching decisions in matters as important electorally as unemployment. Just how important the decision was can be seen from subsequent events. Immediately after it with an election pending, legislation was passed by the Conservative government to cope with the situation which might arise as a result of the decision and to provide compensation to any firms forced to reduce their capacity (the Cotton Industry Act 1959)".[101]

VI. *Some aspects of the application of both legislations*

The scope of this contribution does not permit to survey all the decisions taken by the competent authorities either in the Community or in the United Kingdom. Another reason not to do so is the consideration that each case decided upon has its own particular circumstances so that generalisation seems not feasible. Some main "policy" lines of thought, however, may be detectable from the decisions of the authorities concerned. Exclusive agency contracts, patents and licences will not be dealt with as these categories of agreements are being discussed in other parts of this book[102] and as far as the United Kingdom legislation is concerned profit largely of exemptions from registration. Nor are the reports of the Monopolies Commission and the

99. I.A. MacDonald, *op.cit.*, note 23, 361.

100. Yarn Spinners' Agreement 1959, L.R.1.R.P. 118, cited by I.A. MacDonald, *op.cit.*, note 23, 366.

101. Cited from I.A. MacDonald, *op.cit.*, note 23, 367.

102. See the contribution of Professor Snijders on exclusive dealing arrangements, *infra*, 52-83, and that of Wertheimer on patents and licences, *infra*, 160-227.

action taken on these reports by the Board of Trade and the Department of Trade and Industry being considered, as both the monopoly and merger legislation in the Common Market have only started in their actual application.[103]

The scope of this review of decisions thus being narrowed down, it will be attempted to give hereunder a survey of

1. decisions by wich Article 85 para. 1 was applied;
2. judgments by which an agreement was declared to be contrary to the public interest;
3. decisions by which an agreement was admitted under Article 85, para. 3;
4. judgments by which an agreement was considered not to be contrary to the public interest.

1. Under the E.E.C. rules of competition in connection with Regulation No. 17, price-agreements, agreements to limit production or markets and market-sharing agreements have in not a single case been exempted from the ban of Article 85, para. 1. Also systems aiming at national protection of the market have been condemned without exemption.

It is hardly surprising that agreements on prices between manufacturers in different member-States which replace the insecurity of market conditions by the security of a common price often based on average costs, restricts competition and may affect trade between member-States. Nor is it doubtful that such an agreement cannot be justified under the conditions of Article 85 para. 3. In particular when the price-agreement has as a complement an agreement to share markets. Such was the case e.g. with the international quinine agreement which was condemned by the Commission and upon whose members because of aggravating circumstances fines were imposed.[104]

Less apparent is the situation from the viewpoint of Article 85, para. 1, in cases where only within one member-State a price-agreement has been entered into by manufacturers and importers of the goods concerned. Also in cases like these the Commission did not lift the ban of Article 85, para. 1.[105]

103. Article 86 has been applied twice:

a. concerning GEMA=a German office for the exercise of musical copy-rights: improper use of monopoly. Decision of June 2, 1971, O.J. 1971, L 134/15; [1971] CMLR, D 35 *et seq.*

b. concerning Continental Can Company–American firm in monopolistic position taking over a Dutch company. Decision of December 9, 1971, O.J. 1972, L 7/25; [1972] CMLR, D 11 *et seq.*

104. Decision of July 16, 1969, O.J. 1969, L 192/5; [1969] CMLR, D 41 *et seq.* uphold by the Court of Justice: judgment of July 15, 1970, Cases Nos. 41, 44 and 45/69 (ACF Chemiefarma, Buchler, Boehringer v. Commission) *Recueil* XVI, 661, 733 and 769.

105. Decision on the V.C.H.=Vereniging van Cementhandelaren (Association of wholesale-dealers in Cement) December 16, 1971, O.J. 1972, L 13/34. Uphold by the Court of Justice, judgment of October 17, 1972, Case No. 8/72, *Recueil* XVIII, 977.

Among other arguments the Commission considered that under these conditions the realisation of one single market between member-States could be endangered. Exemption from the prohibition of Article 85 para. 1 could not be taken into consideration as there was no indication—exceptional situations left aside—that elimination of competition on whole-salers level should be a better instrument than competition itself to safeguard a regular stocking of the market under favourable economic circumstances.

Protection of the national market may also be reached by two other categories of agreements: the national collective exclusive agency contracts and the aggregated rebate agreements. Both categories of agreements have been condemned by the Commission. The collective exclusive agency contracts, as these contracts have the effect of splitting the market into two parts: one part of those manufacturers parties to the contract and their buyers, bound by the contract to deal exclusively with these manufacturers, the other part being formed by the manufacturers not being parties to the agreement and their buyers. This artificial splitting up of the market has as a consequence that manufacturers from other member-States are unable to enter the market for which the agreement has been entered into.

In this case the manufacturers-parties to the agreement—have a predominant influence and their buyers form the majority of the whole of distributors, agreements of this kind maintain an isolation of the sector concerned within the Common Market.[106]

National aggregated rebate agreements prompt buyers to purchase all they require from the national manufacturers in order to obtain a maximum rebate.

By forcing them to do so the agreement is liable to affect the freedom of buyers to import rival products made by manufacturers in other member-States and hampered access by the latter to the national market concerned. Such was the situation in the Ceramic Tiles case.[107] The Commission did not find that the agreement in question entailed, by comparison with the grant of individual rebates, substantial improvements in the production or distribution of goods offsetting the serious restrictions of competition involved. The agreement therefore failed to meet the first of the conditions laid down in Article 85, para. 3.

Joint-selling agencies in a national market may only then get a negative clearance in case these agreements comprise a considerable number of the national

106. See e.g. the recommendation, on the basis of Art. 3 of Regulation No. 17 in the case of the "Convention faience", 7th General Report on the Activities of the Community (1965), No. 67.

107. Decision of December 29, 1970, O.J. 1971, L 10/15; [1971] CMLR, D 6 *et seq*.

manufacturers, when they do not impede the expansion of exports to other member-States. In two cases the Commission found that this could be reached by no longer letting the agencies concern themselves with export to other member-States, which means that manufacturers themselves will then be free to deliver directly to buyers in other member-States without any intervention of the agency. [108]

It must be added, however, that in order to contribute to cooperation between small and medium-sized enterprises the Commission admitted joint-selling agreements when the agreement does not represent an appreciable restriction of competition.[109]

2. In the United Kingdom the Registrar in his report on restrictive trade agreements covering the period of July 1, 1966 to June 30 1969.[110] referred to a statement made in the earlier report that the mass of price-fixing agreements registered under the 1956 Act had been dismantled and that there was no backlog of important cases awaiting reference to the Restrictive Practices Court. Very few major agreements involving price-fixing or discriminatory dealing in a substantial part of a trade or industry are now being made and registered, according to the Registrar in his last report and comparatively few have now to be referred to the Court.

In an appendix to a paper[111] A. Sutherland gives a survey of judgments in the Restrictive Practices Court, since 1956 and up to September 1964, in contested cases involving "the public interest" provisions in the Act. From this annex can be seen that of 23 contested cases explicitly dealing with one kind or another of price-fixing 8 were considered to be not contrary to the public interest.

Since then as far as could be ascertained no price-agreement was upheld by the court.

In several cases in which the Court did not uphold the agreement, parties to the agreement seeking to justify their agreement under the general gateway(b)[112] often tried to prove that price fixing promoted price stability and

108. Two Decisions of November 6, 1968 concerning two joint-selling agencies Cobelaz (Belgian) and C.F.A. (French) of firms in the industry of straight nitrogenous fertilizers. O.J. November 14, 1968, L 276/13 and L 276/29; [1968] CMLR, D 45 *et seq.* and D 68 *et seq.*

109. Decision of December 16, 1971 concerning Safco (Société anonyme des fabricants des conserves alimentaires) (French preserve manufacturers), O.J. 1972, L 13/44; [1972] CMLR, D 83 *et seq*

110. Cited in the XV Anti-Trust Bulletin 1970, 563.

111. A. Sutherland: "Economics in the Restrictive Practices Court", 17 Oxford Economic Papers 1965, 385-426.

112. A. Hunter, "*Competition and the Law*" (London 1966), 122, calls paragraph(b) "an open invitation to respondents to demonstrate the superiority of collusion and collaboration over competition".

therefore contributed to specific benefits, such as preservation of capacity to meet fluctuations in demand, prevention of quality debasement, ensuring availability of supplies when demand revived and convenience for the consumers.

This argument of price stability through price-fixing was often rejected by the Court. So in the Yarn Spinners' case [113] the Court found that "price stabilisation which in isolation would be a benefit, should be considered not in isolation, but as an alternative to a free market".

In the case concerning the "Agreements about the Scottish Bread"[114] by which recommendations were made as to the price of "standard" bread, which were defended with the argument that removal of these recommendations would deny to the public the benefit of the maintenance and improvement of the quality of bread, the Court held that there was no reason why freedom from restriction in price should in general lead to reduction in quality of the product. Finally with regard to the argument that stability of prices would maintain adequate stocks, in the judgment concerning the Agreement of the Linoleum Manufacturers' Association, the Court[115] did not consider that such price movement as would result from price competition would result in adequate stockholding or alter stockholding habits to an extent sufficient to amount to a denial to the public of substantial benefit.

With regard to agreements limiting the entry to the market, the Court did reject the argument by the parties in the case of the Newspaper Proprietor Association and National Federation of Retail Newsagents agreement[116] –to control the number of retail outlets–that new entrants would lead to a decline in profitability per outlet.

3. Apart from negative clearances–by which as a consequence of the fact that the restrictions in the agreements involved did not appreciably restrict competition in the Common Market and therefore did not fall under Article 85, para. 1–the Commission of the European Communities has admitted, although not without certain limitations, agreements under Article 85, para. 3 with regard to cooperation. In particular those agreements which foster cooperation between small and medium-sized enterprises. Three categories of forms of cooperation may be mentioned here: specialisation agreements, research agreements and agreements regarding conditions as to the quality of the product.

– The ban of Article 85, para. 1 as far as specialisation agreements are concerned might be lifted as these agreements lead to an expansion of production

113. Judgment of January 29, 1959, L.R. 1. R.P. 118.
114. Judgment of July 23, 1959, L.R. 1. R.P. 347.
115. Judgment of June 22, 1961, L.R. 2. R.P. 395.
116. Judgment of July 27, 1961, L.R. 2. R.P. 453.

lines, to a decrease of production costs and thus to an increase of productivity. The increased capacity to compete will, it is assumed, benefit the consumers. Attention, however, should be paid that the bounds necessary to achieve the improvement sought should not be exceeded, that is that the specialisation should not impede effective competition (for instance when the number of manufacturers on the market of the goods concerned is too much reduced) while also at the stage of distribution the maintenance of competition should be sufficiently assured.[117]

– Research agreements as such may restrict competition but not in general endanger it when small and/or medium-sized enterprises enter into such an agreement. The situation becomes different when the research agreement concerns a market for technically homogeneous products and the number of sellers is limited or concerns a market where each of the parties is already specialised "in his own right" in respect of the goods concerned. Care should then be taken according to the Commission that as a consequence of the research agreement each of the parties to the agreement does not get an inadmissibly preferential position in its own market from the viewpoint of competitive conditions and, furthermore, that import of the goods concerned remains possible.[118]

– Agreements having as object a common label to designate a certain quality restrict competition when they are connected with obligations regarding prices or other conditions of sale such as the obligation to sell any products of the guaranteed quality. Only when the agreement does not restrict the freedom of manufacturers parties to the agreement to sell other products, an exemption from the prohibition of Article 85, para. 1 will be considered.[119]

A border case of exemption in this field represents the Decision with regard to the Transocean Marine Paint Association[120] where restrictions of compe-

117. See Decisions of the Commission:
a. of July 22, 1969 (Clima-Chapée/Buderus, air-conditioning equipment), 1969, L 195/1; [1970] CMLR, D 7 *et seq.*
b. of December 20, 1971 (Sopelem and Langen), O.J. 1972, L 13/47; [1972] CMLR, D 77 *et seq.*

118. Decisions of the Commission:
a. of July 17, 1968 (ACEC/Berliet, electrically-driven busses). O.J. 1968, L 201/7; [1968] CMLR, D 35 *et seq; cf. Wertheimer, infra,*190–191.
b. of December 23, 1971 (Henkel/Colgate, textile-detergents), O.J. 1972, L 14/14; cf. Wertheimer, *infra,* 192-194.

119. Decisions of the Commission:
a. of June 25, 1969 (V.V.V.F. a Dutch association of exporters of paint and varnish). O.J. 1969, L 168/22; [1970] CMLR, D 1 *et seq.*
b. of June 29, 1970 (electrically-welded steel tubes), O.J. 1970, L 153/14; [1970] CMLR, D 31 *et seq.*

120. Decision of the Commission of June 27, 1967, O.J. 1967, No. 163/10; [1967] CMLR, D 9 *et seq.*

tition of a considerable extent were considered to be outweighed by the necessity to collaborate in order to compete with other international groups in the market.

It may be recalled that in as far as the restrictions in the field of specialisation and joint research are concerned the Commission has been empowered under Regulation No. 2821/71[121] to grant category-exemptions when these agreements enter into the scope of Article 85, para. 1 and that Regulation No. 2821/71 exempts from notification by giving quantitative criteria, some other agreements in these fields.[121a]

4. Under the Restrictive Trade Practices Act 1956 it is still more difficult to trace more or less general lines than under the E.E.C.-rules of competition, the judgment of the Court being based on the circumstances of the case. With this reservation two cases will be mentioned under which the parties succeeded in convincing the Court. The first one will be the case of the Cement Makers Federation.[122] The main restrictions were a scheme for common delivered prices in general arrived at on the multiple basing point system, together with common margins to approved merchants, standard terms and conditions of sale and an aggregated rebate system for large users. The Federation claimed that the pricing system would be justified under the general gateway (b) as under the restrictions the prices of cement would be cheaper than would be the case without the agreement. Arguments for this claim were: operation of industry was efficient, profit margins were modest, the overall capacity was expanded in proper relationship to increasing demand and excess of capacity was avoided. The Court was satisfied[123] by these claims and accepted in its balancing operation the arguments of the Federation, apart from those in support of the aggregated rebate system which the Court declared to be contrary to the public interest because among other things the rebates had the positive disadvantage of discouraging purchasers from buying cement from non members of the federation.[124]

The second case to be mentioned is the Glazed and Floor Tiles Home Trade Associations Agreement.[125] By this agreement the members agreed to sell their standard tiles at prices set out in the Association's price list, all other tiles must be sold at not less than 25 per cent in excess of the nearest standard tile or at actual cost of manufacture, whichever is the greater. The

121. O.J. 1971, L 285/46; [1972] CMLR, D 4 *et seq.*

121a. In December 1972 the Commission passed an implementing regulation with regard to specialisation agreements. See *supra*, 26.

122. Judgment of March 16, 1961, L.R. 2. R.P. 241.

123. See for a detailed analysis of the case: A. Sutherland *op.cit.*, note 11, 386-398.

124. Cf. the Decision of the Commission in the Ceramic Tiles case. See *supra*, 34.

125. Judgment of January 17, 1964, L.R. 4. R.P. 239.

respondents claimed under gateway (b) that without the price discrimination against non standard tiles there would be an erosion of standardisation and in consequence higher production costs and higher prices. The Registrar contended that the degree of standardisation was not due to the prices fixed under the agreement. The Court held, however, that the agreement was necessary to maintain the degree of standardisation as this degree would not have been maintained if left to the individual commercial judgment of each manufacturer. It found no countervailing detriment to the public and declared accordingly that none of the restrictions were contrary to the public interest.

VII. *The rules of competition in the European Coal and Steel Community.*

Not only the E.E.C. but also the E.C.S.C. contains rules of competition. Although in the latter Treaty–the Treaty of Paris of April 18, 1951, entered into force July 25, 1952–competition is also the basic principle, the way in which these rules are applied differs considerably from that of the E.E.C.-Treaty. Only the executive body, first the High Authority and after the integration of the executive bodies of the E.E.C.-Treaty, the E.C.S.C.-Treaty and the Euratom-Treaty the Commission of the European Communities is empowered to give decisions, with exclusion of any other authority except a decision of the Court of Justice in cases of appeal from decision of the executive body. Actually these rules are of less importance than the ones in the E.E.C.-Treaty as they only are applicable to enterprises in the coal and steel sector. Article 80 in conjunction with Article 79 of the Treaty specifies which enterprises fall under the scope of the E.C.S.C.-rules of competition which are laid down in the Articles 60, 65 and 66 of the Treaty.

Article 60 prohibits unfair competitive practices and discriminatory ones. To counteract these practices it contains provisions which regulate the conduct of enterprises on the market: a situation not existing under the E.E.C.-rules. Three basic principles come into play: publication of price-schedules, the possibility open to a producer to deviate from his published prices and align his quotation on a lower price quoted by a competitor and equality of prices for comparable transactions. On this last point the Commission made a proposition to the Council tending to undo the existing connection between the obligatory publication of prices and the prohibition of discrimination.[126]

126. See in detail: First Report on Competition Policy, Annex to the 5th General Report on the Activities of the Communities (Brussels/Luxembourg, 1972), 92 *et seq.* The description of what is to be considered as a discriminatory practice has been given in the decision of the Commission of December 22, 1972, O.J. 1972, L 297/39.

Article 65, para. 1 prohibits agreements between enterprises, decisions of associations of enterprises and concerted practices tending directly or indirectly to prevent, restrict, or distort the normal operation of competition within the Common Market, Article 65, para. 2 provides that under certain specified conditions authorisation shall be given to agreements to specialise in the production of, or to engage in the joint buying or selling of specified products. The latest case in which the Commission on specialisation-agreements decided was the agreement in the German Steel industry.[127] The Commission refused to prolong the authorisation for the joint selling agency given in 1967. The parties then submitted a rationalisation agreement to solve problems of restructuration then prevailing on the German market. Originally the parties had devised a system of production quotas. The Commission found this system contrary to the Treaty: such a sytem would have fixed the market position of each of the manufacturers and therefore would not contribute to a real improvement of the production.[128]

Article 66 has two rather distinct parts. Paragraphs 1 to 6 contain provisions to control the creation of mergers, while paragraph 7 is directed against the improper use of dominant positions. Mergers to be made are subject to prior authorisation unless the size of their assets lies below a certain level (paragraph 2 and 3). Para. 4 gives the Commission far reaching powers to obtain information while paragraph 5 and 6 provide for a series of measures and sanctions (even divestiture) to enable the Commission to have their policy enforced.[129] The minimum size above which Article 66, para. 3 is applicable has been fixed quantitatively in a general decision of the Commission.[130]

Article 66, para. 7 is directed against private and public enterprises which have or acquire a dominant position. The Commission may address recommendations to prevent the use of such position for purposes contrary to those of the Treaty.

127. Decision of the Commission of July 21, 1971, O.J. 1971, L 210/1.

128. In January 1970 the Commission published a memorandum: "*Main lines of a competition policy in relation to the structure of the iron-and steelindustry*", O.J. 1970, C 12. In this memorandum the Commission states that although in the past combination plans have been endorsed, the maintenance of effective competition will in future pose a problem. Therefore the upper limit in the share of production in the Common Market to be acquired has been fixed at 12 to 13% of total crude steel production. Effective competition is thought to be safeguarded as long as at least ten independent producers exist in the Common Market.

129. See First Report on Competition Policy, *op.cit.*, note 126, 87 *et seq.* for a description of that policy.

130. Decision 25-67 of the Commission of June 22, 1967, O.J. 1967, No. 154/11.

VIII. *Final remarks.*

In this chapter some remarks will be made on generalities coming to the mind when trying to survey the whole field. Secondly an unfortunately too short review will be given of the main implications for competition legislation and policy of United Kingdom entry into the Common Market.

1. As far as restrictive agreements are concerned both legislations follow the rule in their application that in general there is not a prohibition per se of these agreements but that on the basis of criteria–varying under the Common Market rules of competition from rather general in nature in criteria under the United Kingdom legislation rather specified in nature–restrictive agreements are to be assessed against these prohibitions. Initially one might have thought, that the prohibition of Article 85, para. 1, should have been more severe but judgments of the Court of Justice pertaining to the creation of validity of agreements until the Commission's decision–have taken away much of this expected severeness. On the other hand the directly applicable prohibitive character of Article 85, para. 1 comes more into light when one compares the situation that an infringement of Article 85, para. 1 has been dealt with by the Commission, with the situation that the Restrictive Practices Court declares an agreement to be contrary to the public interest. Under Community law apart from the ensuing nullity of Article 85, para. 2, heavy fines may be imposed–and experience shows that indeed these fines may be considerable[131] –the Commission furthermore announcing its intention to pursue this way of proceeding against prohibited restrictions. (In this respect the Commission's activities have shown and, as announced, will show that the expectation voiced in 1963 that the Common Market approach "is more ostensibly ferocious, but perhaps less likely to be effective in its bite"[132] is in its turn likely to be belied.

The effect of the judgment of the Restrictive Practices Court is that the restriction, declared to be contrary to the public interest, is null and void. The Court may then, upon application of the Registrar, make such orders as appear to be necessary for restraining the parties to the agreement, restrictions which are null and void, from giving effect to the agreement in respect of the restriction and from making any other agreement, whether with the same parties or with other parties, to the like effect. Usually the Court requires an undertaking instead of giving an order. Only after this undertaking or order, as

131. cf. Decision of the Commission of July 16, 1969 (Kinine), O.J. 1969, L 192/5; [1969] CMLR, D 41 *et seq*. Decision of the Commission of July 24, 1969 (Dyestuffs), O.J. 1969, L 195/11; [1969] CMLR, D 23 *et seq*.

132. D. Walker-Smith and L. Gombos, "Restrictive Practices and Monopolies; a comparison of British and Common Market Law", III Virginia Journal of International Law, 1963, No. 1.

the case may be, is deliberately not observed, the Court, upon application of the Registrar, may punish for contempt of court, which either entails the imposing of fines or imprisonment. The British system of "prohibition" works in phases but may in the end be more severe.

Despite the rather specified criteria laid down in the gateways of the British system, which might theoretically induce one to think that the working of the precedent rule should not be overemphasized, the results show that the interpretation of the Restrictive Trade Practices Court of these gateways has had a considerable deterrent effect leading to the abolition of many restrictions without any attempt to contest before the Court the findings of the Registrar.

Under Common Market Law a deterrent effect of decisions taken to such an extent as in the United Kingdom cannot be shown. There is a certain amount of cases in which the Commission has successfully brought to an end the procedure without having to take recourse to a formal decision, as the Commission indicated in its First Report on Competition Policy earlier mentioned. But given the fact, that for those agreements, which are subject to notification and which have been notified, validity may be claimed, at least for the "existing" ones, as long as the Commission does not decide, it does not seem very probable that parties to such agreements would abandon voluntarily their agreements. Unless the Commission makes use of Article 15, para. 6 of Regulation No. 17, which leads to the loss of validity.[133]

With regard to monopolies legislation the Common Market application is so far only in its beginning. This has the advantage, from the law-making point of view, that all possibilities are still open. In how far the British attitude may contribute to find a satisfactory solution is perhaps not so open a question. Although it may be considered to be an advantage that the British approach is essentially ad hoc, certain disadvantages of the system should also be mentioned. First there is the one-third criterion. One may wonder if positions of market power could not exist, and not have adverse effects, in a market situation below the level of one-third supply of the market. Secondly attention should be paid to the fact, that there is a complete discretion for the Department of Trade and Industry to decide whether there should be a reference or not. And thirdly the criteria by which the Monopolies Commission has to decide if and to what extent the public interest is involved are rather vague as to the role competition should play.

The scope of reference of mergers to the Monopolies Commission is wider than that of the reference of monopolies and oligopolies. But there also is valid, that once it is satisfied that a merger is covered by the legislation, the

133. See No. 31 of the Report-Berkhouwer, European Parliament Rules of Competition and the position of European enterprises in the Common Market and in the economy of the World, Documents E.P.-session 1969, No. 197.

Department of Trade and Industry may, only if it thinks fit, refer to the Commission.

In the European Parliament a proposition was made[134] that with regard to mergers by which a certain size or a certain market share is reached, an obligation of preliminary notification should be introduced and, secondly, that such a merger could only be admitted after the Commission had made it known within a period to be fixed that there were no objections against the merger.

The Commission, however, although in principle in agreement with this proposition, stated[135] that legal objections based on interpretation of the Treaty, in particular Articles 86 and 223 of it, were so well founded that it would not make such a proposition unless by way of a modification of the Treaty itself. According to the Commission such a system of notification would be equivalent to a system of prior authorisation, a system not provided for in the E.E.C.-Treaty.

2. The implications of the accession of the United Kingdom into the European Economic Community as to the form have been regulated from the side of the United Kingdom by section 10 of the European Communities Act [136] of which the principal provision is to relieve the Register of his duty to refer to the Restrictive Practices Court agreements rendered void or authorised in community proceedings. The Restrictive Practices Court is given a similar discretion not to proceed with such agreements.

From the side of the Community, nothing more was necessary than to adapt time limits for notifications to be made by British enterprises.[137]

Materially, the accession of the United Kingdom means that E.E.C.-rules of competition become directly applicable and become part of the United Kingdom Law. As to the kind of agreements covered by these rules differences exist compared with the kind of agreements registrable under United Kingdom Law, which poses the question to examine the need to notify as provided for by Regulation No. 17. As to the application of monopolies and mergers legislation under United Kingdom Law, it would seem that the question of the relevant market–both the geographical and the product market–would have to be one of the main questions to take into account

134. O.J. 1971, C 66/11.

135. Discussions European Parliament June 7, 1971, p. 23/24. Statement by Mr. Borschette, member of the Commission of the European Communities.

136. [1972] CMLR, D 119.

137. See Annex I, p. 110/11 of the list mentioned in Article 29 of the Treaty of Accession, O.J. 1972, L 73/92; adaption of Regulations Nos. 17, 19/65, 1017/68 and 67/67 (Commission). On the basis of Article 153 of the Treaty an adaption of Regulation No. 2821/71 is provided for.

when deciding to make a reference to the Monopolies Commission as it is conceivable that the effect of some monopolies or mergers would not be confined to the internal market of the United Kingdom.

More in general, it may be said that experience in the member-States of the existing Community shows that there still is room for application of national legislation. A question which in this context has been widely discussed is whether differences between national legislations on competition might lead to distortions of competition and whether for that reason these national laws should be harmonised. The counter argument then was that as far as the parties to an agreement are engaged in trade between member-States–that being the situation in which distortions of the kind expected should mostly occur–the E.E.C.-rules on competition would apply, safeguarding equal treatment. The question would then be narrowed down to the question if under a certain national legislation distortions might occur when it should prohibit agreements having been authorised by the Commission. It is not possible to review here this question. It must suffice to refer to the judgment of the Court of Justice of the European Communities of February 13, 1969[138] stating among other things that "the application of national law may not detract from a thorough and uniform application of Community Law and of the actual authority of its implementation".

As this article is prepared for press the government of the United Kingdom introduced into Parliament (December 1, 1972) a Fair Trading Bill. The proposals laid down in 121 clauses,

a. create a new office that of Director of Fair Trading and confers upon the holder duties in conncetion with the protection of consumers. They also transfer to him the function of the Registrar of Restrictive Trading Agreements and invest him with certain duties in connection with monopoly situations and mergers;

b. provide for the establishment of a Consumer Protection Advisory Committee and empower the Secretary of State to make orders prohibiting or regulating practices in connection with consumer transactions which the Advisory Committee have found to have adverse effects upon the economic interests of consumers. They empower the Director to bring proceedings before the Restrictive Practices Court against persons who persistently maintain a course of conduct which is unfair to consumers and detrimental to their interest;

c. replace with revised provisions the Monopolies and Mergers Acts 1948 and 1965;

138. Case 14/68, Recueil XV, 1 *et seq*; [1969] CMLR, 100 *et seq.*

d. make amendments to the Restrictive Trade Practices Acts and, in particular, make provisions for the application of Part I of the Act of 1956 to agreements and arrangements between suppliers of services which involve restrictions upon the supply or acquisition of services other than services of a professional nature.

As far as the acts are concerned dealt with in this article the proposals coincide to some degree with those points about which observations have been made in this paper.

The proposals as far as restrictive trade practices, monopolies and mergers are concerned, comprise in essence:

a. with regard to restrictive trade practices legislation:

– to extend the scope of the legislation to services, not including professional services

– to bring within the ambit of Part I of the 1956 Act agreements relating to the recommendation of resale prices and agreements relating to patent and design pooling

– to extend the powers of the Restrictive Practices Court to make interim orders in relation to agreements which it does not think can be shown to be defensible by reference to any of the so-called "gateways" of section 21 of the 1956 Act;

b. with regard to monopolies:

– to reduce the proposition of the market by reference to which monopolies are defined from 33 1/3 per cent to 25 per cent;

– to create a novel form of reference which requires the Commission–to be called Monopolies and Mergers Commission–if they find a monopoly exists, thereafter to consider only whether the acts of the monopolist in respect of a specified matter e.g. prices operate or may be expected to operate against the public interest;

– to allow monopoly references in relation to the supply or acquisition of goods and services being generally or in certain circumstances the subject of a statutory monopoly or regulated by a statutory body;

– to impose a time limit to the Monopolies and Mergers Commission for a report on any reference.

c. with regard to mergers:

– to empower the Secretary of State to make temporary "stop" orders, while a merger is under investigation;

– to make a reference requiring the Commission if they consider the relevant merger qualifies for investigation to consider only whether certain elements or certain possible consequences operate or may be expected to operate against the public interest.

This survey is inevitably too short and does therefore not sufficiently give credit to the different other clauses in the Bill which represent interesting modifications in the existing legislation in the field of competition. By way of

preliminary comments the following remarks of a necessarily too cursory nature are made.

It may be recalled that in the paper the exclusion of services from the restrictive trade practices legislation and the exclusion of public monopolies from possible references to the Monopolies Commission represented according to the opinion of the author drawbacks. On these points the proposals when adopted, will bring the British legislation into line with the EEC-rules on competition.

A cautious step in this connection has been taken in relation to patents. Only patent pooling agreements are brought within the ambit of Part 1 of the 1956 Act.

On the other hand no provision has been proposed to change the legal situation, as far as the Act of 1956 is concerned, in relation to exclusive sales agreements. These agreements remain exempted. Perhaps the argument is that no explicit provision will be necessary since the accession of the United Kingdom to the European Communities, gives the policy the European Commission elaborated on this point.

Apart from the proposals already mentioned, to which may be added the proposal to extend the scope of the 1956 Act to recommended resale prices the Bill seems mainly to tend to create a machinery in order to accentuate the position of the consumer. As to the competition policy properly speaking no new changes were proposed e.g. in relation to the criteria to be used either by the Restrictive Practices Court or by the Monopolies Commission when determining the public interest. One is inclined to ask whether the introduction of new legislation would not have provided the opportunity by re-wording these criteria to underline more explicitly a commitment to competition. That also would have made "an important contribution to the fair and open operation of the free market" as Sir Geoffrey Howe, Minister for Trade and Consumer Affairs, said when moving the second reading of the Bill in the House of Commons. (December 13, 1972).

APPENDIX A

Section 21 of the 1956 Act

For the purposes of any proceedings before the Court under the last foregoing section, a restriction accepted in pursuance of any agreement shall be deemed to be contrary to the public interest unless the Court is satisfied of any one or more of the following circumstances, that is to say:

a. that the restriction is reasonably necessary, having regard to the character of the goods to which it applies, to protect the public against injury (whether to persons or to premises) in connection with the consumption, installation or use of those goods;

b. that the removal of the restriction would deny to the public as purchasers, consumers or users of any goods other specific and substantial benefits or advantages enjoyed or likely to be enjoyed by them as such, whether by virtue of the restriction itself or of any arrangements or operations resulting therefrom;

c. that the restriction is reasonably necessary to counteract measures taken by any one person not party to the agreement with a view to preventing or restricting competition in or in relation to the trade or business in which the persons party thereto are engaged;

d. that the restriction is reasonably necessary to enable the persons party to the agreement to negotiate fair terms for the supply of goods to, or the acquisition of goods from, any one person not party thereto who controls a preponderant part of the trade or business of acquiring or supplying such goods, or for the supply of goods to any person not party to the agreement and not carrying on such a trade or business who either alone or in combination with any other such person, controls a preponderant part of the market for such goods;

e. that, having regard to the conditions actually obtaining or reasonably foreseen at the time of the application, the removal of the restriction would be likely to have a serious and persistant adverse effect on the general level of unemployment in an area, or in areas taken together, in which a substantial proportion of the trade or industry to which the agreement relates is situated;

f. that, having regard to the conditions actually obtaining or reasonably foreseen at the time of the application, the removal of the restriction would be likely to cause a reduction in the volume or earnings of the export business which is substantial either in relation to the whole export business of the United Kingdom or in relation to the whole business (including export business) of the said trade or industry; or

g. that the restriction is reasonably required for purposes connected with the maintenance of any other restriction accepted by the parties, whether under

the same agreement or under any other agreement between them, being a restriction which is found by the Court not to be contrary to the public interest upon grounds other than those specified in this paragraph, or has been so found in previous proceedings before the Court;

h. that the restriction does not directly or indirectly restrict or discourage competition to any material degree in any relevant trade or industry and is not likely to do so (as added by section 10 of the 1968 Act);

and is further satisfied (in any such case) that the restriction is not unreasonable having regard to the balance between those circumstances and any detriment to the public or to persons not parties to the agreement (being purchasers, consumers or users of goods produced or sold by such parties, or persons engaged or seeking to become engaged in the trade or business of selling such goods or of producing or selling similar goods) resulting or likely to result from the operation of the restriction.

APPENDIX B

The Monopolies and Restrictive Practices (Inquiry and Control) Act 1948

Section 14. The public interest

In determining whether any conditions to which this Act applies or any things which are done by the parties concerned as a result of, or for the purpose of preserving, any conditions to which this Act applies, operate or may be expected to operate against the public interest, all matters which appear in the particular circumstances to be relevant shall be taken into account and, among other things, regard shall be had to the need, consistently with the general position of the United Kingdom, to achieve:

a. the production, treatment and distribution by the most efficient and economical means of goods of such types and qualities, in such volume and at such prices as will best meet the requirements of home and overseas markets;

b. the organization of industry and trade in such a way that their efficiency is progressively increased and new enterprise is encouraged;

c. the fullest use and best distribution of men, materials and industrial capacity in the United Kingdom; and

d. the development of technical improvements and the expansion of existing markets and the opening up of new markets.

APPENDIX C

Article 85

1. The following shall be deemed to be inconsistent with the common market and shall be prohibited, namely: all agreements between firms, all decisions by associations of firms and all concerted practices likely to affect trade between member-States and which have the object or effect of preventing, restraining or distorting competition within the common market, and in particular those which:

a. directly or indirectly fix buying or selling prices or other trading terms;

b. limit or control production, markets, technical development or investment;

c. effect the sharing of markets or sources of supply;

d. apply to trade partners unequal conditions in respect of equivalent transactions, thereby placing them at a competitive disadvantage;

e. make the conclusion of a contract subject to the acceptance by trade partners of additional goods or services which are not by their nature or by the custom of the trade related to the subject matter of such contract.

2. Any agreements or decisions prohibited by this Article shall be automatically null and void.

3. The provisions of clause 1 may nevertheless be declared inapplicable

- to any agreement or category of agreements between firms
- to any decision or category of decisions of associations of firms or
- to any concerted practice or category of concerted practices

which contributes to improving the production or distribution of goods or to promoting technical or economic progress while reserving to users a fair share in the profit which results, without

a. imposing upon the firms concerned any restriction which is not essential for the attainment of these objects, or

b. giving such firms the power to eliminate competition in respect of a substantial part of the products in question.

Article 86

It shall be inconsistent with the common market and prohibited so far as the trade between member-States may be thereby affected for one or more firms to abuse a dominant position in the common market or any substantial part thereof.

The following practices shall in particular be deemed to be an abuse:

a. the direct or indirect imposition of buying or selling prices or other unfair trading terms;

b. the limitation of production, markets or technical development to the prejudice of consumers;

c. the application to trade partners of unequal conditions in respect of equivalent transactions, thereby placing them at a competitive disadavantage;

d. subjecting the conclusion of a contract to the acceptance by trade partners of additional goods or services which are not by their nature or by the custom of the trade related to the subject matter of such contract.

Chapter 2

EXCLUSIVE AGENCY, RESALE PRICE MAINTENANCE AND SELECTIVE SELLING

by *Prof. Mr. W. L. Snijders*

I. *Introduction*

1. *Cartels and other restrictive agreements*

Among the several types of private agreements and arrangements, in which clauses are figuring, that are restrictive of competition in some or other way, the cartel is the most characteristic phenomenon, albeit not the one occurring most frequently.

Cartels may be defined as agreements and arrangements, that solely or mainly restrict competition between the parties to the agreement or arrangements (or between these parties and third parties) and thus are aiming at influencing the conditions under which transactions are concluded in the market concerned, to the benefit of the partners to the agreement or arrangement.

An effective cartellization is only feasible, if the big majority of enterprises of any importance on the market concerned are prepared to act in conformity to the cartel agreement, although they must not necessarily be partners to the agreement in a formal sense. For practical purposes this means, that cartels constitute collectivities of firms, the size of which bears a relationship to the number of firms in the market concerned. Furthermore, cartels inasfar as they are functioning effectively, necessarily embody an important degree of market dominance with regard to the object of the cartel agreement, f.i. prices, conditions, output, sales, choice of distribution outlets etc. The aforementioned definition implies, that restriction of competition is the sole or at least the main content of a cartel agreement and is aimed at for its own sake; that is to say the benefits which the partners to the cartel hope to derive from its operation, are a direct consequence of the restriction of competition.

It may be, however, that a number of enterprises sets out to undertake certain economic activities (e.g. buying, selling, production) on a joint basis (either one they previously exercized individually, or a new one) and in connection therewith agrees to accept certain limitations to their individual freedom of business behaviour. Such limitation may for instance be required

to ensure, that the costs of the technical-organisational apparatus, that is necessary for the joint activity, will be adequately covered and more generally to ensure that each participant, while taking part in the benefits from the join activity, bears his fair share in the financial or other burdens, accompanying that activity. In such a case, the restrictions agreed upon are of an accessory and at the same time instrumental nature with regard to the joint activity, which in itself is not restrictive of competition.

In such cases, the cooperating enterprises will constitute a collectivity as well as the enterprises parties to a cartel agreement, but the size of that collectivity will be determined by the requirements of a sufficient plan for the joint activity, rather than by the extent of the market concerned. Nonetheless there are also cases where the cooperating firms, rather than to compete with others on the basis of financial-economic advantages, acquired by their joint activity, seek for domination of the market concerned, e.g. by the device of a central selling agency. In such a case, their cooperation must be deemed to be of the nature of a cartel. It may also happen that a joint activity, that originally was competitive, by international growth or by merger with other units acquires a dominant position on the market.

Hitherto we have seen that clauses, which are restrictive of competition, may occur in the framework of cartels (restrictions which are collective and non-accessory) and in the framework of joint economic activities (restrictions which are collective but, except in certain borderline cases, accessory and instrumental to those joint activities). However, contractual clauses which restrict in some or other way the freedom to compete, also occur in the framework of transactions or commercial relationships between small numbers of (in most cases only two) enterprises. In this connection, one may think of restrictive clauses in labour contracts or going along with the transfer of a business, in licensing contracts concerning patents, trademarks or know-how, in contracts between public houses and breweries, in which the public houses against a loan received from the brewery undertake to sell only beer supplied by that brewery, in exclusive agency[1] contracts, by way of tie-in clauses and by way of resale price maintenance.

Inasfar as such restrictive clauses occur in connection with some relationship, which in itself is not restrictive of competition, those restrictions are accessory and they may also have an instrumental function in connection with the main content of those relationships. In bilateral relationships, as those mentioned above, to attain an equilibrium of benefits and burdens that is satisfactory to both parties, or to reduce certain risks to acceptable proportions, it may be useful and even necessary to add certain restrictions of the economic freedom of one or both parties to the positive obligations,

1. For the purposes of this paper the word "agent" is taken to mean "independent distributor".

which they undertake towards each other. For instance, an employer may be exposed to unacceptable risks, if his employee, having in his job acquired a special knowledge of confidential matters in the enterprise concerned, would be entirely free after termination of the labour contract, to enter into the service of a competitor of his former employer or to start himself a business firm in the same branch. The buyer of a trade business may only be sure to get everything which he has been paying for, if the former owner undertakes to refrain from engaging himself into similar economic activities in the area of operation of the transferred enterprise. For comparable reasons, an instrumental character may be ascribed to the claim that is inherent in the position of an exclusive agent, that he be the only one in the area assigned to him to whom the other party may make direct deliveries: economically speaking, he could not fulfill the special obligations of exclusive agents as sales promotion, keeping stocks, providing service to clients, if his exclusive position would not ensure that the benefits of any sales in the area concerned will accrue to him, thus enabling him to recoup the outlays caused by the fulfilment of those obligations.

Other restrictions of an accessory nature in bilateral contracts may as well have an instrumental character in the aforementioned sense, thus the obligation of the public house owner to buy beer only from the brewery that has granted him a loan and the obligation of a retailer to observe resale prices fixed by his supplier, as the fixing of resale prices may be an instrument for the producer or the importer to effectuate a sales policy vis à vis the consumer, with whom he may not enter in a direct commercial relationship. The so-called competition clause in exclusive agency contracts, by which the exclusive agent accepts restrictions with regard to his freedom to deal in goods from other suppliers than his partner in such contract, may also have an instrumental character: the supplier, who by leaving the sales activities with his goods to the exclusive agent makes himself dependent on the latter, may feel the need for stronger guarantees of that agent devoting himself sufficiently the sale of his goods than may be obtained by imposing positive obligations on the latter. However, one should also be aware of the possibility, especially if the contract concerns goods for which an established demand already exists, that it is just the attractiveness of the exclusive agency that enables the supplier to get a competition clause inserted in the contract.

Also in other cases–for instance with regard to restrictive clauses in licensing agreements–a case to case approach to a certain relationship, should be deemed instrumental to the proper functioning of that relationship and in certain accessory restrictions, such an intrumental character will only seldom be found; thus so-called tie-in clauses will in most cases only be deemed to be the consequence of a strong market position of the supplier concerned.

Although the presence or absence of an instrumental character to restrictions, which are accessory to bilateral economic relationship, is surely relevant

to the appreciation of such restrictions, other aspects should also be taken into consideration when such restrictions are being assessed from a point of view of social economic policy in general and, more specifically, from a point of view of competition policy.

First of all the circumstance, that certain restrictions have from their nature an instrumental character with regard to the relationships to which they are accessory, does not mean that the degree or the extent of such restrictions will always be proportional to the interest determining their instrumental character. Thus a competition clause in a labour contract may excessively restrict the freedom of the employee to change over to an other employer or to establish himself a business in the branch of his former employer and the duration of the obligation of a public house owner only to buy beer from the brewery that has granted him a loan may be out of proportion to the duration of the loan.[1a]

Furthermore, when accessory restrictions as mentioned before are generally permissible, it may occur that such restrictions are introduced into specific contracts because they are customary, without parties asking themselves, if these restrictions are really necessary which regard to their specific relationship. It is also feasible that an interaction between restrictions takes place; one party is easily inclined to accept a certain restriction on behalf of the other party, as he finds the other party prepared to accept a restriction on his own behalf. With regard to such situations it is important from a point of view of competition policy that restrictive clauses in bilateral contracts sometimes rather affect the position of third parties in an unfavourable sense than that of the contracting parties themselves. Such a situation may for instance present itself in connection with competition clauses in exclusive agency contracts on behalf of suppliers, which may foreclose the access of other suppliers to the market concerned.

The position of competing traders and buyers of the goods concerned may be unfavourably affected exclusive agency contracts affording a far reaching protection to the exclusive agent in the area assigned to him. This example may also serve to illustrate another aspect that may present itself with regard to contracts, that in a formal sense are concluded between only two parties: when a series of such contracts is concluded between one entrepreneur (e.g. a producer) with a number of other parties (e.g. traders) who are each other's competitors, the aggregate effect of those parallel contracts may come near to that of a horizontal cartel agreement between the several traders, who have each concluded a bilateral contract with the supplier of the goods concerned. This aspect of a series of bilateral contracts is found in resale price

1a. The part of the Dutch Civil Code that is devoted to labour contracts holds a provision, enabling the courts to mitigate restrictions, imposed on employees. Excessive restrictions in beer delivery contracts are subject to control by the courts under the doctrine of undue influence.

maintenance in the first place and it is also found in connection with exclusive agency and with licensing agreements; especially with regard to resale price maintenance that aspect is particularly striking; one may even say that that aspect is an essential feature of resale price maintenance. If a supplier wants to apply resale price maintenance he must necessarily impose the same resale prices on all distributors who sell to the same category of buyers. It may be mentioned in this connection, that the close economic relationship, that exists between obligations to observe a certain resale price, imposed in individual contracts with several traders by the same supplier, is in some countries (in Germany for instance) recognized in civil jurisdiction as far the enforcement of resale price maintenance-contracts is concerned: the supplier may only enforce the resale price maintenance with regard to individual traders, who have undertaken to adhere to the fixed prices, if he takes adequate measures to ensure that this resale price maintenance is generally observed.

One may say that, even if with regard to a resale price maintenance contractual relationships only exist between the supplier who practises resale price maintenance and the distributors concerned–in other words, even if the resale price maintenance is from a legal point of view purely individual–from an economic point of view still the collective-horizontal aspect of the resale price maintenance is more important than its bilateral-vertical aspect. This situation has also other consequences: resale price maintenance is from the legal point of view an obligation, incumbent on the distributor on behalf of the supplier; nevertheless, in certain circumstances, especially if competitors of the supplier concerned apply resale price maintenance, the freedom of decision of that supplier with regard to application and enforcement of resale price maintenance–and with regard to the determination of the trade margin, resulting from the resale prices in connection with his own selling prices–will be only a limited one.

2. *Methods of regulation of cartels and other restrictive agreements*

If one takes the view, that cartels are detrimental to competition to such an extent, that they should be subject to a prohibition without possibility of exemption–the point of view prevailing in the U.S.A–it is quite evident that such a solution cannot generally[2] be applied with regard to accessory restrictive clauses in bilateral contracts. The reason for this is, that accessory restrictions in bilateral relationships as mentioned before cannot be prohibited generally, without possibilities for exemption; such a prohibition

2. It may be applied with regard to specific restrictions e.g. tie-in clauses and resale price maintenance.

would, in view of the importance of such relationships, severely impair the functioning of economic life.

If on the other hand–more in line with views prevailing in Western Europe–cartels are made subject to a more or less stringent supervision, but not to a per se prohibition, the problem may arise, if it is possible and recommendable to make cartels on the one hand and the aforementioned bilateral relationships on the other hand subject to mainly the same substantial and procedural rules of restrictive practices law.

With regard to this problem, the following aspects appear to be of some importance.

Cartels may be suitably assessed in individual cases on the basis of criteria for granting exemptions from a general prohibition or for taking action in the framework of a system of abuse supervision. The reasons for this are the following. Cartels do not occur in very great numbers, they are individually of some importance and they are relatively durable and stable phenomena. Furthermore, decisions on cartel agreements, even if they cause such agreements to be eliminated or thoroughly modified, do not necessarily affect the economic activities, which are regulated by the cartel. On the other hand, in as far as economic activities may be affected by taking action against a cartel agreement concerning such activities, the effect on those activities may be foreseen and thus be taken into account in deciding on the cartel.

The aspects, mentioned in the preceding alinea, are rather different with regard to restrictive clauses figuring in bilateral contracts. Such restrictions of competition occur very frequently and in most cases they are individually of little importance. This has the consequence, that neither criteria for exemption from prohibitions, nor guidelines for an abuse control may be applied convincingly, as the microcharacter of the individual case will make as well the eventual damage to competition, caused by the restriction, as on the other hand the eventual positive aspects of the restriction hardly discernible. Furthermore, deciding on numerous cases which are individually of small importance will easily cause a disproportional administrative encumbrance for the governmental agency that has to handle the cases, as well as for the enterprises that are concerned with them. Finally, the existence and the application of a legal regime, that subjects restrictions in bilateral contracts in general to a somewhat stringent system of control, may have impredictable consequences with regard to the transactions and relationships in which such restrictions are figuring.

Thus with regard to a system of regulation of restrictions of competition, embodied in bilateral contracts as mentioned before, a smaller number of options is practically available than with regard to cartels. Especially systems of control, that would require that in individual cases the nature and extent of restrictions of competition be appreciated with regard to their necessity for realizing the aims of the contract as a whole and be weighed against the

positive aspects of the contract as a whole, are hardly practicable.

The remaining options comprise firstly control systems, based upon the abuse principle. However, in view of the limitations to which a system of abuse control is anyhow subject, such a control with regard to bilateral contracts only makes sense in cases, that do not show the micro-character, that is in most cases inherent to bilateral contracts as such. Thus an abuse control may only have any practical effect, firstly in cases where restrictions in individual contracts show the consequences of a dominant position of one of the contracting parties or, eventually of both of them and secondly in cases, where the aggregate effect of a set of connected bilateral contracts comes near to that of a cartel agreement.

Finally, there is the option of regulating restrictions in bilateral contracts by means of prescriptions of a general nature. However, such prescriptions must have a selective character, that is to say, they should only forbid specific types of accessory restrictions, or certain modalities of such restrictions, in order not to impair too much the possibility of applying restrictions which have an instrumental function.

Thus a general prohibition of resale price maintenance will not cause essential difficulties for a suitable build-up of relationships between suppliers and traders: as far as the instrumental function is concerned which resale price maintenance may have in connection with the circumstance that the supplier addresses himself directly to the consumer, other devices may in general function as adequate substitutes, e.g. advices concerning the resale prices, and requirements concerning the non-price aspects of the behaviour of distributors. On the other hand, exclusive agency clauses in bilateral contracts can hardly be subjected to a general prohibition, as such a prohibition would amount to abolish the exclusive agency, being a widely used means of organizing the sales of suppliers who want to refrain from direct activities in the distribution field, while securing the promotional activities of independent traders with regard to the marketing of their products. It was mentioned already, that even a general prohibition of exclusive agency clauses with the possibility of individual exemptions is hardly practicable. However, certain sub-types of such clauses may without excessive inconvenience be subjected to a general prohibition, e.g. the aggravated type of exclusivity, which in the E.E.C. is called "absolute territorial protection" of exclusive agencies, may be subjected to a prohibition, from which exemptions are not granted at all or only in very exceptional cases.

3. *Regulation of exclusive agency and resale price maintenance in some countries of Western Europe*

In the Netherlands the notion of "regulation of competition" as defined in Article 1 of the Economic Competition Act, covers any contract or private

arrangement (cartels and other agreements and arrangements) in as far as they are binding in law, which comprise any clause which restricts the freedom of competition. Thus exclusive agency contracts as well as contracts, pertaining to resale price maintenance, are regulations of competition. Regulations of competition are in principle subjected to compulsory registration, but bilateral exclusive agency contracts, as well as resale price maintenance contracts (in as far as the resale price maintenance is agreed upon between one supplier and one distributor) are exempted from the obligation to register.

Application of the Economic Competition Act (or of the preceding legislation) with regard to bilateral exclusive agency contracts has until now never taken place, nor has it ever been considered.

In April 1964, an Order in Council was issued concerning resale price maintenance. By this Order, which was based on Article 10 of the Economic Competition Act,[3] any collective types of resale price maintenance were declared not legally binding. The main such types are cartel agreements, that either oblige suppliers to apply resale price maintenance or provide for a system of collective enforcement of individual resale price maintenance.

By a supplementary Order of 31 august 1964 individual resale price maintenance in a series of sectors of durable consumer goods, which were characterised by the fact that the system of resale price maintenance was prevailing, was also declared legally non-binding. The goods were: radio and television sets, record-players and tape-recorders, some important electrical household goods (a.o. refrigerators, vacuum cleaners, washing-machines), cars, photographical apparatus, records. Also for parts of those goods resale price maintenance was declared non-binding.

From the Order, declaring collective resale price maintenance non-binding, a number of exemptions have been granted. When the Order on individual resale price maintenance was prepared, the sectors concerning which it was felt that there was some reason not to forbid individual resale price maintenance (e.g. books) were left out beforehand, so it was felt not to be necessary to insert a possibility of exemptions into this Order.

The Order of April 1964, together with the supplementary Order concerning individual resale price maintenance would have expired on June 15, 1969, but shortly before its expiration the Government lodged with the Social-Economic Council a request for advice on a permanent legislation concerning resale price maintenance while the existing Order was provisionally prorogated for a term of 3 years. The advice was rendered in December 1970, a slight majority of the Council recommending a system of abuse control coupled

3. "When it is required to Our opinion by the public interest, may be decided by Order in Council that stipulations in regulations of competition of a nature or tendency indicated by that Order are not legally binding".

with obligatory registration,[4] while the minority recommended a prohibition of resale price maintenance with the possibility of exemptions. No action was taken on the basis of this advice as the new government that appeared on the scene in the summer of 1971 decided to embark upon a radical reform of the Economic Competition Act. A request for advice about such a reform was lodged with the Social-Economic Council in October 1971. As the preparation of such a reform will take a long time, it was envisaged, as an interim measure, to pass legislation concerning as well horizontal regulations on prices (price cartels) as resale price maintenance. An advice of the Council on such legislation is expected towards the beginning of 1973. In connection with the developments mentioned, the Order of 1964 concerning resale prise maintenance has been prorogated for another three years, so that it will now expire June 15, 1974.

In *Belgium* on the basis of the Act of 1960 for protection against abuse of economic power action could be taken against exclusive agency contracts or against resale price maintenance in cases where persons or corporate bodies, that hold a position of economic power, would by such restrictive practices damage the public interest. However no such action has until now taken place.

An Act of 1961 offers protection to exclusive agents in case of termination of their contracts at short notice. Restrictions imposed on public house owners by beer delivery contracts are subject to rules, embodied in a private regulation, entered into by the organisations of the breweries and the public house owners respectively. That regulation has been declared generally binding and has thus acquired the status of a legal prescription under a Royal decree of 1935.

In the *Federal Republic of Germany,* both resale price maintenance and exclusive agency contracts are subject to specific provisions of the Act against restrictions of competition. According to paragraph 16 of the Act, resale price maintenance is only permissible if certain material and formal requirements are met; moreover, resale price maintenance is subject to an abuse supervision. The material requirements are that goods concerned must be products of the publishing trade or branded goods, which are in price competition with similar products of other producers or dealers and whose delivery is guaranteed in an equal or improved quality. As to branded goods there is moreover the formal requirement of notification with the Federal Cartel Office as a precondition for the validity of the resale price maintenance under civil law. The notifications, which next to the resale prices

4. As the Economic Competition Act already holds provisions for obligatory registration and abuse control, one may ask why special provisions concerning resale price maintenance would be necessary. The answer is that the existing substantial and procedural provisions concerning the exercise of abuse control are suitable for control of individual resale price maintenance.

must also comprise particulars like trade margins and supply restrictions, are entered into a register that is open to public inspection.

The abuse supervision over resale price maintenance has been provided for in paragraph 17. This paragraph empowers (and in certain cases obliges) the Federal Cartel Office to take action against a resale price maintenance if the requirements of paragraph 16 are not or no longer fulfilled, if one has taken improper advantage of the resale price maintenance or if it causes undesirable economic effects, especially if the prices of the goods concerned are unduly made to increase or if a lowering of prices is prevented.

The Federal Cartel Office has rather vigorously exploited the above mentioned possibilities to take action against resale price maintenance. It has deemed resale price maintenance to be abusive, if it does not meet the conditions for its enforcement which have been developed in civil jurisprudence, especially the condition of completeness ("*Lückenlosigkeit*"). As will be mentioned in more detail later on, the condition of completeness has led to an interesting interplay between national (civil and restrictive practices) law and EEC-restrictive practices law in connection with the fact that EEC-law does not allow national sales systems to be sealed off against influence from abroad by export and re-import prohibitions.

Other bilateral vertical restrictions, especially exclusive agency contracts and tie-in clauses are dealt with in paragraph 18. Apart from the formal requirement, that they must be in writing, such agreements are only subject to an abuse supervision, that is to say the Federal Cartel Office may take action against such agreements either if they unfairly ("*unbillig*") restrict the access of other enterprises to the market, or if they substantially restrict competition in the market for the same or other products or services. In cases, where only the relationship between the contracting parties is at stake, restrictions may be attached in as far as they would be contrary to general principles of civil law, but no control by the Federal Cartel Office may take place. The powers under paragraph 18 have only in a few cases been used.

There is no uniform opinion in Germany with regard to the question, if paragraph 18 applies to contracts with commercial agents. In the 1964 report of the Federal Cartel Office such applicability was denied, but from the 1967 report it appeared that the Office had changed its mind. In the 1971 report mention is made of a conference of restrictive practices experts, held under the aegis of the Federal Cartel Office, which was devoted to problems concerning a.o. paragraph 18. In this conference, the opinion prevailed that paragraph 18 should be deemed to be applicable to contracts with commercial agents, as such contracts may as well as contracts with independent traders restrict the access of third parties to markets.

In *France* Article 37, sub 4 of the Price Ordinance of June 30, 1945 holds a general prohibition to fix minimum prices or margins with regard to goods and services. Thus the prohibition does not only cover the fixation of resale

prices, while on the other hand it is not forbidden to fix only maximum resale prices. Temporary exemptions may be granted on the grounds, inter alia, of the novelty of goods or services, of exclusive rights under a patent, licence or registered design or of the requirements of a specification which includes a warranty of quality or condition or of an initial publicity campaign.

As far as resale prices are concerned, exemptions were in force at October 1, 1972 with regard to perfumes and electrical household apparatus.

Rather than by the prohibition of cartel agreements which is comprised in Article 59 bis of the afore mentioned Ordinance, the permissibility of exclusive agency contracts is governed by Article 37, 1,a, prohibiting (with several qualifications) refusal to sell and sales at discriminatory prices and conditions. In a ministerial circular of March 31, 1960 (the so-called Fontanet circular) the prohibition was construed to the effect that an exclusive agency contract which makes the grantor of the concession the sole supplier of the grantee and the latter the sole client of the former, in a given area and for a given product, may be involved as reason to refuse deliveries. It may be added that the *Cour de Cassation* with regard to exclusive agency contracts adopted a position, that is essentially in line with the view expressed in the aforementioned circular.[5]

According to French jurisprudence an exclusive agent is entitled to sue for unfair competition (*"concurrence déloyale"*) traders who knowingly encroach upon the exclusive agent's position by selling the goods concerned in the area, assigned to the latter. Thus a legal effect against third parties (*"opposabilité aux tiers"*) is conferred by French law upon an exclusive agency. As we shall see, EEC restrictive practices law, while imposing certain restrictions on the protection of exclusive agents by contractual arrangements, restricts as well the possibility to invoke an exclusive agency against third parties.

In *Great Britain*,[5a] under the Resale Prices Act of 1964, contractual conditions and arrangements intended to maintain minimum resale prices are unlawful and unenforceable, but suppliers may recommend minimum resale prices. It is unlawful under the Act for a supplier to withhold goods from a dealer or to offer them on discriminatory terms on the grounds that a dealer has not been observing minimum resale prices. A supplier is, however, allowed to withhold goods from a dealer who has recently been using goods of the same or a similar type as "loss-leaders". Exemption may be granted by the Restrictive Practices Court for any class of goods, if it appears that in default of resale price maintenance the quality of the goods, or the number of retail

5. Decisions of July 11, 1962 and October 22, 1964, *Recueil Dalloz* 1962-497, 1963-206, 1964-753, 1966-114.

5a. Cf. the contribution of Ham, *supra*, 1-51.

outlets would be reduced, or the prices would be increased, or necessary services would no longer be provided to the detriment of the public, or if the goods would be sold under conditions causing danger to health or misuse. Exemptions have only been granted for books and for medicaments.

Section 8,3 of the Restrictive Trade Practices Act of 1956 causes exclusive agency contracts not to be subject to the obligatory registration and to the pursuant investigation by the Restrictive Practices Court. Thus exclusive agency contracts are exempted from the legislation on restrictive practices of the nature of "cartels". However, in far as such contracts are practised by "monopolies", they may be subject to control under section 10 of the Monopolies and Restrictive Practices (Inquiry and Control) Act 1948 and section 3 of the Monopolies and Mergers Act 1965. In some cases, which have been investigated by the Monopolies Commission, it has made recommendations concerning such agreements.[6]

II. *Exclusive agency, resale price maintenance under the EEC-rules on competition*

1. *Exclusive agency contracts*

Neither the prohibition, which is comprised in Article 85(1) of the EEC-Treaty, nor the conditions for exemption from that prohibition, mentioned in Article 85(3), make any distinction between different types of agreements and arrangements, that hold elements which are restrictive of competition. Thus it appears–and it has been confirmed with regard to exclusive agency contracts by the Court of Justice of the European Communities–that bilateral agreements, comprising restrictive clauses next to elements which are not restrictive of competition, may as well as cartels come under that provision.

Bilateral exclusive agency contracts as well as agreements, embodying resale price maintenance, appeared for the first time in an official document concerning the competition provisions of the EEC-Treaty in October 1960. At that time in the EEC-Commission submitted to the Council of Ministers a proposal for a First Regulation, to be based on Article 87, implementing Articles 85 and 86 of the Treaty.

In Article 5 of that proposed regulation, agreements which would exist on the moment of the regulation coming into force, were made subject to a compulsory notification; however, bilateral exclusive agency contracts as well

6. Report on supply of wallpaper, 1969, London HMSO Cmnd No 59 Report on the Supply of Petrol to Retailers in the United Kingdom, 1965, London HMSO, Cmnd No. 264.

as agreements embodying resale price maintenance would be exempted from the obligation to notify.[7] In the explanatory memorandum accompanying the proposal, the exemptions were motivated by the incalculable number of the agreements concerned. However it also appeared from that memorandum, as well as from Article 18, which provided for a review of the proposed exemptions, that these were not considered by the Commission as definitive.

In the definitive version of the Regulation, as it was adopted by the Council, with regard to resale price maintenance the exemption from compulsory notification was maintained, but with regard to exclusive agency contracts, concluded between residents of two different member States, the exemption was dropped under French and German pressure.[8]

Rather soon, this decision appeared to entail far-reaching administrative consequences, in view of the number of exclusive agency contracts, that first of all would have to be notified and afterwards would have to be decided on by the Commission. The term for notification of agreements in existence on the day on which Regulation No. 17 came into force,[9] which originally was generally fixed on November 1, 1962, was with regard to bilateral contracts postponed till February 1, 1963. The Commission tried to utilize the delay thus created by furthering measures to stem the flood of expected notifications. Thus a proposal was published of a decision to apply Article 85(3) for a group of exclusive agency contracts, which was defined with the help of abstract criteria. A similar decision was envisaged with regard to restrictive clauses in patent licensing agreements. Moreover the Commission announced its intention to issue publications to the effect that exclusive agency contracts with commercial agents (not being independent traders) and certain clauses in patent licensing agreements do not come under the prohibition of Article 85 (1) and thus would not need to be notified under Regulation No. 17.[10]

7. It should be noted, that in the original proposal of the Commission the compulsory notification and the requirements of seeking application of art. 85(3) were distinguished, while the two were melded together in the definitive version, that became Regulation No. 17. According to the original proposal, the exemption from notification left intact the requirement of application for exemption on the basis of Art. 85(3), but the delay for making such application was rather longer (3 years) than with regard to those agreements, that were subject to notification. Practically this meant that agreements, exempted from notification, would at least for a number of years have the benefit of the provisional validity, which was provided for in the original proposal, except in cases where the Commission would take an early decision on its own initiative.

8. The French government feared that an exemption would, in connection with the territorial applicability of the prohibition in France of refusal to sell (see *supra*, 62) favour foreign suppliers and encourage the transfer of sales activities from France to other countries. The attitude of the German government seems to have been inspired by a preoccupation at that time of the Federal Cartel Office with vertical restrictions.

9. March 13, 1962. O.J. 204/62.

10. The announcements, mentioned here, of decisions and publications, appeared in 2627-29/62.

These attempts to reduce the number of contracts, notifications of which would be necessary, met with only very partial success. Especially the proposed exemptions concerning categories of contracts did not succeed, as several objections were voiced against these projects, apart from objections against their content, they were criticized, especially from the side of the member-States, as being premature as well as lacking a suitable legal basis, Regulation No. 17 being only devised for individual decisions on the application of Article 85(3).

Eventually, the Commission dropped the proposals concerning application of Article 85(3) for categories of contracts. Instead, as far as exclusive agency contracts were concerned, a simplified system of notification was introduced for roughly speaking those contracts, for which the Commission previously contemplated a category-exemption. The Commission issued furthermore revised versions of the previously announced publications to the effect that exclusive agency contracts with commercial agents and certain clauses in patent licensing agreements do not come under the prohibition of Article 85 (1). The Commission's view on such contracts rested on the ancillary nature of the function of commercial agents, from which it was deduced that restrictive clauses concerning their activities could not be deemed to impair competition in the sense of Article 85(1). It was stated however, that that view was valid only under the assumption that the commercial agent would not fulfil functions, which are characteristic of independent traders, such as keeping stocks of any size, being responsible for providing customers with service, or fixing himself prices or other conditions.

Shortly before February 1, 1963 a great numer of notifications of bilateral agreements took place, that is to say about 32000 concerning exclusive agency contracts (of which 12000 by means of the simplified notification system, introduced in December 1962) and about 4000 concerning licensing agreements.[11] Thus the Commission was finally confronted with the "mass problem", which had been impending from the moment of promulgation of Regulation No. 17, and which the Commission had in vain sought to avert by its proposal to apply Article 85(3) for exclusive agency contracts as a category. For the time being, attempts to solve the mass problem were postponed. In February 1964 the Commission submitted to the Council a proposal for a regulation, empowering the Commission to apply Article 85(3) with regard to categories of agreements of whatever type. As the Council declined such a widely framed power, the proposed habilitation was restricted to the two types of agreements, the notification of which had brought about the "mass problem", namely exclusive agency contracts and licensing agreements. Having thus been modified, and having undergone other alterations,

11. cf. Wertheimer, *infra*, 176-178.

the proposal was adopted and was published in March 1965 as Regulation No. 19/65.[12] By this regulation the Commission was empowered to apply by way of executive regulation Article 85(3) with regard to categories of agreements of the type mentioned. Of course the categories to be exempted should be defined in such a way that the fulfilment of the conditions of Article 85(3) would be guaranteed. Furthermore it was indicated in the motivation of Regulation No. 19/65, that the Commission should only exercize its powers after sufficient experience would have been gained in the light of individual decisions.

In the meantime, the Commission had in September 1964 taken a decision in the case of the exclusive agency contract between Grundig and its French exclusive agent Consten.[13] This contract held in connection with other contractual relationships an absolute territorial protection of Consten's exclusive agency, as Grundig forbade German traders and exclusive agents in other countries to export Grundig products to France. Moreover, a connected agreement enabled Consten to use the Gint trademark to prevent undesired imports in France.

The Commission decided that the exclusive dealing contract and its annex concerning the Gint trademark infringed Article 85(1) and refused application of Article 85(3). This refusal was essentially based on the absolute territorial protection: the Commission reasoned concerning the second condition of art. 85(3) that the absolute territorial protection stood in the way of an adequate participation of French consumers in the eventual improvements, caused by the contract,[14] as the sealing off of the French market prevented an adaptation of prices in France to lower prices abroad. Concerning the third condition of Article 85(3) the Commission said, that the absolute territorial protection could not be deemed indispensable for eventual improvements of the distribution, as these could as well be realized on the basis of an exclusive agency without absolute territorial protection.

Grundig and Consten, as well as the German and the Italian government, appealed from the decision with the Court of Justice and the suit lasted until the middle of 1966. In the meantime, the Commission applied Article 85(3) in favour of four exclusive agency contracts[15] without absolute territorial protection, concluded between suppliers and dealers in different member-States. Thereby the Commission paved the way for the future application of Article 85(3) for exclusive agency contracts as a category; it was mentioned already, that the Council when it adopted Regulation No. 19/65, had vented

12. O.J. 533/65 cf. Wertheimer, *infra,* 168-169.

13. Decision of September 23, 1964 O.J. 2545/64; [1964] CMLR 489 *et seq*. cf. Wertheimer, *infra*, 204-208.

14. No decision was taken about the presence or absence of such improvements.

15. DRU-Blondel, O.J. 2149/65, Hummel Isbecque, O.J. 2581/65, Jallatte-Voss and Jallatte-Vandeputte, O.J. 37/66.

the requirement of such decisions as a precondition for the application of Article 85(3) on behalf of a category of contracts. In the present decisions, the Commission said that the exclusive agency restricted competition in the sense of art. 85(1), because the contracts concerned articles of an individualized character (appearing from the use of trademarks), for which consumers' preferences exist; thus the contracts were deemed not only to affect the position of the contracting parties, but also to affect perceptibly the position of third parties. One of the contracts [16] also held an exclusive agency clause on behalf of the supplier; it was said, that this clause restricted the access of competing suppliers to the Belgian market, as the number of traders, in possession of the special technical knowledge, required for the trade concerned, was somewhat restricted. Furthermore, the restrictions in the contracts were deemed to be able to affect trade between the member-States, as they caused that trade to develop under other circumstances than would have prevailed without those contracts.

The fulfilment of the first condition of Article 85(3) was motivated by the improvement of the distribution of the goods concerned, arising from the exclusive agency. With regard to each of the three other conditions, the absence of absolute territorial protection played a role in the reasonings, by which their fulfilment was established.

Viewed in themselves, the decisions mentioned clearly demonstrate, that in cases that are individually of little importance neither the applicability of the prohibition, nor the fulfilment of the conditions for exemption, can be convincingly established. The individualized character of the goods concerned appears to be hardly sufficient for deeming the exclusive agency restrictive of competition, as the decisions indicated the presence, with regard to the goods concerned, of polypolistic circumstances; these may very well go along with lively competition; in fact, it was stated that there was an effective competition with respect to the categories of goods concerned. Furthermore the advantages, that were ascribed to the exclusive agencies to establish the fulfilment of the first condition of Article 85(3), left room for the hypothesis that, without those contracts, the goods concerned would have penetrated to a lesser extent into the national market of the exclusive agent or even would not have appeared on that market at all.

Thus the Commission, in taking individual decisions, aimed at demonstrating that application of Article 85(3) for exclusive agency contracts without absolute territoral protection as a category was defensible, rather overshot the mark: the cases selected were so innocent, that negative clearances would have been appropriate as well or even more.

In the meantime, next to the already mentioned appeal lodged by Grundig and Consten against the Commission's decision of September 1964, two other

16. Jallatte-Vandeputte.

cases concerning exclusive agency contracts had been brought before the Court of Justice. In a lawsuit, in which an exclusive agency contract between a German producer of bulldozers and a French trader, coupled with a sales contract, was at stake, a French Court requested a prejudicial decision on the applicability of Article 85(1) with respect to exclusive agency contracts without absolute territorial protection and with respect to the separability of "composite" contracts with regard to the nullity sanction of Article 85(2).

The Italian Government after the adoption of Regulation No. 19/65 lodged an appeal for annulment of that regulation, which was essentially based on the contention that the Council, in adopting that regulation, had infringed (amongst others) Articles 85-87: according to the Italian Government vertical agreements did not come under Article 85 but eventually, if a dominant position was involved, under Article 86. Furthermore, it was a.o. contended, that the Council should have defined the scope of the prohibition of Article 85(1) before defining the conditions for exemption from that prohibition; it was also contended that by adopting Regulation No. 19/65 the Council had preempted the decision on the applicability of Article 85 with respect to the contracts with which that Regulation is concerned.

The Court of Justice rendered the three decisions almost simultaneously.[17]

The main points of the decisions, as far as relevant to the object-matter of this paper, are the following.

The Court strongly rejected any contentions, that vertical bilateral agreements could not come under Article 85(1). On the other hand, it appeared that the Court was not prepared to deem the granting of an exclusive agency with regard to economically differentiated goods to be restrictive of competition for the sole reason, that the concessionaire obtains a preferential position vis à vis other traders, who cannot compete with him on an equal footing in the area concerned.[18]

17. Judgment of June 30th, 1966, case no. 56/65 (LTM-MBU), *Recueil* XII, 337 *et seq*; [1966] CMLR, 357 *et seq*.
Judgment of July 13th, 1966, cons.cases nos. 56 + 58/64 (Grundig/Consten), *Recueil* XII, 429 *et seq*; [1966] CMLR, 418 *et seq*.
Judgment of July 13th, 1966, case no. 32/65 (Italy-Commission), *Recueil* XII, 563 *et seq*. [1969] CMLR, 39 *et seq*.

18. Cf. the following considerations, devoted to the criterion of restriction of competition in the L.T.M.-M.B.U. decision ([1966] CMLR, 375-376):

"The competition in question should be understood within the actual context in which it would occur in the absence of the agreement in question. In particular, the alteration of the conditions of competition may be thrown in doubt if the said agreement appears precisely necessary for the penetration of an undertaking into an area in which it was not operating. Therefore, to judge whether a contract containing a clause "granting an exclusive right of sale" should be regarded as prohibited by reason of its object or its effect, it is necessary to take into account, in particular, the nature and the quantity,

Thus it seems that the reasoning, followed by the Commission in respect of the criterion of restriction of competition in the aforementioned cases of application of Article 85(3), was (implicitly) deemed to be insufficient.

The fact that the Court annulled the Commission's decision that the Grunding-Consten agreement came under Article 85(1) in as far as the decision was bearing on the agreement as a whole (and not only on the absolute territorial protection), although based on the formal point of lack of motivation, also suggests that the Court is reluctant to admit the applicability of Article 85(1) in respect of "simple" exclusive agency contracts.

With regard to the criterion of being likely to affect trade between member-States, it was mentioned already, that the Commission had employed a formula, according to which any perceptible influence on trade between member-States, arising out of a restriction of competition, would fulfil this criterion. That formula would for instance allow for deeming a purely national minimum price cartel to be likely to affect trade between member-States, if such a cartel would provoke imports from other member-States that would not have occurred without the presence of the cartel.

In the cases L.T.M. vs M.B.U. and Grundig-Consten vs Commission, the Court defined the criterion in such a way that the influence on trade between member-States must be such that the realization of a single market between member-States may be hindered. This formula, that is rather more specific, [19] has subsequently been employed consistently by the Commission in decisions on the applicability of Article 85(1).

In the decision, rendered in the case 32/65 the Court rejected any contentions which had been put forward by the Italian government. It was said, o.a., that the Council could, without infringing upon any provision of the Treaty or upon any principle of law, adopt a regulation, providing for exemptions, on the basis of Article 85(3), for certain categories of agreements, without having defined exhaustively the scope of Article 85(1). Furthermore, the Court pointed out, that the definition of a category of agreements to be exempted eventually and the enumeration of conditions for

---

whether limited or not, of the products which are the object of the agreement, the position and size of the grantor and concessionaire on the market for the products concerned, the isolated nature of the agreement in question or, on the contrary, its position in a series of agreements, the severity of the clauses aiming at protecting the exclusive right or, on the contrary, the possibilities left for other commercial currents upon the same products by means of re-exports and parallel imports".

Pursuant to this decision of the Court of Justice, the French Court (Cour d'Appel de Paris, decision of February 22, 1967) decided that the exclusive agency agreement between L.T.M. and M.B.U. did not come under Art. 85(1).

19. It is true that in the L.T.M.-M.B.U. decision, one also finds a passus that seems rather related to the formula previously employed by the Commission. However, from the subsequent consideration it appears, that that passus is not an exhaustive description of the criterion, but rather indicates some basic requirements for its fulfilment.

such exemption did not preempt the question if any specific contract, coming under such definition—be it in compliance with the conditions for exemption or not—would individually come under the prohibition of Article 85(1).

Article 5 of Regulation No. 19/65 stipulates that before adopting a regulation to apply Article 85(3) in respect of a category of agreements, the Commission shall publish a draft thereof and invite all persons concerned to submit their comments within such time limit, being not less than one month, be fixed by the Commission.

The Advisory Committee on Restrictive Practices and Monopolies, that has been set up under Article 10 of Regulation No. 17, must be consulted by the Commission before a draft regulation is published and, again, before a definitive regulation is adopted.

A draft regulation, devised to apply Article 85(3) for a category of bilateral exclusive agency contracts, was published shortly after the above-mentioned decisions of the Court of Justice had been rendered.[20]

With regard to the content of the draft regulation I confine myself here[21] to one aspect of paramount importance. Article 2 stipulated, that exclusive agency contracts would only have the benefit of the exemption, if six conditions were fulfilled. Some of these conditions amounted to making the validity of agreements dependent on the observance by parties to the agreements of vague rules, the consequences of which in specific cases would be rather unpredictable. For instance, the exclusive agent should not "without valid reasons" exclude groups of buyers from delivery.

Furthermore, there were also conditions, which, apart from comprising vague notions, made the validity of an agreement dependent rather on its economic environment than on the behaviour of the parties concerned. For instance, the goods to which the agreement related should be subject to effective competition from similar goods.

Especially the inclusion in the draft regulation of conditions as mentioned here provoked lively criticisms. It was pointed out that, if such conditions were maintained in the definitive regulation, the consequence would be a lack of legal security, which would force parties to exclusive agency contracts in many cases to demand the requesting of individual exemptions from the prohibition of Article 85(1). Thus the envisaged regulation would not contribute appreciably to solving the "mass problem", that had arisen as a consequence of the big number of individual notifications of exclusive agency contracts.

In article 1 par. 1 of the definitive regulation, that was adopted by the Commission on March 22nd, 1967,[22] the agreements to be exempted were

20. O.J. 2863-66/66; [1966] CMLR, D 9 *et seq.*
21. Some points will be mentioned when Regulation No. 67/67 is being discussed.
22. O.J. 849/67; [1967] CMLR, D 1 *et seq.*; cf. Wertheimer, *infra*, 169-170.

described in essentially the same way as in the draft regulation, that is to say as:

> "agreements to which only two undertakings are parties and:
> *a.* in which one party undertakes, as against the other, to deliver certain products only to the other with a view to their resale within a given part of the territory of the Common Market; or
> *b.* in which one party undertakes, as against the other, to purchase certain products only from the other with a view to their resale; or
> *c.* in which there have been concluded between the two undertakings, with a view to resale, exclusive undertakings of delivery and sale as set out in subsections (a) and (b) above.

In Article 1, paragraph 2, it was stipulated that agreements to which enterprises from one member State only are party and which concern the resale of goods within that member State do not come under the exemption. In the motivation of the regulation, that restricting of its applicability is explained by saying that exclusive agency agreements concluded within a member State do not normally affect trade between the member State, that is to say, do not come under Article 85(1).

The granting of an exclusive agency by a supplier outside the common market to a trader within that market is covered by the regulation.

Among the cases, decided on individually by the Commission and among those that came before the Court of Justice, there was none of the type b, mentioned in Article 1, paragraph 1, sub b. (obligation of a dealer to buy exclusively from a certain supplier, while no corresponding exclusive agency is granted to that dealer). Thus it is somewhat surprising, that restrictions of type b are covered by Regulation No. 67/67. The consequence is that restrictive clauses on behalf of suppliers, occurring in contracts that from an economic point of view are rather different from exclusive agency contracts, may have the benefit of this exemption.[23]

Of the aforementioned six conditions for the applicability of the exemption that had figured in the draft regulation, only two remained in the shape of criteria, that could be invoked before the Courts. In Article 3 of the definitive regulation it was provided, that the exemption does not apply firstly where manufacturers of competing goods entrust each other with exclusive agency in those goods and secondly where the parties to the contract make it difficult for intermediaries or consumers to obtain the goods concerned from other agents in the common market, especially by invoking industrial property rights or other rights (e.g. the aforementioned "*opposabilité aux tiers*" of exclusive agency).[24] These are rules, that make the

23. E.g. exclusive agency clauses in beer delivery contracts.

24. Cf. Judgment of the Court of Justice of November 25th, 1971, case no. 22/71 (Béguelin), *Recueil* XVII, 949-964 at 960-961; [1972] CMLR, 81-99 at 96-97, submissions adv. gen. Dutheillet de Lamotte, *Recueil* XVII, 969-970; [1972] CMLR, 91-92.

validity of the exemption in respect of a given contract only dependent on the behaviour of the contracting parties, while the criteria embodied in those rules are sufficiently determined to allow for reasonable legal security.

From the last mentioned rule it follows, that a supplier, party to exclusive agency contracts in respect of several areas, may not forbid his exclusive agents to sell goods outside their respective areas. This does not mean however, that the supplier may in no way restrict commercial activities of his exclusive agents outside their respective areas; Article 2, paragraph 1, mentions a few restrictive clauses which may be added to the fundamental restrictions, mentioned in Article 1, without invalidating the exemption. One of those additional restrictive clauses is the obligation for the exclusive agent to refrain from activities which may be summarized as actively promoting sales outside the territory assigned to him.

As the six conditions, mentioned in Article 2 of the draft regulation, were designed for ensuring that the agreements, which came under the exemption, would normally fulfil the conditions of Article 85(3), it was impossible simply to strike out most of them. In fact, next to those which were maintained, three others reappeared in another legal shape. Article 7 of Regulation No. 19/65 empowers the Commission, where it finds that in a particular case an agreement exempted under an executive regulation has effects which are incompatible with the conditions of Article 85(3), to withdraw the benefit of the executive regulation and instead issue a decision in accordance with Articles 6 and 8 Regulation No. 17. This means that the Commission may impose on parties with the agreement concerned specific obligations and conditions, which they should comply with in order to retain the benefit of being exempted from the prohibition of Article 85(1).

In Article 6 of Regulation No. 67/67, three types of cases, corresponding to conditions which were figuring in Article 2 of the draft regulation, were deemed to warrant application of Article 7 of Regulation No. 19/65. Those cases come down to, roughly speaking:

a. lack of competition in respect of the goods concerned;

b. barring the access of other suppliers to the market concerned;

c. abuse of the exemption by refusal to sell to categories of purchasers, or by selling at excessive prices.

Thus what were in the draft regulation conditions for the applicability of the exemption were transformed into criteria for exercizing the control of the fulfilment in specific cases of the conditions of Article 85(3), which has been provided for in Article 7 of Regulation No. 19/65.

For the sake of completeness it may be mentioned, that the retroactive effect, which in pursuance to Article 6 of Regulation No. 17 may be given to decisions for application of art. 85(3) and the possibility of "covering the bad past" of an agreement, provided for in Article 7 of that regulation, have inspired the makers of Regulation No. 19/65 to include analogous provisions

in this Regulation.[25] These provisions are in turn reflected in Articles 3 and 4 of Regulation No. 67/67. As the provisions mentioned here have until now not appeared to have an appreciable practical importance, no attention will be paid to their content.

Regulation No. 67/67 has proved to be an effective instrument to solve the mass problem that had arisen as a consequence of the large number of notifications of exclusive agency contracts, that had been effected in 1963. From the general reports, that were published after the promulgation of that regulation, a steady decline of the number of files concerning such contracts becomes apparent, as an increasing number of them was adapted to the requirement of Regulation No. 67/67. In paragraph 48 of the first report on competition policy[26] that was published in April 1972, it was mentioned that the original number of about 30.000 files concerning notified exclusive agency contracts, 4500 of which contained export prohibitions, had been reduced to 1500. Among the enterprises, who feel as yet unable to give up export prohibitions, figuring in their exclusive agency contracts, are importers of motorcars and producers of perfume. Recalling a statement to the same effect, which was made in the first general report on the activities of the Communities (1967),[27] the Commission says in paragraph 50 that a temporary authorization of absolute territorial protection may be considered in favour of exclusive agency contracts, by which a new producer should enter into a market. The Commission also says, that this opinion is in conformity with the feeling, expressed by the Economic Committee of the European Parliament. However, it appears from the document concerned[28] that the Economic Committee felt that absolute territorial protection might be justified as well in other cases (complicated products, small producers) than the one, mentioned by the Commission.

Until now, no exemptions have been granted or envisaged in cases, where this might be possible according to the opinion of the Commission, while on the other hand the Commission has recently taken steps to eliminate absolute territorial protection from exclusive agency contracts in the motor trade.[29]

A rather familiar restriction, figuring in exclusive agency contracts, is the obligation imposed on the agent, to pay a certain fee or commission to another exclusive agent, in case of sales effected by the first agent in the area,

25. Arts. 3 and 4 respectively.

26. Pursuant to a request, expressed by the European Parliament in a resolution of June 7th, 1971, the Commission has undertaken to publish annually a report, that is specifically devoted to the competition policy.

27. In point 44.

28. European Parliament doc. 197, 1969/1970, par. 38.

29. In 18 A.W.D. 1972, 419-421 the content of a letter is published in which the Commission takes objection against export prohibitions in exclusive agency contracts concerning the sale of Citroen Cars.

assigned to the latter. Dependently on the amount of the fee in connection with the circumstances of the case, its effect may vary from only slightly discouraging sales outside an assigned area to completely preventing such sales, but even if their effect is only slight, the imposition of such fees appears not to be covered by Article 2, 1, b of Regulation No. 67/67.

The Commission has never made mention of this type of restriction, but it seems rather probable, that it occurred with some frequence in the exclusive agency contracts that were notified in 1963 and afterwards. It would be interesting to learn, to what extent such restrictions are figuring in the 1500 cases mentioned in the 1972 report, that are still waiting for individual decisions. And, of course, it will also be interesting to learn the view, that will eventually be adopted by the Commission in respect of such restrictions.

Until now, the Commission has not in any case, either on the grounds, mentioned in Article 6 of Regulation No. 67/67, or on any other ground, used its power under Article 7 of Regulation No. 19/65 to withdraw the benefit of exemption under the Regulation No. 67/67.

The latter would in its original version have expired by December 31st,1972, but recently its validity was extended until December 31st,1982, without any alteration of its contents. [30]

After the publication of Regulation No. 67/67 some prejudicial decisions have been rendered by the Court of Justice, in which the Court has more clearly defined the position of exclusive agency contracts under Article 85 and the regulations for the implementation of that provision.

In a judgement of July 9, 1969 [31] the Court said that even an exclusive agency contract comprising an export prohibition may because on the weak position of interested parties on the market of the products concerned escape the prohibition of Article 85(1).

This view was confirmed in a judgement of May 6th, 1971. [32]

In a judgement of June 30th, 1970 [33] the Court said that, if a standard exclusive agency contract has come into existence before Regulation No. 17 came into force and has been duly notified, the ensuring provisional validity [34] holds good as well in respect of contracts which have been concluded afterwards but which are identical with the standard agreement. The Court also said, that exclusive agency contracts, that are specimens of a group of parallel contracts with several agents, should nevertheless be considered as contracts to which two enterprises only are parties. The latter view, although

30. Reg. No. 2591/72, O.J. 1972, No. L 276/15.

31. Case 5/69 (Volk-Vervaecke), *Recueil* XV, 295 *et seq*; [1969] CMLR, 273 *et seq*.

32. Case 1/71 (Cadillon-Höss), *Recueil* XVII, 351 *et seq*; [1971] CMLR 420 *et seq*.

33. Case 1/70 (Rochas-Bitsch), *Recueil* XVI, 515 *et seq*; [1971] CMLR, 104 *et seq*.

34. which has been proclaimed in the judgment of April 6, 1962, Case 13/61 (Bosch), *Recueil*, XIII, 89-111; [1962] CMLR, 1 *et seq*; cf. the contribution of van der Wielen, *infra*, 140-159.

rendered in respect of Article 5 of Regulation No. 17, should be deemed to hold good as well in respect of Regulations Nos. 19/65 and 67/67, which are applicable only to contracts to which two enterprises only are parties.

Finally in a judgement of 25th November 1971 [35] the Court said, that an exclusive agency contract between a producer in a non-member State and an agent within the Common Market may come under the prohibition of Article 85, when the contract prevents the agent in fact or in law to re-export the products concerned to other member-States or if it prevents others than the concessionaire to sell products concerned, which come from other member-States, in the area, assigned to that concessionaire. The latter situation must be deemed to occur especially if the concessionaire should utilize the national legislation on unfair competition to block parallel imports, more specifically the "*opposabilité aux tiers*" on exclusive dealing contracts which, the case having presented itself in France, had been invoked by party Béguelin.

With regard to this "*opposabilité aux tiers*", the Court says in consideration 14 that an exclusive agency contract meets the criteria of Article 85(1) if the combined effect of the contract and a national legislation on unfair competition enables the exclusive dealer to block parallel imports from other member-States.

The Court says then in consideration 15 "that therefore the exclusive agent can only invoke such legislation, if the pretended unfair character of his competitors' behaviour can be based on other elements than their having effected parallel imports"

This consideration may be construed in two ways. Firstly, it may be conceived as expressing the reasoning, that if the exclusive agency contract is unlawful because of infringement of Article 85(1), there is no basis under French civil law to invoke the "*opposabilité aux tiers*". According to this construction (which is also compatible with the wordings of consideration 14) the action against the parallel imports would just not be backed by national law, but would not in itself constitute an infringement of Article 85(1).

Secondly, consideration 15 may be construed in such a way, that the fact that the contract is prohibited by virtue of Article 85(1) not only and not primarily makes it impossible under national civil law to invoke the "*opposabilité aux tiers*", but rather causes this activity to be directly prohibited by Article 85(1) and therefore to be liable to be enjoined by the Commission under Article 3 of Regulation No. 17 and to be subject to penalties under Article 15 and 16 of that regulation.

In my opinion, the second construction (that is as well as the first one compatible with the wordings of considerations 14 and 15) is most in line

35. See note 24.

with views, expressed by the Court in earlier judgements.

In the Grundig/Consten judgement [36] and in the Sirena/Eda judgement [37] the Court extended the prohibition of Article 85(1) to activities (the blocking of parallel imports on the basis of trademark rights) which historically could be traced back to agreements, coming under Article 85(1), but which legally were rather founded on national trademark law and which at any rate could not be deemed to be of the nature of the exercise of rights or the fulfilment of obligations under the agreements concerned. In the Grundig/Consten case, the agreement on the basis of which Consten had got the right to use the Gint trademark in France could still be deemed to be in existence and the use of that trademark by Consten could be deemed to have been envisaged by parties to the agreement. In the Sirena/Eda case however, the agreement concerned had been definitely executed when the Prep trademark was transferred to Sirena as long as ago as 1937 and thus could not reasonably be deemed to be in existence any more at the time at which the Prep trademark was invoked to block parallel imports of products under that trademark into Italy.

With regard to the question, under what circumstances an agreement comes under Article 85, the Court repeated the criteria which had been mentioned in the LTM/MBU judgement.[38] Thus it must be assumed that the Court has not reversed the Völk-Vervaecke [39] and Cadollin-Höss [40] judgements, according to which even import and export prohibitions do not per se come under Article 85(1).

The Court said furthermore that, as export prohibitions do not figure among the restrictions, which may be imposed on the exclusive agent according to Article 2, alinea 1 of Regulation No. 67/67, the presence of such a prohibition in an exclusive agency contract causes the contract not to be exempted by virtue of that regulation.

2. *Resale price maintenance, selling organizations*

The policy of the Commission with regard to exclusive agency contracts is in its present phase, which started with the publication of Regulation No. 67/67, well established and uncontroversial. The major problems of the past have been solved in a way which is nowadays rather generally accepted and substantial changes in that policy seem rather unlikely. However, the way that has led up to the present situation has been an eventful one: certain

36. See note 17; cf. Wertheimer, *infra*, 204-208.

37. Judgment of February 18th, 1971, case 40/70, *Recueil* XVII, 69 *et seq*; [1972] CMLR, 260 et seq.; cf. Wertheimer, *infra*, 210-215.

38. See *supra*, 68-69.

39. See note 31.

40. See note 32.

measures taken have brought about unwelcome side effects, certain solutions embarked upon have proved to be blind alleys, issues have been hotly debated in literature and in the Court and, at certain stages at least, the element of passion and intrigue has not been lacking.

It has also been necessary, in order to attain satisfactory solutions, to draw heavily upon the arsenal of legal instruments available. Thus next to individual decisions, the instrument of exemptions for categories of contracts had to be brought into play, causing the adoption of legislative measures by the Council and by the Commission. Also a rather impressive series of decisions of the Court of Justice of the Communities has been devoted to exclusive agency contracts.

In comparison with the rather spectacular aspects of the policy concerning exclusive agency, the policy on resale price maintenance and on vertical agreements, aiming at organizing and promoting the sale of products in other ways than by the device of exclusive agency, offers quite a modest picture. Hardly any serious controversies in literature, no spectacular lawsuits, no measures of legislative nature but only a restricted number of decisions in individual cases, the main features of which are traceable back to the principles, which have been evolved in respect of exclusive agency contracts.

Those principles amount to accepting certain restrictions of competition, subject to the condition that the operation of corrective influences, originating from other parts of the common market than those where the restrictions are practised, must not be prevented.

For instance, the benefit which, in case of exclusive agency without absolute territorial protection in several parts of the Common Market, each agent may derive from his exclusive position, is limited by the possibility that, if he charges prices that are appreciably higher than those charged by other exclusive agents, his customers may address themselves to other exclusive agents or to customers of the latter, who may feel able to offer the products concerned at competitive prices in the area, assigned to the first exclusive agents.

Thus the restrictions, that have been deemed admissible are so to speak, kept within bounds, the participation of the consumers in the benefits, accruing from those restrictions is ensured[41] and the functioning of the Common Market as an internal market, unimpaired by national or other boundaries, is safeguarded.[42]

The example illustrates that among the motives underlying the Commission's policy in respect of exclusive agency contracts, considerations about the functioning of the price mechanism in a way, consistent with the basic principles of the common market, played a paramount rôle.

41. in conformity with the 2nd condition of Art. 85(3).
42. Cf. First Report on Competition Policy, para. 48.

One should also bear in mind that the factual situations, that at an earlier stage confronted the Commission with the problem of exclusive agency, reinforced by absolute territorial protection, were precisely characterized by price differentials, which inspired parallel importers to overcome the absolute territorial protection against the opposition of the official agents.

Thus it is not surprising that, when the Commission started to tackle the problems connected with resale price maintenance, it could mainly rely on principles and solutions, which had already been evolved in respect of exclusive agency contracts.

The approach, adopted by the Commission in respect of resale price maintenance inasfar as practised by individual suppliers, has from the outset on been a reluctant one.

In Article 4(2)(a) and 5(2) of Regulation No. 17, individual resale price maintenance was exempted from compulsory notification, even in cases where the contracts concerned are concluded between enterprises of different member-States.[43]

When the Commission in 1966 drew attention to the desirability of notification of certain agreements, concluded between enterprises of one member-State, horizontal agreements on the resale price of imported products were mentioned but not resale price maintenance-contracts concerning imported products.[44]

In answering questions of a member of the European Parliament about resale price maintenance, the Commission said that the obligation imposed on trading to observe fixed resale prices does not normally affect trade between the member-States within the meaning of Article 85(1).[45] So the Commission did not distinguish between the fixing of resale prices of goods, produced within the member-State concerned and the fixing of resale prices of goods, imported from other member-States. This is rather remarkable, as resale price maintenance concerning imported goods normally binds a series of resalers and thus is very similar economically to a horizontal agreement concerning the resale price of imported goods, which in the view of the Commission comes under Article 85(1).

The Commission added however that it sees to it, that traders and consumers are not deprived of the possibility to obtain their goods anywhere in the Community at the most favourable conditions. The latter phrase depicts the essence of the policy, pursued by the Commission in respect of resale price maintenance.

43. It may be mentioned that such cases are exceptional; when resale price maintenance is applied with regard to imported goods, it is normally imposed by the importer.

44. 10th General Report on the Activities of the Community, para. 47.

45. Written Question 247/71, O.J. 1971, C 115/5. Essentially the same view was voiced in para. 55 of the First Report on Competition Policy of April 1972.

Resale price maintenance as such is not attacked under Article 85(1) but no devices are tolerated, which would aim at insulating national resale price maintenance-systems from influences from abroad. Thus they are subject to the prohibition of Article 85(1)–export and reimport prohibitions, as well as clauses, providing for the resale of goods, in case of export to a country where resale price maintenance is practised, at the resale prices.

It seems utterly improbable, that such clauses will ever get the benefit of exemption under Article 85(3), as until now the Commission has persistently condemned them, even without the reservations for exeptional cases that have been mentioned in respect of exclusive agency contracts.

About the consequences which the prohibition of the abovementioned clauses will have with regard to the continuation of resale price maintenance in member-States, where this practice is still generally permissible[46] as far as the national legislation is concerned, the following remarks may be made.

In the Federal Republic of Germany the doctrine of completeness (*Lückenlosigkeit*) prevents the enforcement of resale price maintenance contracts, if the resale price maintenance is not (theoretically and practically) "complete". Moreover, the Federal Cartel Office takes action on the basis of Article 17 of the *Gesetz gegen Wettbewerbsbeschränkungen* against the continuation of an incomplete resale price maintenance.

In other member-States, the requirement of completeness does not play such a big rôle in respect of the enforceability of resale price maintenance contracts. However, another matter that is relevant to the legal protection of resale price maintenance is the possibility to take action against agents, who by utilizing breach of contract of buyers of goods, sold under resale price maintenance, have obtained those goods without having undertaken the obligation to sell only at the fixed prices. In such cases, the requirement of completeness plays again a rôle at least in Germany and in the Netherlands.

Thus the impossibility to apply export and reimport prohibitions within the Common Market in several cases prejudices the legal protection of national systems of resale price maintenance. Moreover, even in cases where that legal protection remains to some extent upright, the circumstance that the resale at free prices of goods, identical to those sold under resale price maintenance but originating from parallel import or re-import, may not be blocked, may affect seriously the attractiveness of resale price maintenance to suppliers as well as to traders.

46. In Italy opinions are divided in respect of the possibility to take action against third parties who disturb a resale price maintenance system. In Belgium such possibility exist but opinions differ as to their legal construction. In France, as far as resale price maintenance is permissive in this country, it may be protected legally against disturbance by third parties, without completeness being a precondition to such protection. Cf. E. Ulmer, *das Recht des Unlauteren Wettbewerbs in den Mitgliedstaaten der EWG*, Band 1 (Köln, 1965), Nos. 332-342

It seems rather probable, that which regard to goods, that are sold in several countries of the Common Market, suppliers who want to continue operating resale price maintenance-systems will have to fix the several national price levels and trade margins in such a way that the incentives for parallel imports and reimports are minimized. Practically this means that the lowest level of prices, prevailing for commercial reasons in any member-State, will as well determine the price-levels in other member-States, as these cannot be appreciably higher on penalty or provoking parallel imports from the first state. And even national resale price maintenance-systems, that have been adapted to these requirements, will lead a more precarious existence than at a time when they could be sealed off against influences from abroad.

It may be added that the principles, laid down in the Sirena/Eda judgement[47] and the DGG/Metro judgement[48] of the Court of Justice operate in the same direction as the Commission's policy with regard to export and re-import prohibitions, in as far as those principles do not allow for the sealing off of national markets on the basis of trade-mark rights and of rights, akin to the copyright respectively. In both cases, the lawsuits before national courts, which occasioned the judgements of the Court of Justice, originated from attempts to block the importation and resale of goods at substantially lower prices than were practised by the firms, which sought to protect their national price level by invoking the rights concerned.

In a number of cases, the selling organisations of big companies have been adapted to the aforementioned principles concerning export prohibitions, which have been developed by the Commission.[49]

A negative clearance was granted[50] in favour of the uniform conditions applied by several daughter companies in the member-States with regard to the sale of Kodak products, after elimination of export-prohibitions, which were formerly comprised in those conditions. Moreover, it was stipulated, that those companies would, in case of export to other member-States, apply no higher prices than those prevailing in their home-country.

In this decision, also other aspects of selling organisations of big companies were tackled.

Provisions limiting the resale of Kodak-products to agents, meeting objective requirements, which were calculated to ensure a proper handling of

47. See *supra*, 76.

48. Judgment of June 8, 1971, case 78/70, *Recueil* XVII, 487 *et seq*; [1971] CMLR, 631 *et seq*.

49. Thus the selling conditions of companies of the Agfa-Gevaert group, as well as those of Zeiss-Ikon-Voigtländer were adapted. Cf. First Report on Competition Policy, para. 55.

50. O.J. 1970, L 147/24; [1970] CMLR, D 19 *et seq*. See para. 54 of the First Report on Competition Policy, where also the elimination of export prohibitions in the general conditions of Philips is mentioned.

Kodak-products were as such not deemed to come under Article 85(1); it was said that there was no reason to fear that those provisions would be used illegally to curtail deliveries to traders, who would have exported the products concerned to, or imported those products from other member-States.

In the case of the Omega sales organization,[51] the Commission also required, that the appointed importers of Omega-watches in the several member-States, as well as other traders, belonging to that organization, should be free to export the products concerned to or to import them from other member-States at prices to be determined freely. The meeting of that requirement did not, however, pave the way for a negative clearance, as the admittance of retailers was not (as in the Kodak case) dependent on objective and uniform criteria. Rather a quantitative limitation of the number of retailers was practised. This limitation was deemed to be restrictive of competition and to affect trade between the member-States, as it limited the number of selling points, available for the sale of products concerned, that would be imported from other EEC-countries.

Not only measures, aiming at protecting national systems of resale price maintenance by regulation of transnational transactions–such as export and re-import prohibitions–are deemed by the Commission to come under Article 85(1) and not to fulfil normally the conditions for exemption on the basis of Article 85(3). Rather, measures pertaining to transactions within the member-State concerned are judged in the same way, as far as the resale of products imported from other member-States is concerned. Thus in the Aspa-decision,[52] the Commission condemned a system of collective exclusive agency, set up by a Belgian organisation in the branch of perfumes and toilet articles, which was used a.o. to ensure the observance of resale price maintenance, practised by the members of the organization.

In the case mentioned, the collective exclusive agency was also used to protect traders, who had been appointed as exclusive agents, against parallel imports and this aspect of the Aspa-rules was also condemned. A similar position was adopted in respect of an agreement between a Dutch and a Belgian organization in the automobiles, spare parts and accessories trade, that created an absolute territorial protection to the benefit of exclusive agents, members of the respective organizations.[53]

51. O.J. 1970, L 242/22; [1970] CMLR, D 49 *et seq.*
52. O.J. 1970, L 148/9; [1970] CMLR, D 25 *et seq.*
53. Fourth General Report on the Activities of the Communities, para. 28.

3. *Evaluation of the EEC policy on exclusive agency contracts, resale price maintenance and selective selling*

An evaluation of the policy of the EEC concerning bilateral exclusive agency contracts, as it is reflected in regulations and individual decisions as well as in judgements, rendered by the Court of Justice, may be summarized by saying that all is well that ends well. The introductory phase, characterized by the bringing about of the mass problem of over 30000 notifications and by the abortive attempt, mentioned hereabove [54] to solve that problem by exempting exclusive agency contracts as a group on the basis of Regulation No. 17, was distinctly unfortunate. In the next phase, highlighted by the Grundig/Consten decision of the Commission and by the adoption of Regulation No. 19/65, things improved as attention was rightly focused on the paramount significance of absolute territorial protection, while an adequate legal instrument was forged to solve the mass problem. In this period, the Commission still clung to a somewhat rigid interpretation of the criterion of restriction of competition in Article 85(1), but in the three judgements, rendered in 1966 [55] the Court of Justice introduced a more realistic interpretation of that criterion, while on the other hand backing the Commission's point of view in respect of absolute territorial protection, as expressed in the Commission's Grundig-Consten decision. [56]

Finally, with the adoption of Regulation No. 67/67 [57] a set of rules was created, that provided ample room for exclusive agency and offered sufficient legal security to enterprises utilizing that instrument of sales promotion, while on the other hand due weight was given to the necessity of counteracting any use of that instrument to insulate parts of the Common Market. Regulation No. 67/67 also proved to be an adequate means finally to solve the mass problem, as the number of notifications requiring individual decisions was within a few years reduced to manageable proportions.

Regulation No. 67/67 also meets the requirements, set out in the introductory part of this paper, that should be observed in respect of reglementation of bilateral agreements: it contains clear-cut rules, that leave ample room for the utilization of the instrument of exclusive agency and it reduces to small proportions the need for individual decisions.

The judgements of the Court of Justice in respect of exclusive agency contracts in general deserve favourable comment. It should be noted, however, that the opinion, expressed in the Völk/Vervaecke and the Cadillon/Höss judgements, [58] according to which even a contract embodying absolute

54. See *supra*, 65 *et seq.*
55. Especially in the LMT/MBU judgment, see *supra*, 68-69.
56. See *supra*, 69.
57. See note 22.
58. See notes 31 and 32.

territorial protection may escape the prohibition of Article 85(1), in case of a notably weak position of the parties concerned, hardly provides the national courts with useful criteria to assess the eventual occurrence of such a situation. It would seem recommendable, that national courts, when called upon to decide upon this problem in specific cases, pay attention to the quantitative criteria, that are to be found in the Notice of the Commission, according to which agreements of minor importance may be deemed not to come under the prohibition of Article 85(1). [59]

Notwithstanding the fact, that there is reason to comment favourably on the present EEC-policy concerning exclusive agency, it would be interesting to learn how suppliers and exclusive agents have fared with contracts, that have been adapted to meet the requirements of Regulation No. 67/67. Also it would be interesting to learn about the experiences of concerns, that have been obliged to do away with import and export restrictions in respect of their selling systems within the Common Market, and to what extent the necessity to abandon absolute territorial protection has caused firms, that previously utilized the instrument of exclusive agency to change over to organizing their sales by means of branches or dependent firms.

An investigation of these and similar matters would however surpass the scope of this paper.

The favourable comment, vented above in respect of the present shape of the EEC-policy concerning exclusive agency, may be extended to the policy, which has been developed in later years in respect of the related matters of resale price maintenance and selective selling.

In respect of national resale price maintenance-systems, the Commission has adopted an ingenious roundabout approach, that leaves the decisions on the admissibility of resale price maintenance as such to the national authorities and only counteracts practices, eventually accompanying or reinforcing resale price maintenance in such a way that the functioning of the Common Market is affected.

The policy of the Commission concerning resale price maintenance and selective selling has essentially the same merits as the policy on exclusive agency, inasfar as on the one hand ample room is left for the practices concerned, while on the other hand care is taken, that those practices do not take on shapes or are accompanied by devices, that would be contrary to essential principles of the competition system of the Common Market:

59. O.J. 1970, C 64; [1970] CMLR, D 15 *et seq.*

Chapter 3

"PER SE" RULES UNDER ARTICLE 85 EEC?

by *Willy Alexander*

In its judgment Völk-Vervaecke of July 9, 1969,[1] the Court of Justice of the European Communities ruled:

> "It is therefore possible that an exclusive concession agreement, even with absolute territorial protection, may, in view of the weak position of the parties on the market in the products in question in the territory which is the subject of the absolute protection, escape the prohibition set out in Article 85(1)".

This judgment was repeated in Cadillon-Höss.[2]

In the present contribution we intend to develop the argument that EEC competition policy would have been better served by a decision that agreements of the type defined by the Court are *per se* unlawful under Article 85(1) of the Treaty.

The argument contains three elements: (1) following the American example of developing *per se* prohibitions is desirable, (2) such rules are acceptable under paragraph 1 of Article 85, and (3) the case Völk-Vervaecke offered an excellent opportunity for defining a first rule of this kind.

Rule of Reason and "per se" rules in American Antitrust Law

Section 1 of the Sherman Act declares illegal "every contract . . . in restraint of trade . . .". This prohibition has not been qualified by the possibility of an exemption. It is applied by the federal courts.

It has been held, since 1911,[3] that the construction of the statutory prohibition requires the observance of a Rule of Reason. This standard permits the decision whether a certain conduct is "significantly and unreasonably anticompetitive in character or effect". In this way, the Sherman Act grants a certain latitude to the courts, the limits of which we need not explore.

1. Case No. 5-69, *Recueil* XV, 295 *et seq.* (1969) CMLR, 273 *et seq,* at 282.
2. Judgment of the Court of Justice of May 6, 1971, Case No. 1-71 (Cadillon v.Höss), *Recueil* XVII, 351 *et seq.*; (1971) CMLR, 420 *et seq*.
3. Standard Oil Co. of New Yersey v.United States, 221.U.S. 1; United States v.American Tobacco Co., 221 U.S. 106.

The significance of the later definition of *per se* violations of the Act was that they relieve the judge of the necessity of studying the exact character and effect in the case under review of practices falling within the scope of these rules. According to the words of the Supreme Court:[4]

> ... there are certain agreements or practices which because of their pernicious effect on competition and lack of any redeeming virtue are conclusively presumed to be unreasonable and therefore illegal without elaborate inquiry as to the precise harm they have caused or the business excuse for their use. This principle of *per se* unreasonableness not only makes the type of restraints which are prescribed by the Sherman Act more certain to the benefit of everyone concerned, but it also avoids the necessity for an incredibly complicated and prolonged economic investigation into the entire history of the industry involved, as well as related industries, in an effort to determine at large whether a particular restraint has been unreasonable–an inquiry so often wholly fruitless when undertaken. Among the practices which the courts have theretofore deemed to be unlawful in and of themselves are pricefixing ... divisions of markets ... group boycotts ... and tying arrangements.

An amount of discretionary powers has been sacrified to the desire of having clear cut rules, i.e. to a requirement of legal security. In the American example the solution works to the benefit of those who suffer from the practice under attack.

Rule of Reason in EEC-competition law

According to the Court of Justice, Article 85(1) does not prohibit certain types of agreements. The competent authority or judge must always examine the actual effect of the contract under review in the light of the ascertained economic and legal facts. The judgments L.T.M.-M.B.U.,[5] Brasserie de Haecht[6] and Völk-Vervaecke enumerate a number of circumstances which may be relevant for such an investigation. One of these is the market share of the contracting parties.

Whenever the conditions which make Article 85(1) applicable have been fulfilled, the Commission may exempt the agreement from its prohibition. Such an exemption is warranted under certain conditions enumerated by Article 85(3). One of these is that the agreement offers appreciable advantages for the production or distribution of goods or for the promotion of technical or economic progress which compensate the disadvantages resulting from the restraint of competition.[7]

4. Nothern Pacific Railway Co. v. United States, 356 U.S. 1 (1958).
5. Judgment of the Court of Justice of June 30, 1966, Case No. 56-65, *Recueil* XII, 337 *et seq.*; (1966) CMLR, 357 *et seq.*
6. Judgment of the Court of Justice of December 12, 1967, Case No. 23-67, *Recueil* XIII, 525 *et seq.*; (1968) CMLR, 26 *et seq.*
7. Judgment of the Court of Justice of July 13, 1966, Cons. Cases Nos. 56 and 58-64

A comparison with the American Rule of Reason is dangerous, not in the least because there are conflicting views, in the case law and in the legal literature of the U.S.A., about the exact significance of this standard.[8] But taking up the terms used in the quoted passage from the Northern Pacific Railway judgment we submit that an application of Article 85(1) to certain practices requires "an inquiry as to the precise harm they have caused", while an application of Article 85(3) requires, inter alia, a test of "the business excuse for their use".

Our main proposition is that the Court of Justice should have made it possible that the experience gained through a case-by-case application of Article 85(1) would produce the definition of agreements or clauses which are so contrary to the EEC competition policy that they may only be tolerated by grant of an exemption. This very exempting power makes the formulation of *per se* prohibitions under Article 85(1) less dramatic than it may be under Section 1 of the Sherman Act.

Effectiveness of the prohibition and legal security

Article 1 of Regulation No. 17[9] states that agreements referred to in Article 85(1) of the Treaty shall be prohibited, no prior decision to this effect being required. The advantages of such a system of prohibition are the same as those attached to the self-executing character of other provisions of the Treaty: the goals of the Treaty are sooner reached because–to use the argument contained in the Van Gend & Loos judgment[10]–the vindication by interested parties of their rights adds an efficient control to the enforcement assigned to the Commission. Its disadvantages stem from the state of uncertainty about the legality of certain agreements in which contracting and third parties may remain.

This uncertainty bears both upon the difficulty of ascertaining whether the conditions for an application of Article 85(1) have been fulfilled and upon the possibility that the resulting prohibition be declared inapplicable under Article 85(3) by a decision having retroactive effect.

(Ets. Consten S.A.R.L. and Grundig-Verkaufs-G.m.b.H. v. EEC-Commission), *Recueil* XII, 429-507, at 502, (1966) CMLR, 418-481, at 478.

8. Cf. Joliet, *The Rule of Reason in Antitrust Law* (The Hague 1967), 5-7.

9. O.J., p. 204/62.

10. Judgment of the Court of Justice of February 5, 1963, Case No. 26-62, *Recueil* IX, 1-29, at 25; (1963) CMLR, 105-132, at 130.

In its judgments Bosch,[11] Portelange[12] and Bilger-Jehle[13] the Court of Justice has developed certain solutions for the latter problem. The effectiveness of the prohibition of restrictive agreements has to a large extent been sacrificed to the need for legal security. The provisional validity of agreements which have been duly notified or which are exempt of notification, determined by the aforesaid decisions, operates to the detriment of those who suffer from practices which may violate the provisions of the EEC-Treaty. It is hoped that the Court may reverse its case law which is difficult to accomodate with the system of Article 85 and its implementing Regulation No. 17.[14]

As to the former problem, the formulation of *per se* rules under Article 85(1) would provide clearness to the national jurisdictions who are charged with its application and to the interested parties. The prohibition of restrictive practices would gain in effectiveness without harm to legal security. We do not fear major inequities from such a method if it takes the form of generalizing the experience acquired in the course of individual decisions. The policy towards exclusive dealing contracts for parts of the Common Market can be used to illustrate our point.

Absolute territorial protection of the exclusive agent

The term "absolute territorial protection" is used when third parties are prevented from importing the products under contract into the territory assigned to the exclusive dealer. The Commission has made it clear, by its decisions Grundig-Consten,[15] confirmed on this point by the Court of Justice, D.R.U.-Blondel,[16] Hummel-Isbecque[17] and Jallatte-Vos and Vandeputte,[18]

11. Judgment of the Court of Justice of April 6, 1962, Case No. 13-61, *Recueil* VII, 89 *et seq.*; (1962) CMLR, 1 *et seq.*

12. Judgment of the Court of Justice of July 9, 1969, Case No. 10-69, *Recueil* XV, 309 *et seq.*

13. Judgment of the Court of Justice of March 10, 1970, Case No. 43-69, *Recueil* XVI, 127 *et seq.*

14. Cf. Ulmer, Europäsches Kartellrecht auf neuen Wegen?, A.W.D. 1970 193-198; Van Gerven, Over voorlopige of definitieve geldigheid en over nietigheid met of zonder terugwerkende kracht van kartelafspraken, S.E.W. 1970, 361-362; Ulrich, Anmerkung zum Urteil des Gerichtshof der Europäischen Gemeinschaften von 18 März 1970 (Rechtssache 43/69), G.R.U.R. Int. 1970, 382; Joliet, Prix imposés et droit européen de la concurrence, Cah. dr. europ. 1971, 50; Waelbroeck in:Mégret-Louis-Vignes-Waelbroeck, *Le droit de la CEE*, Vol. 4 Concurrence (Brussels 1972), 172. Cf. Van der Wielen, *infra*, 140-159.

15. O.J., p. 2545/64; (1964) CMLR, 489 *et seq.*; cf. Snijders, *infra*, 63-76.

16. O.J., p. 2194/65; (1965) CMLR, 180 *et seq.*

17. O.J., p. 2581/65; (1965) CMLR, 2 *et seq.*

18. O.J., p. 37/66; (1966) CMLR, D1 *et seq.*

as well as by its Regulation No. 67/67,[19] that monopolies based on contracts for the resale of goods in a part of the Common Market are contrary to the goals of the EEC-Treaty.

As far as we remember, commentators have essentially accepted this policy. Objections against the Grundig decision which may be said to concern the question whether Article 85(1) should be deemed to apply took the ground that an exclusive dealer of branded goods does not enjoy a monopolist's protection whenever there exists interbrand competition. With regard to this argument the Court held that competition at the distribution level in goods of the same brand deserved to be stimulated, since this would urge traders to greater efforts which might have a strong effect on distribution cost. It was further objected against the Commission's policy, that the efforts required from and the risks shifted on to the exclusive dealer make it necessary—generally or in special circumstances—to allow him a further protection. But this is an argument which could very well be considered in handling a request for an exemption.

The judgment Völk-Vervaecke does not reverse the principles of the Commission's policy towards exclusive dealing contracts. The Court has only limited the extent to which it applies by judging that such an agreement, even if the exclusive dealer enjoys absolute territorial protection, may escape from the prohibition of Article 85(1) when it has only a minor effect on market conditions because of the parties' weak position on the relevant market. In other words, under certain circumstances a restraint of competition, unacceptable as a matter of principle, may, as a matter of fact, be so insignificant that the Community's interest is not sufficiently involved.

This implicit reference to the rule "*de minimis non curat praetor*" might have taken the form of a pure policy statement to the extent that in such minor cases there would be no grounds for action on the part of the Commission. This enforcement agency might perhaps even have considered whether it would be prepared to commit itself to inaction in such cases by granting a negative clearance under Article 2 of Regulation No. 17, without excluding application of the prohibition by domestic courts. But the Commission itself went much further by suggesting, in its statement presented in the Völk-Vervaecke case, that there is no violation of Article 85(1) where the agreement has no significant effect on market conditions because of the small market share held by the contracting parties. This has caused the Court to render the judgment quoted at the beginning of this paper.[20]

19. O.J., p. 849/67; (1967) CMLR, D1 *et seq.*

20. See note 1. For this distinction between motives of expediency of an enforcement agency and interpretation of the law by the competent court the author is indebted to Michel Waelbroeck, who has, in the meantime, developed this idea in: *op.cit.*, note 14, 20-22.

Long range judicial policy and equitable decisions

The judgment handed down in the Völk-Vervaecke case constituted an incident in a German law suit, where a German manufacturer held his Belgian exclusive dealer liable because the latter had not taken delivery of the stipulated quantities. The German court had indicated that its decision depended on the question whether the agreement was null and void under Article 85(2) EEC-Treaty, or not.

When taking this setting into account, one is left with the impression that the Court of justice could not accept that a contracting party might escape from its obligations by relying on Article 85 of the Treaty in a case where the interests protected by this article were hardly affected.

Quite apart from the question whether this would have been the inevitable consequence of a different judgment by the Court of Justice, we hold that the fairness of its individual judgments is not only standard by which case law should be measured. The long range consequences of the solutions handed down deserve to be kept in mind and they require even more consideration when the Court's competence is limited to clarifying points of law. The process of making law by judicial determination operates necessarily at the expense of either of the contending parties.

The main consequence of Völk-Vervaecke is that national courts and private parties have lost a simple standard to go upon. They can no longer conclude that Article 85(1) is applicable where an exclusive dealer enjoys absolute territorial protection. Instead, they have to delve in a factual inquiry guided by criteria which are difficult to handle and which may have varying influences on the appreciation of an agreement according to the developments on the relevant market.

In order to be of some help, the Commission has published in 1970 its Notice on agreements of minor importance which are not covered by the provisions of Article 85(1) EEC. [21] In this Notice the Commission proposes the application of two tests–market share of the contract products and aggregated turnover of the contracting parties–for the assessment of whether an agreement has a "noticeable effect" on market conditions. The interpretation of this document raises many questions. [22] It is, moreover, doubtful to what extent it may be relied upon, since the Commission itself has already suggested that Article 85(1) may be applicable in a case where neither threshold is exceeded. [23]

Another consequence has been pointed out by Waelbroeck: Article 85 would no longer grant a right to individuals to the suppression of restrictive

21. O.J. 1970, No. C 64/1.
22. See Waelbroeck, *op.cit.*, note 14, 18-20.
23. Statement submitted in Case No. 22-71 (Béguelin), *Recueil* XVII, 956.

clauses and practices which hinder them; it would, at most, guarantee that some competition within the Common Market will always be preserved.[24] In this way, private enforcement of Community law is being jeopardized.

Has Völk-Vervaecke been overruled by Béguelin?

After this paper had been written, the Court of Justice has ruled in its Béguelin judgment of November 25, 1971:[25]

> "An exclusive agency agreement concluded between a producer belonging to a non-member country and a distributor established in the Common Market fulfils the two criteria (of Article 85(1)) when it obstructs, in law or in fact, the distributor re-exporting the products in question into other member-States or the products being imported from other member-States into the protected zone, and there being distributed by persons other than the concessionaire or his customers".
>
> This condition is met "where the concessionaire can prevent parallel imports from other member-States into the conceded territory by means of a combination of national law of the agreement with the effects on unfair competition".

This is exactly the type of judgment which would comply with our proposition: Absolute territorial protection brings the exclusive dealing contract for part of the Common Market within the prohibition contained in Article 85(1).

Read by itself, this would come down to an overruling of Völk-Vervaecke. It is, however, rather unlikely that the same Court, after having explicitly confirmed its former judgment in Cadillon-Höss, would now six months later overrule it implicitly. The Court's reasoning contains no indication to this effect. On the contrary, it more or less quotes its general judgment in L.T.M.-M.B.U., of which Völk-Vervaecke seemed to be a specific application.

What then is the explanation of the ostensible deviation from a previous case law? It is to be found by an analysis both of the type of situation in which a litigant party invoked the nullity of Article 85(2) and of the market conditions in the case at issue. In L.T.M.-M.B.U., Völk-Vervaecke and Cadillon-Höss, on the one hand, exclusive agents each time tried to free themselves from their commitment of taking delivery of the product. This implies that its marketing in the protected area was not very succesful. In Béguelin, on the other hand, the party that invoked this Treaty provision was a parallel importer. This implies the existence of a sufficient demand for the product in the protected area. In the latter case the Commission had, moreover, declared before the Court of Justice that the aggregated turnover of the Japanese supplier and its distributors exceeded the threshold mentioned in its 1970

24. *Op. cit.*, note 14, 21-22.
25. Case No. 22-71, *Recueil* XVII, 949-964, (1972) CMLR, 81-99, at 96.

Notice and that the European markets for lighters revealed oligopolistic structures.

Although the Court of Justice may have been influenced by these indications, we think that the fact that Article 85 was invoked by a parallel importer was decisive. It may be recalled that the prevention of parallel imports was also the main theme in Grundig-Consten. In that case the Court saw no reason for an analysis of the exact effects of an agreement which intended to grant absolute territorial protection to the exclusive dealer.

This view on the case law permits the reconciliation of apparently conflicting judgments relating to exclusive dealing contracts with absolute territorial protection: Where parallel imports appear to be interesting, the Treaty prohibition becomes operative.

If we are right, the legal status of this absolute territorial protection of exclusive dealers under Article 85(1) EEC is comparable to that of a price fixing clause contained in a patent licensing agreement under the Sherman Act. Although it has not been defined as being illegal *per se*, it appears to be forbidden anyway in those cases where a contracting party may want to have it.

Chapter 4

THE ECONOMICS OF CONCERTED PRACTICES (COLLUSION)

by *Dr. H. W. de Jong*

1. *Introduction: Concepts*

What are "concerted practices"? In what sense does the term differ from terms like "cooperation", "agreement", "coordination", "cartellike" and so on? At first sight, there seem to be wide divergencies: everybody likes to be called "cooperative"; to be in agreement and to coordinate sound much more neutral, whereas collusive or concerted behaviour (or practice) have sinister undertones. But even if ethical or legal judgments may be involved when these expressions are used, the economist has no such fine antennas for measuring the differences. For him there are conceptually only two seperate classes of the behaviour of firms in the market: on the one hand rivalrous or competitive behaviour, on the other hand cooperative or coordinated behaviour. The last category can be further divided into cooperation based on expressly written agreements called cartels or restrictive practices on the basis of tangible documents, and parallel behaviour where no such written agreements are involved. But whereas parallel behaviour is thus rather clearly defined, it still covers a variety of business attitudes which are of the utmost importance to distinguish from the viewpoint of competition policy.

In order no to beg the question, the terms "collusion" or "concerted practice" will be reserved for coordinated behaviour between enterprises which is intended to and has proved to be succesful in eliminating unwanted rivalry. Parallel behaviour therefore differs from collusion or concerted practice in that it does not unvariably aims at the setting aside of competition, but it accords with both in that it does not represent competition or rivalry in the ordinary sense.

This division of terms has several advantages. First, it more or less accords with daily language, which is an advantage because the artificial loading of terms with contents which are not in agreement with daily practice, leads to confusion. Machlup for example designates all behaviour which is not competitive as "collusive" and then adds that for him this terms has no pejorative connotation.[1] Such a procedure is at variance with ordinary understanding.

Second, it allows an unprejudiced analysis of non-competitive, non-cartellike behaviour of firms in markets, which may or may not be collusive. Only in case such behaviour turns out to have aimed at suppressing existing or potential competition without achieving express agreements will we speak of collusion or concerted practice. Third, this division of terms also allows a theoretical clarification, which is urgently necessary. The practical business man and the lawyer understand by "competition", the rivalry between firms for suppliers or customers. But the theoretical economist has, during the past half-century, applied the term to a particular kind of market structure, viz. perfect competition. This is the kind of market structure under which there are so many sellers in a market for homogeneous goods that none of them is able to influence the market price through his behaviour.

The perfectly competitive firm takes the market price as something given and moreover sells undifferentiated products. This idea may be all right for theoretical economics but it has certainly added to confusion in respect of policy questions. And, because perfectly competitive markets in the theoretical economists' sense are nowadays hard to find, it would seem to clarify things if this kind of "competitive behaviour" is simply considered as a variety of parallel behaviour without the collusionary connotation. It follows that "parallel behaviour" can, but need not be "collusive" behaviour, and that "collusive behaviour" or "concerted practice" is something which is in disagreement with (American or European) competition law. Fourth, the distinction draws the attention to the criteria by which the two forms of non-agreed, coordinated behaviour can be distinguished. At least for competition policy purposes concepts should be operative.[2]

2. *The determinants of parallel behaviour*

Is oligopolistic behaviour of business firms always intended to achieve a monopoly-price or near-monopoly price? This idea has gained currency since E.H. Chamberlin said in the early thirties that any small number of sellers of homogeneous goods cannot avoid the interdependency-situation. Price-cutting is, under the stipulated conditions, no longer sensible. Of firms in such situations it was said:

"If each seeks his maximum profit rationally and intelligently, he will realize that when there are only two or a few sellers, his own move has

1. F. Machlup–*The Economics of Sellers' Competition* (Baltimore 1956), 419 *et seq*.

2. Here we differ again from Machlup, who designates by the term "collusion" all kinds of restrictive behaviour: both very loose forms of understanding between firms without contacts or the exchange of information as well as the most complete and complex forms of agreements.

a considerable effect upon his competitors, and that this makes it idle to suppose that they will accept without retaliation the losses he forces upon them. Since the result of a cut by any one is inevitably to decrease his own profits, no one will cut, and, although the sellers are entirely independent, the equilibrium result is the same as though there were a monopolistic agreement between them".[3] Chamberlin recognized that "the factor of uncertainty on the part of one seller as to what the other is going to do" will play a role. I.e. the monopoly price resulting from uniform control over all sellers or a binding agreement between them would have to be lowered with a certain percentage, owing to the fact that collusionary behaviour would be liable to uncertainty. Such uncertainty could easily arise in case:

(1) the degree of intelligence and far-sightedness of sellers would differ, leading up to different price-behaviour.

(2) different cost conditions of the various producers would induce different behaviour with regard to price.

(3) the price-cutter would not know in advance to what extent the others would follow suit–or let their market share slip.

(4) the price-cutter would be in doubt *when* his competitors would follow suit, which suffices, however, to make him uncertain as to what to do in the first place.

Despite these restrictions, due to uncertainties, it was emphasized that when sellers are few and recognize mutual interdependence, collusionary behaviour–that is, without formal agreements existing between sellers–is bound to follow from the very structure of the industry. In other words, an oligopolistic industrial structure would bring forth collusionary behaviour, of the participating firms, provided the uncertainty which prevails due to the factors mentioned is not too strong. This doctrine heavily influenced later economic thinking. It meant the adoption by economists of the idea that monopoly or quasi-monopoly-pricing could occur in an industry consisting of several firms without the requisite of explicit agreements between the firms being present.

The conclusion would then have to be drawn that structure determines behaviour and in particular that firms in (tight) oligopolistic market structures could be excused from monopolistic practices if together they fixed their prices at a (quasi) monopolistic level or at least a level, higher than normal competitive practice would bring forth. This doctrine reappears in the dyestuffs-case[4] when parties state as their central objection to the E.E.C. Commission's Decision (see apparative clause No. 57 I.C.I.): "The E.E.C.

3. E.H. Chamberlin–*The Theory of Monopolistic Competition* (Cambridge (Mass.) 1947), 48.

4. Judgment of the Court of Justice of the European Communities of July 14, 1972, case Nos 48, 49, 51-57/69, *Recueil* XVIII, 619 *et seq.*; [1972] CMLR, 557 *et seq.*

Commissions's Decision is based on an insufficient analysis of the market in the products in question and on an erroneous view of the concept of concerted practice, since it identifies the latter with the consciously parallel behaviour of the participants in an oligopoly whereas this behaviour was due to the autonomous decisions of each enterprise determined by objective economic necessities and particularly by the need to redress the unsatisfactory level of profitability in the manufacture of dyestuffs".[5] Is there any merit in this argument? The weakness in the theory that structure determines behaviour lies in the leaving out of account of the qualifications with regard to the uncertainties mentioned by Chamberlin and other economists. And, in my opinion, these qualifications go so far as to dismantle the theory altogether, as far as real life cases are concerned. Perhaps the most important qualification of the structure-behaviour theory relates to its exclusive and static nature. As long as it is assumed that only the number of competitors, present at a given time in the market, determines firm behaviour, the derived conclusion that prices will be fixed by oligopolists at a higher than competitive level is well-nigh inescapable. But, in criticism of this position, it can be upheld that:

(1) Not only the number of competitors, but also other variables are important in determining behaviour. Among such variables are relative size of sellers, barriers of entry to the market existing for newcomers, the transparency of market transactions, the difference in cost prices between competing firms, the degree of explicit organisation existing within the branch, the kind of product traded in, and so on. Some of such variables have to be considered as part of the structural make-up of an industry, and together they influence market behaviour as much as (and sometimes more than) the number of enterprises.

(2) The degree of expansion or stagnation of market sales also has its role to play. This factor clearly refers to influences deriving from the lapse of time. It should surprise nobody that a fast-growing industry offers more scope for rivalrous behaviour of companies with respect to price than a stagnating branch of industry.

For in such cases, individual firms have sufficient room for cutting their prices without encroaching too heavily upon the sales of their competitors. Therefore the other oligopolists would be less inclined to match the prise cut –a fact which the price-cutting oligopolist would realize. Whereas in a stagnating market, producers sticking to an accepted price level of their products in the face of price competition by other sellers would have to suffer declining absolute sales, in a fast growing market only their relative market shares would fall. Also, new competitors could more easily enter the market and their number need to be high. A single "maverick" among the

5. *Recueil id.*, 657-658; [1972] CMLR, 622.

latter might upset the established price pattern.

The Court's judgment takes these considerations into account. It clearly points the intermittent existence of competitive behaviour between the dyestuffs companies, which had a bearing not only on the quality of the products supplied and the technical services rendered, but also on the importance of the rebates, given individually to the principal buyers.

This occurrence of price competition rests on several basic factors, characterising the market:

- the interchangeability of at least the standard colours
- the different cost structures of the manufacturers
- the overall demand for dyestuffs which is constantly growing.

It will be seen that these are mainly factors exerting a long-term influence. They account for the drifting back towards rivalrous behaviour of companies. On the other hand, short-term factors pulling towards parallel behaviour are: the small impact of the price of aniline colours in the final price of the product of the buying company, the technical adaptation of the product to the needs of each individual buyer and the splitting-up of the Common Market by the main companies. It is not at all unusual to find such a mixture of forces promoting both competition and parallel behaviour. In general parallel behaviour will be stimulated by the following factors and the degree in which they are realised;

(1) The higher the degree of absolute concentration in the market, that is the higher the share of a small number of sellers in a given market, the greater will be the propensity to collaborate.

(2) The higher the degree of relative concentration, that is the more sales of the industry are unevenly divided between sellers, the more parallel behaviour will be seen as inevitable.

(3) The more cost prices per unit of output are equal among enterprises the more a tendency towards parallel behaviour will be discernible.

(4) The more market transparency will be in evidence the more parallel behaviour will be promoted. If producers are perfectly aware of what passes with the transactions of their competitors they will not be able to achieve even temporary gains. And this will hamper a competitive conduct, for any advantages from price reductions gained by an initiating firm will immediately be matched by others.

If, on the contrary, a price cutter can get away with the results from his initiatives, due to the fact that others will not be aware of his gestures, the lure to take action is always present.

3. *Collusionary behaviour: aims and motives*

It follows from the foregoing that collusionary behaviour can not be simply deduced from market structures, but has to be deduced from direct or

circumstantial evidence. Direct evidence will be provided by documents indicating that the participants in parallel conduct are expressly intended on avoiding or suppressing competition. Such kind of evidence is often hard to detect—if it exists at all. But the dyestuffs case illustrates that the search may nevertheless be rewarding: to find written evidence that the companies concerned raised prices for identical products, with identical percentages within a matter of minutes or hours, constitutes ideal proof. Circumstantial evidence or indirect proof requires more intensive study of company behaviour within the context of a particular market. One of the important questions encountered in such studies concerns the goal(s) of coordinated behaviour.

In the course of the development of cartel theory a shift in thinking about the aims of cartel agreements has appeared. Early economic thinking emphasized the monopoly element: the fact that agreements were made, eliminated competition so that a monopolistic situation would arise. But this position proved untenable in the face of refined economic analysis.

For, a monopolistic price would be one which maximizes the profits of the monopolistic seller.

If a cartel were such a monopolistic seller, it would have to be assumed that all firms participating in the cartel agreement were able to achieve maximum profits by means of eliminating the competition between them. This is an assumption which is seldom fulfilled. Costs differ between firms, also after the formation of a cartel, so that profits will continue to vary. Each individual firm will therefore attain its maximum profit level, given its costs, only perchance if a common cartel price is set. Moreover not all competition will in fact be eliminated: in a simple price cartel, firms can change their quantity of sales or the conditions of supply. This often leads to more elaborate forms of cartels—in fact the combination of price agreements with stipulations regarding sales conditions and sales quantities are often to be found. Thus, only in the limiting case where a cartel would be able to fix both the price and the cost conditions of all supplier firms on a more or less uniform basis and at the same sime could prevent members from "breaking out", the cartel price could indeed be identified with a monopolistic price. The conditions mentioned, however, do indicate that such cases will only occur in strictly organized syndicates, with effective control over output, investments, sales etc. Economists have therefore come to the conclusion that the price which cartels are as a rule able to fix will not be a monopoly price, but will lie somewhere between the competitive price and the monopolistic price. The cartel will at best be a "quasi-monopoly", and the price which will result from its actions will be one which lies below the pure monopoly price and above the competitive price. It necessarily follows that a similar conclusion applies—but with still more force—to concerted practices. Collusionary behaviour among firms which are not bound by agreements will only in

limiting cases result in the fixing of a monopoly price.

If it is concluded that collusion practically never leads to monopoly and monopolistic price behaviour, it can safely be deduced that these effects will not be the goals of the business firms concerned.

For businessmen are far too practical to strive after goals which, in the overwhelming majority of cases, are ephemeral.

What other goals then do they have in view? When the analytical economic explanation of cartel prices in terms of monopolistic behaviour failed, cartel theory degenerated into an empirical research for motives and obstacles. Descriptions appeared, in which psychological, sociological and organisational moments prevailed. At the extreme end the position was taken up that a theoretical economic explanation was harmful, because it reduced the reality of manifold cartel aims and forms to a simplified scheme. Though this movement unearthed a large amount of materials relevant to cartels and other coordinated practices, no light was shed on the central problem: how the common element in such practices was to be explained. That is, we have to know what motivates businessmen to collude on prices, how they are determined and what the effects will be.

A new impulse towards explanation was provided by the Chamberlinian theory of monopolistic competition; the main advances came however in post-war years.[6] Much more attention came to be paid to the implicit assumptions which Chamberlin had adopted.

Fellner in particular struck at the heart of the problem when he noted that oligopolists will, save in exceptional circumstances, not attain the perfect collusion because they value above all their independence. Because of the unwillingness of the individual oligopolist to give up his sovereignty of decision making, the collusive price can practically never be identified with the monopoly price. Generalized, the Fellner thesis may be stated as follows:

An oligopoly consisting of a few, independently controlled firms has members with conflicting motives. On the one hand there is the urge to share in the largest possible profit result which the industry as a whole can secure. Cooperation, whether in the form of cartels, tacit agreements or "implicit bargaining" (offers to agree and the responses via public communication channels) is the road towards joint profit maximization, but requires for its complete achievement the fulfillment of some conditions (a.o. agreement on the non-price dimensions). The most obnoxious condition is the relinquishment of independent, sovereign behaviour. This condition squarely collides with the other prime notive of an oligopolistic seller: the achievement of individual maximum profits or the enlargement of his market share, even to the detriment of other oligopolists. Individual action, whether via price cuts

6. In particular: W. Fellner–*Competition among the Few* (1949); J.S. Bain–*Barriers to New Competition* (1956).

on list prices, secret rabates, easier selling conditions or some other means is the road towards the achievement of this aim. But, of course, independent action requires individual power of decision making. Psychologically speaking, oligopolists are therefore split personalities.

They desire both the one and the other, sometimes at the same time, sometimes alternatively. It follows that sovereignty of action will ultimately be preserved, the more so if competition laws prevent the enforcing of restrictive contacts. In the course of development of economic thinking the factors responsible for the oligopolist's choice between rivalrous and collusive behaviour came to the fore. They proved to be closely related to the (broad) structural and dynamic traits of the markets in which oligopolists operate. Bain (1956) laid stress on seller concentration, product differentiation and entry barriers. That is, he emphasized structural characteristics. Other writers[7] have in more recent times paid attention to market dynamics. We need not repeat such determinants, enumerated under 2. It suffices to underline the fact that the relative strength of both motives depends on the specific characteristics of an oligopolistic market and cannot be generalized in advance. The European Court in the dyestuffs judgment has acknowledged this idea, by stating (in apparative clause No. 68, ICI). "Attendu que la question de savoir s'il y a concertation en l'espèce, ne peut donc etre appréciée correctment que si les indices invoqué par la décision attaquée sont considérés non pas isolement, mais dans leur ensemble, compte tenu des caracteristiques du marché des produits en cause".[8]

4. *Collusionary behaviour: forms and degrees*

There are different forms and degrees of collusion. To describe them all would require a book. A few of the more prominent specimen may suffice however. Degree of collusion refers to the amount of information necessary to convey a collusionary message to competitors and the expectation that the message will be understood. Firms abstaining from reducing their prices or penetrating other market areas, when market conditions would make such actions possible, in the expectation that other oligopolists would behave likewise, show a light degree of collusionary behaviour.

Even a negative signal is sufficient here to induce collusion. Higher degrees involve "warning actions", information concerning other competition parameters besides price, such as customers, delivery terms, product qualities, etc.; still higher degrees require price lists together with extra's and rebates

7. E. Heuss–*Allgemeine Markttheorie* (1956); H.W. de Jong–Aspects économiques du comportement parallèle sur la Marché, Cah. dr.Eur. 1971, 550-561. Also: Dynamische concentratie-theorie, (1972) 120-130.

8. *Recueil, id.*, 659 [1972] CMLR, 623.

which are exchanged among competitors in the expectation that they will take note, and so on.

Forms of collusion concern the bases on which the expectations that competitors will fall in line, depend. On what traditions, customs, agreements and organisations does collusion depend for its functioning? The higher forms are all more organised than lower forms and are much less easy to break away from. The more pronounced the form, the more collusionary behaviour shows constancy.

Degree and form of collusion do not run parallel however. High-degree collusion, involving many variables and other information which is being communicated, may require only minimal organizational form, for example when tradition is strong or only casual meetings take place. In reverse, a complicated organisational apparatus may be necessary to achieve a low degree of information and understanding. In the first case the efficiency of collusionary behaviour will consequently be high; in the second case it will be low.

Forms therefore do not determine the efficacy of concerted practices and the old idea that express agreements or at least a "meeting of minds" is required to make collusion work has been abandoned.

The main forms of collusion, apart from loose unwritten agreements among more or less equal partners are price-leadership and information associations. Both forms have been dealt with in the literature so that only a few remarks will do.[9]

Price leadership may be based on low unit costs pertaining to the leading firm. In such a case the price-leader may either reap high benefits by keeping other firms alive through a raised price-level, or he may restrict them to a fringe of market transactions by setting a lower price. The course to follow will depend on several variables a.o. whether the market will grow or stagnate. It easily follows that the first variety will as a rule have more detrimental effects for society. Price-leadership may also be based on market power, deriving for example from multi-market operations, from financial means or the pre-emption of customers. Competitors will not dare to undercut the price-leader for fear of being "punished". In such cases high prices in well-established markets may go alongside "fighting-prices" in particular or special markets where small competitors will have to be brought into line or destroyed. To deal with such kind of situations, Heuss has advanced the interesting proposal that large, market power possessing firms should be forbidden to

9. See a.o. J.W. Markham–The Nature and Significance of Price Leadership, in: Readings in Industrial Organization and Public Policy, American Economic Association, 1958; D.P. O'Brien and D. Swann–*Information Agreements, Competition and Efficiency* (London 1968). Particularly interesting cases are assembled in the collection of essays edited by W. Adams–*The Structure of American Industry* (1971).

undercut small competitors. Only defensive price-cuts (of the alignating type) should be allowed.

The proposal would give small firms and new entrants the chance to undercut big firms without fear of retaliation or punishment. The big firm could defend itself by aligning its price. Whether the idea would also be a practically sound proposal remains to be seen however.

A third form of price-leadership is mostly much more innocent: barometric price-leadership assumes that particular firms respond much more quickly and aptly to market changes than others. The competitive firms then follow suit, mostly after some delays and/or some erroneous endeavours.

The innocence of this form of price-leadership wears off, however, in case the leading firm: (a), is always the same one,[10] (b) price changes and dates of change tend to become uniform and (c) price changes are first announced to competitors instead of to customers. In some cases seemingly innocent barometric price-leadership approaches outright collusion.

Information associations, another form of collusion, often coming into existence when an anti-cartel policy is strictly enforced, mostly flourish on the basis of larger numbers of competitors in markets which are not so transparent. An elaborate organisation is set up to assemble and disseminate information concerning prices and other variables. They mostly lose whatever innocence they may possess, when transgressors of agreed lines of behaviour are publicly exposed and even penalized. Thus, in order to ensure conformist behaviour, an informative and corrective mechanism is necessary. In such cases, collusionary behaviour rests on an advanced measure of organized action. The degree and form of collusion will then go hand in hand.

Degrees of collusion have a habit of intensifying once the concerted practices get started. The logic of collusionary action will drive towards higher degrees because competitive action in non-agreed fields will be countered; and retaliation or its fear will in turn prompt further agreements.

Practical histories therefore show very often that initial attempts at collusive behaviour get frustrated, only to be followed by more elaborate and formal agreements. With some exaggeration it might be said that collusion often ends in cartels, as well as that cartels often end in mergers and take-overs. This proposition is not meant to deny that stable collusionary structures may persist: if markets have crystallized into small numbers of well organized, strong companies, valuing their independence, collusion may well be a long-lived phenomenon.

10. or the same duet, as in the U.S. cigarette industry. c.f. Tennant, 239/40.

5. *Effects of Collusion*

When the American Tobacco Trust was split up (in 1911) into four successor companies of sufficient strength to stand on their own, price competition was not reinstalled (save for the introduction of new brands). Each firm had to count on the continued existence of its competitors. It therefore needed to take into consideration the effect its actions must have on the others, and "in a mature market judicious self-restraint can eliminate price competition as efficiently as explicit agreement among them".[11] The example is interesting from several points of view. It shows that a very often heard opinion stating that collusion is little harmful and at best temporary or short-lived, is erroneous. In cigarettes, tacit price restrictions have now lasted for more than 60 years; in automobiles, "the pattern of interfirm behaviour–under General Motor's leader-ship–has become largely a function of industry custom, convention and tacit understandings";[12] in containers, oil, steel and many other American industries, parallel behaviour is pervasive.[13]

There is an important warning for Europe implied in these findings. Because American business had earlier opportunities to develop to a large size (and to consolidate) in a market of continental dimensions, absolute and relative concentration have progressed further on the other side of the Atlantic than in Europe. In many American branches of industry tight oligopoly is the rule, whereas in the European market (the inclusion of Britain and Scandinavia reinforces the Case!) loose oligopolies prevail at least for the time being. With the continuing merger wave in Europe, much tighter oligopolistic positions will probably be created in the future and the collusive threat may therefore come to loom larger.

Another inference is that collusion will be most durable and harmful in mature industries. Now, a mature industry as a rule deserves this qualification because its products are widely diffused. A majority of consumers or industrial users buys the mature product, whether because of its inherent qualities or because of standard which have become customary in society. This means, that the injury society will undergo because of the collusion will be large, even if a collusive price usually cannot be identified with the monopoly price.

If, as is generally recognized, pure monopolies are rare, and a strong anticartel policy is maintained, it would seem to be a fair deduction that the majority of deviations from competitive prices are ascribable to the wide field

11. R.B. Tennant–The Cigarette Industry, in W. Adams (Ed.) *op.cit.*, note 9, 241.
12. R.F. Lanzilotti–The Automobile Industry, in W. Adams, (Ed.), *op.cit.*, note 9,274.
13. See the other essays in the Adam's book.

of restrictive business behaviour called collusion. Several estimates of the public losses traceable to the absence of competition in oligopolistic industries have been made in recent years. All of them apply to the United States economy and are therefore not directly relevant to European circumstances. They may nevertheless be instructive as to the welfare losses which may result from heavily concentrated industry structures showing collusionary behaviour.

Ralph Nader estimated the costs of the various forms of "monopoly" (in the loose usage of the term) at more than $ 100 billion or over 20 per cent of every dollar spent. Senator Hart, who presided over the U.S. congressional hearings of the sixties has put the figure at 35-40 per cent, or $ 170-230 billion per year. As traditional monopoly theory indicates, part of these "losses" represents a lowering of standards of living through a wastage of resources. Another part represents a shift of income from small industries to monopolized business, from labour to capital.

Two leading industrial economists have made separate estimates by means of more refined techniques. They have found much lower figures than the ones quoted above, though still substantial, William Shepherd found that:

a. prices tend, on the average, to be from 10 to 30 per cent above the competitive level in the intermediate and tight oligopoly industries.

b. costs tend to be increased by some five per cent (on average) where concentration is pronounced.

c. market power appears to double or triple the margin of excess profits (that is the margin of profitability over the minimum competitive profit rates of six to eight per cent.).

For the economy as a whole, Shepherd estimated the lost output or "welfare loss" at about 2.5 per cent of the national income.[14] This percentage does not account for the redistribution of income resulting from quasi-monopolistic pricing. If this effect is also taken into consideration " the combined loss in efficient resourse-use . . . may range upward toward 5 per cent of national income"[14a]

F.M. Scherer[15] puts the "padding of costs" due to "firms insulated from competition to operate with copious layers of fat" as high as 10 per cent ("not at all uncommon"). Taking into account other social losses (such as excess product differentiation, excess capacity, pricing distortions, etc.) he arrives at a figure of 6.2 per cent of the Gross National Product or some $ 60 billion per year at current values. To this should be added an estimated

14. W.G. Shepherd–*Market Power and Economic Welfare* (New York, 1970), 196-198.

14a. c.f. Shepherd–*id* at 246.

15. F.M. Scherer–*Industrial Market Structure and Economic Performance* (Chicago 1971), 400-411.

3 per cent of the G.H.P. for income redistribution, plus some unquantifiable negative effects on technological developments and the stability of capital investment. The last factor–capital investment–is considered "to be somewhat more volatile in concentrated than in unconcentrated industries.[16] It seems that, even if we restrict our estimates of welfare losses to the more conservative ones, they are far from negligible and collusionary practices may well account for a major share of them. Though European circumstances are not (yet) so inducive to similar practices and losses as American, it would be nevertheless be opportune if policy makers were to sharpen their knives. The Court in Luxemburg has, by pronouncing in the dyestuffs-case in the way it did, at least given them an approving nod.

16. Id. at 410.

Chapter 5

THE INTRA-ENTERPRISE CONSPIRACY PARADOX

by *Prof. Mr. A. van Oven*

For about 30 years now, the concept of intra-enterprise conspiracy has played an important part in antitrust cases before the courts of the United States. It is based on the interpretation–on one particular point–of one of the most elementary provisions of the legislation in this field, *i.e.* Section 1 Sherman Act, which declares "every contract, combination in the form of trust or otherwise, or conspiracy, in restraint of trade or commerce . . . illegal". The provision further states that "every person who shall make any contract or engage in any combination or conspiracy hereby declared to be illegal" will be liable to punishment (Section 1 *in fine*). The term "person" as used in this Act also refers to corporations and associations (Section 8). The prohibition contained in Section 1 thus applies to–natural or juristic –*persons*. For this prohibition to be operative, the practices concerned must involve more than one *person*. Acts done by only one person may also come under the Sherman Act, but only by virtue of Section 2 which deals with (attempted) monopolisation. Section 1 requires several persons as it apparant from notably the terms "contract, combination or conspiracy".

The word "conspiracy" seems to carry a somewhat romantic connotation but, in law, this is of no importance whatsoever. As the American case-books concerning antitrust law have it, "the picture of conspiracy as a meeting by twilight of a trio of sinister persons with pointed hats close together belongs to a darker age".[1] Thus, used along with the term combination, conspiracy hardly possesses independent meaning. The purpose of adding these two concepts to contracts in Section 1 was obviously to make it clear that the law applies to any "concerted action" based upon whatever legal construction and even if not so based at all. For that matter, the courts regard the mere evidence of "implied conspiracy" sufficient: on the basis of circumstantial evidence it is inferred that parallel conduct of competitors is the result of some concert of action. Some uncertainty existed as to whether consciously parallel conduct of competitors alone is sufficient to infer conspiracy, but apparently the courts are not prepared to go to such lengths.[2] However this

1. S. Chesterfield Oppenheim, *Federal Antitrust Laws* (1959), 224.
2. M. Handler, Recent Antitrust Developments–63 Michigan Law Review 1964, 85 *et seq.*

may be, it is difficult to distinguish clearly between cases of concerted action and independent parallel action. In this respect the case-law appears to present a more or less casuistic nature.

The prohibition of Section 1 extends to "every . . . conspiracy in restraint of trade or commerce . . .". In these latter words lies the core of the antitrust philosophy which is to preserve and to protect free competition. However, even if viewed in connexion with this objective, these words by no means offer a clear-cut criterion for answering the question as to which conspiracies are illegal and which are not. For here, too, we are dealing with a broad concept susceptible of many interpretations. And so it has proved to be in the case-law; for instance, all questions relating to the so-called rule of reason are closely bound up with the meaning of this concept.[3] True, subsequent legislation provided more specifically that certain phenomena constitute restraint of trade. But this does not alter the fact that whenever such specific provision does not apply, the court must rely on the general norm of Section 1 Sherman Act (or as the case may be, on the norm of Section 2) and then has to decide whether restriction of trade within the meaning of this provision exists.

The above shows that to a very great extent the shaping of antitrust law lies in the hands of the courts. The wording of the provisions of the Sherman Act accords the courts the greatest possible discretion[4] and it is their task to elaborate, to delimit, further to shape the concepts which underlie the legal system, so as to create a greater certainty as to what is lawful and what is not. We shall now ascertain–be it very summarily–how the courts have performed this task in relation to the problem of intra-enterprise conspiracy.

It is of course quite well conceivable–certainly if the concept is construed in the wide sense as described above–that a conspiracy is set on foot within the walls of a single enterprise even if the latter is run as a single limited company. It is equally conceivable that such a conspiracy may result in restriction of trade. Consider for instance the event that one of the regular suppliers is excluded from future orders as a result of discussions between the director of an enterprise and the manager of one of its divisions. The wording of Section 1 is broad enough to cover this case. And yet one may wonder whether this is actually its purpose. Thus interpreted, pretty nearly all joint decisions within an enterprise might constitute a potential violation of Section 1. It need hardly be argued that antitrust legislation would thus far exceed its purpose. Obviously, if internal consultations within an enterprise

3. M. Handler, *Antitrust in perspective* (1957), 3 *et seq.*

4. Wyzanski, J., United States v. United Shoe Machinery Corp., 110 F. Supp. 295 at 348 (D. Mass. 1953): "In the antitrust field the courts have been accorded, by common consent, an authority they have in no other branch of enacted law".

would be rendered impossible, the entire economic system, based as it is upon free enterprise, would be endangered.

It is remarkable that nevertheless the courts–at least initially– appeared to be prepared to accept the intra-enterprise conspiracy doctrine (sometimes also called the intra-*corporate* conspiracy doctrine) even to this extent.[5] Perhaps the connexion with Section 2 Sherman Act was a contributory factor, for the latter makes not only (attempted) monopolisation illegal, but also "to combine or conspire . . . to monopolize". Monopolisation may be the result of the action of a single enterprise, and the addition of the words "conspire to monopolize" may in that case mean that officers of the enterprise who had internally conspired to monopolise, are liable to punishment together with the monopolising corporation itself. Meanwhile, the fact that internal conspiracy to *monopolise* is punishable under Section 2, by no means implies that internal conspiracy *in restriction of trade* is prohibited under Section 1. For in Section 2 the concept of conspiracy only serves to determine the persons to be punished if an illegal and punishable fact exists, whereas in Section 1 this concept is part and parcel of the illegal conduct itself. This follows from the fact that to monopolise *is unlawful as such*, restriction of trade on the other hand only *as a result of a conspiracy*. The latter concept must therefore be considered to be a separate element of the prohibition. Accordingly, the intra-corporate conspiracy doctrine in the above sense is explicitly rejected in the more recent cases.[6] The authoritative Report of the Attorney General's Committee "to study the antitrust laws" (1955) simply repudiates it.

The more limited version of the intra-enterprise conspiracy doctrine–to which we shall confine ourselves in the following concerns restrictions of trade brought about by an enterprise composed of a number (at least two) of separate legal entities, usually limited companies. In the reality of business intercourse, however, such companies are not autonomous: they cannot determine their own policy since they are jointly controlled by a central management, the top of the enterprise as a whole. Naturally, independence or the lack of it is not always a clear-cut criterion, there may be cases of doubt, cases of a partial or limited autonomy. In the following we shall not concern

5. See on this the Report of the Attorney General's National Committee, mentioned in the text.

6. Nelson Radio & Supply Co. v. Motorola, 200 F2d 911 (1952): ". . . it appears plain to us that the conspiracy upon which plaintiff relies consists simply in the absurd assertion that the defendant, through its officers and agents, conspires with itself to restrict its trade in its own products"; Cliff Food Stores Inc. V. Kroger Inc. 417 F. 2d 203 (C.C.A. 5th, 1969): "The basis of the rule that a corporation cannot conspire with its unincorporated divisions is that there must be at least two persons or entities to constitute a conspiracy, and a corporation cannot conspire with itself any more than a person can"; Ark Dental Supply Co. v. Cavitron Corp., 1971, Trade Cases 73, 539: "As a division of Cavitron, Clev-Dent is not capable of conspiracy, apart from Cavitron".

ourselves with this problem, but rather confine ourselves for simplicity's sake to evident cases of the existence of a central management: a parent-company which is able to influence, in a decisive manner, the business policy of its wholly-owned subsidiaries.

The advocates of the above doctrine are of the opinion that agreements or concerted practices between one or more of the subsidiaries and the parent company or between the subsidiaries themselves should be regarded as conspiracies within the meaning of Section 1. In addition to that a question arises with regard to the meaning of "restriction of trade", *i.e.* can restriction of trade be said to exist if restrictions are effected only on the relations within the corporate family or should the restriction be put upon the freedom of action of third parties, such as competitors, customers or suppliers? If this question has to be answered in the first mentioned sense even internal conspiracy with only internal effects is illegal. In that case, the answer seems to be based upon the notion that the intramural competition–whatever this may be–is protected by law as well as the extramural. If this notion is redupiated, the doctrine is considered to be applicable only in case of external effects: restriction of the competition with (respectively between) third enterprises.

The intra-enterprise conspiracy doctrine is firmly anchored in a series of decisions of the American courts, some of them delivered by the Supreme Court.[7] The answer to the question of whether this doctrine held by the courts also extends to conspiracies which only result in restriction of trade as between the allied companies amongst themselves–restriction of "intra-enterprise competition"–is uncertain. It is often hard to draw the dividing line between external and internal restriction of trade. When for instance the existence of an agreement between allied companies for the purposes of a territorial division of the market has been established, it will be readily inferred that its purpose was also to keep out competitors. In any case, the above Report of the Attorney General's National Committee rejects application of the doctrine (which as such is accepted by the majority of the Committee) to "joint action between members of a corporate family not intended to or resulting in coercive undue restraint on their customers or competitors": "it is obviously unrealistic to expect or to command

7. From the more recent decisions may be mentioned Kiefer Stewart Co. v. Joseph E. Seagram & Son (1951), 340 U.S. 211 and United States v. Timken Roller Bearing Co. (1951), 341 U.S. 593. See also Joseph E. Seagram & Sons Inc. v. Hawaiian Oke Liquors Ltd. (1969) 416 F2d 71: "It is now settled law that if a corporation chooses to conduct parts of its business through subsidiary or affiliated corporations, and conspires with them to do something that independent entities cannot conspire to do under section 1 of the Sherman Act, it is no defense that the corporations are in reality a single economic entity". See for an exhaustive critical discussion of recent American decisions Harms, "Intra enterprise conspiracy?" Eur 1966, 230 *et seq*.

wholly-owned affiliates to compete". And in so far as the courts did indeed accept this consequence, the Report suggests that the Supreme Court review its opinion.

Although therefore the intra-enterprise conspiracy doctrine, at least in so far as such conspiracy results in external restriction of trade, undoubtedly may be said to be generally accepted by the courts, it is by no means uncontested. A minority of the above Attorney General's National Committee peremptorily repudiates it. It is challenged also by the majority of the writers on this subject.[8]

What grounds underlie the intra-enterprise conspiracy doctrine? The court decisions do not provide an answer to this question apart from the often repeated statement "that common ownership and control does not liberate corporations from the impact of the antitrust laws", no grounds whatsoever have been given. This is presumably considered unnecessary since the *wording* of Section 1 is broad enough to cover the intra-enterprise conspiracy doctrine. On the other hand, the *purpose* of the provision–protection of competition–points into another direction. In this connexion it might be inferred that the provision is only intended for those who are capable of determining their competition policy independently. Furthermore it should be pointed out that when this doctrine is put into practice, conduct which is allowed to an enterprise operating through departments or branch offices which are not separate legal entities, is illegal in an enterprise which operates through subsidiaries: an unequal treatment which in fairness seems hardly justified and which furthermore constitutes unwarranted interference with the free use of subsidiaries. Especially in the case of enterprises with establishments abroad the latter may be very prejudicial.[9] It is not clear why these arguments were not allowed to carry weight with the courts. Presumably the wish somehow to pull the antitrust-net so tight as to leave as few loopholes as possible has been the decisive–and rather opportunistic–motive.[10]

It is time to cross the Atlantic and to see whether the intra-enterprise conspiracy doctrine should be accorded a place in the rules of competition of the Common Market. It is well-known that the provisions concerning competition of the EEC-Treaty have been largely patterned after the American example. As in the opinion of the American courts the terms for the application of this doctrine are found in the law, so European antitrust

8. See the literature mentioned in the article by Harms referred to in the preceding note.

9. See in particular United States v. Timken Roller Bearing Co. (1951), mentioned in note 7. Jackson's dissenting opinion relied precisely upon this consideration.

10. It is remarkable that in cases of conspiracy between a subsidiary and a third party the relevancy of the dependent character of the former is acknowledged: for such conspiracy the parent company is deemed responsible. Thus *e.g.* National Dairy Products Corporations v. United States (1965) 350 F2d 321: "In such a situation the court may disregard the legal fiction of corporate entity".

law may be reasonable expected to contain them also. On the face of it this is indeed the case. Although, of course, not identically worded, Articles 85 paragraph 1 and 86 of the Treaty broadly resemble Sections 1 and 2 of the Sherman Act, at least insofar as is material to our subject. Article 85(1) prohibits *joint actions* by enterprises, in addition to agreements (and decisions by associations of enterprises) it mentions also "any concerted practices". The latter should no doubt be taken to mean the same thing as the conspiracy mentioned in Section 1 of the Sherman Act, at least as interpreted by the courts in the broad sense of implied conspiracy. On the other hand, the conduct which is prohibited in Article 86 of the Rome Treaty–*i.e.* improper practices of a dominant position–may very well involve *only one enterprise*, as does monopolisation which is dealt with in Section 2 Sherman Act. Article 85 furthermore mentions prevention, restriction or distortion of competition, which appears to be a somewhat wordy interpretation of the American term "restraint of trade". Finally, both regulations–the European as well as the American– convey that they are intended to protect *interstate commerce*.

Another very important common characteristic is that both regulations are in the nature of a statement of principle: in broad terms and with the aid of elastic concepts some general norms are formulated. Apart from subsequent more specific laws or regulations, these norms are to be substantiated by the courts. In this field, the European courts–in the last instance the Court of Justice of the European Communities at Luxemburg–will thus have to shape law as did their American colleagues.

Meanwhile, along with all the above points which the two systems have in common, there are also differences. One of these could be of pre-eminent importance to our subject, to wit the question of who are affected by the prohibitions. As we have seen the Sherman Act refers to (natural or legal) *persons*. In the relevant articles of the EEC-Treaty, however, *enterprises* are mentioned instead of persons. Article 85(1) refers to agreements between enterprises, Article 86 mentions improper practices of a dominant position by enterprises. When referring to "concerted practices", Article 85 does not explicitly add that practices by enterprises are meant. However in view of the superscription "Rules applying to enterprises" of the Section of which these articles are a part, it is self-evident that here too the conduct of enterprises is contemplated. To what extent the use of the concept "enterprise" in the wording of the Treaty may affect the acceptability of the intra-enterprise conspiracy doctrine will be discussed below. First we shall examine if and to what extent an opinion on the acceptability can be derived from the decisions of the Community organs, to wit the European Commission and the Court of Justice.

Although the Commission is not a judicial body, it is nevertheless repeatedly called upon to state whether in its opinion some agreement is

prohibited under Article 85, for instance because an interested party petitions the Commission for nullity of such an agreement or because the parties to the agreement themselves apply for a socalled "negative clearance".[11] Of recent years several cases such as these were brought before the Commission where the problem of intra-enterprise conspiracy was implied.

At issue in the case of Christiani & Nielsen [12] was an agreement between a Danish parent company and its wholly-owned subsidiary at The Hague. The agreement contained a territorial division and *inter alia* obliged the subsidiary to follow the directives emanating from Christiani & Nielsen, Copenhagen. Subsidiaries had also been set up in other Common Market countries and it appeared that all of them had to abstain from activities in countries where other subsidiaries were situated, Furthermore, the Commission records that within the Common Market a great number of other enterprises exist which engage in activities similar to those of Christiani & Nielsen. In view of this state of affairs, the Commission then considers that the prohibition of Article 85(1) is based on the presumption, that the enterprises concerned are competitors and their competition can be restricted. Whether or not this is the case depends on the subsidiary being capable of independent economic action *vis-à-vis* the parent company. In casu–says the Commission–the Dutch subsidiary is merely an integral part of the economic entity as constituted by the Christiani & Nielsen group. Therefore, the division of the market agreed upon by contract is nothing but a working division within one and the same economic entity. It cannot be demanded that within this entity a part, even though it possesses legal personality, competes with the parent company. For the latter would at all times be entitled to determine the conduct of its Dutch subsidiary, even if no agreement had been concluded. By means of these considerations the Commission arrived at the conclusion that the purpose or the consequences of the agreement at issue were not such as to prevent, restrict or distort competition within the Common Market and that therefore it cannot be concluded on the basis of the available information that the agreement is illegal by virtue of Article 85, paragraph 1.

This decision is obviously based upon an unsound ground. Specifically the opinion that Article 85(1) presupposes competition *between the enterprises concerned* is incorrect. For the prohibition equally applies to agreements which distort competition with and/or between third parties (for instance vertical agreements). And therefore the conclusion drawn from the subsidiary's lack of autonomy, *i.e.* that *consequently* the agreement does not affect competition, cannot be accepted. One gets the impression that the

11. *I.e.* a statement as envisaged in Article 2 of Regulation no. 17 (O.J. p. 204/62), to the effect that the available information provide no grounds for the Commission to take action against the agreement concerned by virtue of Art. 85 para 1.

12. Decision of the Commission of June 18, 1969, O.J., L.165/12; [1969] CMLR, D 36 *et seq*.

Commission was not sufficiently aware of the diversified variations the problem of the intra-enterprise conspiracy doctrine presents. Under these circumstances it may be deduced from the decision that the Commission repudiates the doctrine insofar as internal restriction of trade is concerned, and that is as far as one can go. In this respect the Commission appears to be of the same opinion as the Attorney General's National Committee expressed in its report of 1955.

That the Commission did not intend to repudiate peremptorily the intra-enterprise conspiracy doctrice also in relation to restriction on third parties, seems to be confirmed by a publication the Commission issued some weeks later.[13] This publication concerned the agreement under which the American Sperry Rand Corporation had transferred its trade-mark Remington for electric shavers to its subsidiary Remington Rand Italia as its exclusive agent in Italy. The subsidiary had used this trade-mark for the purpose of opposing the import of Remington products from other Common Market countries. With reference to this use the Commission had informed the companies concerned that the agreement for the transfer of the trade-mark as interpreted and applied should probably be regarded as infringing Article 85(1) because thus applied the agreement guaranteed to Remington Rand Italia a complete territorial protection in restriction of competition on the Common Market. The case was settled amicably after the companies concerned had promised not to make further use of the trade-mark for the purpose of preventing parallel imports from other Common Market countries.

In this affair, a possible restriction on third parties clearly has influenced the Commission's opinion. In this lay indeed the great difference with the casus position in the Christiani & Nielsen case. Meanwhile it remains remarkable that the fact that the issue concerned an agreement between a parent company and a wholly-owned subsidiary apparently did not in any way affect the Commission's anticipation that the relevant agreement would be judged to contravene Article 85(1). On the basis of Article 85(1) the illegality of the intra-enterprise conspiracy is now accepted by the Commission as much as a matter of course as in the Christiani & Nielsen case the reverse was inferred from the same provision.

That the acceptance of illegality in the Remington case was not the result of the Commission's deliberate and fundamental views in regard to the intra-enterprise conspiracy doctrine, became apparent less than a year later. The issue was again an application for a negative clearance this time made by the

13. Bulletin E.G. 1969, No. 8, 40/41. In *re* Scott Paper the Commission has already taken this same view; in view of certain promises by the enterprise concerned, the Commission abstained from taking action in this case (O.J. 1968, C 110/2). See with regard to this affair Wertheimer, Droit des Marques et Concurrence *Cah. dr. Eur.* 1970, 438-472 at 469.

subsidiaries of the American Eastman Kodak Corporation established in five member-States of the E.E.C. [14] These subsidiaries sold their products subject to uniform conditions which imposed certain restrictions on their customers, *inter alia* as regards resale and export. The Commission considers that the subsidiaries are entirely dependent on the parent company and that they are therefore also incapable of independent action in their mutual relations. The Commission infers from this fact that consequently "the uniformity of the sales conditions of the Kodak corporations of the Common Market does not result from an agreement or concerted practices between the parent company and its subsidiaries or between the subsidiaries themselves". Nevertheless the Commission also examines the *contents* of the sales conditions between the Kodak corporations and their customers (the issue in this case is therefore whether *these* agreements infringe the rules of Article 85). As a result the Commission finds that the contents (as subsequently amended) provide no grounds for the Commission to act against the sales conditions.

The reasoning in this case as compared with the Christiani & Nielsen decision presents a startling discrepancy: in the latter case the lack of independence of the subsidiaries led to the conclusion that no restriction of competition existed, in this case that no conspiracy exists. Thus the impression is that the Commission in its last decision deliberately and entirely repudiated the intra-enterprise conspiracy doctrine, at least as regards cases when the subsidiaries are completely dependent. [15] Although as a whole the Commission's policy till now appears to have been not very consistent on this point, after the recent decision of the Court of Justice in the Dyestuffs Cases (mentioned below) it may be expected that the Commission will persist in its rejection.

In November 1971 the Court of Justice of the European Communities had to decide on a case which at least on the face of it offered this body an opportunity (presumbly for the first time) to state its opinion regarding the applicability of the intra-enterprise conspiracy doctrine on the basis of the provisions of the Rome Treaty. At issue was a contract granting to the Belgian Company Béguelin the exclusive right ("concession") to sell the products of a Japanese manufacturer; originally the contract covered both Belgium and France, but later on as to France the right was ceded to a French subsidiary of Béguelin. Before the Trade Tribunal at Nice it was argued that the concession granted to the French subsidiary constituted an infringement of Article 85 of the Treaty and therefore was void, on the ground of the existing affiliation and the common economic interest of Béguelin Belgium

14. Decision of the Commission of June 30, 1970, O.J. 1970, L. 147/24; [1970] CMLR, D 19 *et seq.*

15. A confirmation of this impression is contained–so it seems–in the remarks of the Commission inserted in the decision of the Court of Justice in the Béguelin Case (cited in note 16).

and Béguelin France. The tribunal at Nice decided to ask the Court at Luxemburg for a preliminary ruling on this point (as provided for by Article 177 of the EEC-Treaty). The question put to the latter Court has meanwhile been given a somewhat different wording, *i.e.* the Court was asked to decide whether Béguelin Belgium and Béguelin France would infringe the prohibition of Article 85 if they exploited in their common economic interest the concession granted to one of them (France). In its decision the Court in its turn by implication amended the question by assuming that the question concerned the transfer of the concession by Béguelin Belgium to its French subsidiary, or at least the fact that the Belgian parent company allowed its French subsidiary to acquire the concession. In reply to this question the Court considered that Article 85 prohibits agreements between enterprises which tend to restrict competition or have this effect and that "in the case of a contract conceding exclusive rights of sale that condition is not met, when such concession is in fact partially transferred by a parent company to a subsidiary which, although enjoying a distinct legal personality does not have any economic autonomy". [16]

In the writers opinion it would be wrong to induce from this consideration a repudiation of the intra-enterprise conspiracy doctrine, for it only states a simple truth, *i.e.* that practices which *do not* result in a restriction of trade cannot come under the prohibition laid down in Article 85 merely *on the ground* that they emanate from economically affiliated companies. Indeed, the intra-enterprise conspiracy doctrine precisely concerns the question of whether concerted practices which *do result* in restriction of trade are illegal *in spite* of the fact that they emanate from economically affiliated companies. An American court, examining the Béguelin case in the light of Section 1 Sherman Act, would in all probability have decided in the same sense. From the Court's judgment it may rather be inferred that the Court deliberately wanted to leave a possible adoption of the intra-enterprise conspiracy doctrine open. Otherwise there would have been no need to consider the existence of restriction of trade, since the Court could have confined itself to the consideration that Article 85 paragraph 1 has no bearing on agreements between a parent company and its subsidiaries.

In the recent Dyestuffs Cases the problem of the impact of a company's economic dependency on the applicability of the Common Market rules on competition was brought before the Court once more. The Court decided, that the enterprises involved–most of them situated within E.E.C. territory–had been engaged in concerted practices to increase the price of dyestuffs in the Common Market. Some of the enterprises, respectively situated in the United Kingdom and in Switzerland, denied to have made any sales within

16. Judgment of November 25, 1971, Case.No. 22/71 (Béguelin v. Import Export and Marbach), *Recueil* XVII, 949-964 at 959; [1972] CMLR, 81-102 at 95.

the E.E.C. territory: their products had been sold in the Common Market by their local subsidiaries situated there. The Court, however, ruled on this point: "When the subsidiary does not enjoy any real autonomy in the determination of its course of action on the market, the prohibitions imposed by Article 85(1) may be considered inapplicable in the relations between the subsidiary and the parent company, with which it then forms one economic unit. In view of the unity of the group thus formed, the activities of the subsidiaries may, in certain circumstances, be imputed to the parent company".[17]

As in this case the relations between the subsidiary and the parent company were not at stake, there was no reason for the Court to decide on the acceptability of the intra-enterprise conspiracy doctrine. Consequently, its consideration on this point is to be regarded as an obiter dictum. But in contrast with the Béguelin Case, this time–so it seems–the Court had the intention to take side expressly in the controversy: it clearly rejects the applicability of the prohibition of Article 85(1) on relations of a purely intra-enterprise nature.

Before giving an appreciation of the arguments pro and contra the intra-enterprise conspiracy doctrine on the basis of the EEC provisions, some remarks should be made as to whether and, if so, to what extent the application of this doctrine is *needed* for the purpose of the rules of competition of the Common Market. A definitive answer is hard to give at this stage. The only thing that can be said is that so far such need has not been apparent, except–perhaps–for one specific situation, *i.e.* when a parent company by assigning its trade-marks to its subsidiaries in EEC territory endeavours to affect a territorial division within the Common Market for its products.[18] In view of the territorial character of national trade-mark laws, it is assumed in some member-States[19] that in such cases the subsidiary concerned can succesfully oppose parallel imports from other member States by pleading its exclusive rights, even though the products concerned have been legally marketed in the country of origin (in other words are supplied by the parent company or other subsidiaries). It may be asked whether such restriction of interstate commerce should not be opposed with the aid of the intra-enterprise conspiracy doctrine which could serve as a basis for considering the transfer of the trade-marks an infringement of Article 85, paragraph 1.[20] There

17. Judgment of July 14, 1972, Cases Nos. 48/69, 52/69 and 53/69 (I.C.I. Ciba-Geigy and Sandoz v.Commission), *Recueil* XVIII, 619, 787, 845 at 666 [1972] CMLR, 557-650 at 629.

18. Cf. the casus position of the Remington case mentioned above (note 14).

19. Italy, Belgium and the Netherlands; see on this subject H.W. Wertheimer, 58 The Trademark Report, 258 *et seq* and the cases cited in notes 97, 98 and 101.

20. Cf. Alexander in 61 The Trademark Reporter 1971, No. 1.

appears to be the more reason for this since this method of achieving a territorial division would not be open to an enterprise whose establishments in the member States are not separate legal persons.[21] In relation to Article 85(1) disproportionate advantages would thus accrue from the fact, that an enterprise effects its trade in the E.E.C. countries by means of subsidiaries instead of unincorporated divisions.

In this connexion it should be remarked first and foremost that such unequal treatment of internationally diversified enterprises on the basis of their construction (composed of subsidiaries or not) is a sequel of a questionable application of the principle of territoriality in national trade-mark laws. A trade-mark serves to distinguish the products of an enterprise. And if such enterprise puts its trade-mark into the name of a legally separate subsidiary for a specific country, there is reason from the point of view of trade-mark law to disregard the legal form of the subsidiary. Meanwhile, so long as this is not yet the prevailing opinion in all member States, the danger of incongruity with regard to the application of Article 85(1) is very much alive. But do we need the intra-enterprise conspiracy doctrine in order to cope with this danger? In the writer's opinion there is another, much simpler method, application of Article 86. For we are dealing here with a case in which trade between the member States in products bearing a certain trade-mark is affected. With regard to such products the enterprise concerned undoubtedly enjoys a dominant position and the way in which it manipulates its trade-marks for the purpose of achieving a territorial division appears to be clearly indicative of improper practices of this dominant position. In other cases, too, in which recourse to the intra-enterprise conspiracy doctrine is deemed necessary for the application of Article 85, Article 86 could be expected to offer a simpler solution.[22]

There are some strong arguments for the view that the intra-enterprise conspiracy doctrine should not take root in the rules of competition of the Common Market.[23] The decisive consideration should be that it is the

21. Cf. Snijders, *supra*, 63-76.

22. More often than not, both the Commission and the Court, with the aid of an extremely broad interpretation, regard Article 85 applicable to certain practices whereas application of Article 86, which in the writer's opinion would have been more plausible, is repudiated. See inter alia the judgment of the Court of February 18, 1971, case No. 40/70 (Sirena v. Eda.) *Recueil,* XVII, 69 *et seq*; [1971] CMLR, 260 *et seq;* cf. Wertheimer, *infra,* 210-215.

23. German writers have discussed this matter repeatedly: Ulmer, "Wettbewerbbeschränkende Absprachen" im Rahmen von Unternehmenszusammenschlüssen, *W.u.W.* 1960, 163 *et seq*, Leo, Konzerninterne Marktregelungen im Lichte des E.W.G.-Kartellrechts, 18 *Kartellrundschau* 1966, 11 *et seq*., Treeck, Konzerninterne Vereinbarungen im EWG-Kartellrecht, 15 AWD 1969, 367-368; Huber, Konzerninterne Vereinbarungen im

purpose of the provisions of Articles 85 and 86 to prevent distortion of competition and that is why they can only be intended for persons who are capable of independently determining their policy as regards competition, for a prohibition intended for persons who have no authority as to the object of the prohibition must be regarded as meaningless. Consequently, to be illegal by virtue of Article 85(1) the conduct will have to emanate from persons who carry on business independently and this regardless of the legal form in which these persons engage in their activities. If the legal nature of the forbidden conduct–the conspiracy–is immaterial, so is the legal nature of the performers of such actions. When interpreting the rules which govern business relations, the economic meaning of the concepts rather than the legal form in which the phenomena present themselves, is of paramount importance.

The above implies that not the persons who actually carry out the actions which are prohibited by virtue of Article 85 should be regarded as the performers, but rather the persons who decide whether the actions are to take place and thus are responsible for them. In the case of a parent company with one or more subsidiaries the responsible parties are those in whose hands the overall management lies, the board of directors, of the parent company. For the purposes of the rules of competition, the conduct of the subsidiaries should be regarded as actions of their parent company and as such be examined in the light of the prohibitions.[24] This implies that the rule of Article 85(1) which indeed presupposes participation of more parties than one, can never apply to agreements between or parallel conduct of, subsidiaries, respectively of one or more subsidiaries and the parent company: at least one independent enterprise other than the parent company must be involved.

In the writer's opinion, the above view could be defended quite well as an interpretation of Section 1 Sherman Act, even though the prohibition of this section refers to (natural or juristic) *persons*. On the basis of Article 85(1) this view has an even stronger case since–as has been observed above–this provision is aimed explicitly at *enterprises*. To a certain extent, this is of course a figure of speech; for in law enterprises are objects rather than subjects. Similar personifications are also found in other rules of law, *e.g.* in maritime law; fault of a vessel, responsibility of a vessel. Of course, what is really meant is the (natural or juristic) person or group of persons behind the personified concept, that is in this case the persons who manage the enterprise and are responsible for it, in other words, the owners of the enterprise.

EWG-Kartellrecht nach der Kommissionentscheidung im Fall Christiani und Nielsen, 15 AWD 1969, 429-433; Tessin in: Die Aktiengesellschaft 1969, 294; the last three in consequence of the Decision of the Commission *in re* Christiani and Nielsen.

24. *Cf.* the decision by the American court mentioned in note 10.

For an enterprise which is composed of a number of subordinate companies possessing legal personality, this is the parent company. If each of the subsidiaries were to be regarded as separate enterprises, the legal form would be promoted to a decisive criterion and consequently the concept enterprise would be given a meaning which disregards the purpose of the provision, *i.e.* protection of competition.

Repudiation of the intra-enterprise conspiracy doctrine also has a drawback; it involves the necessity of drawing a dividing line between companies which are not autonomous in the economic sense and those which are. In many cases such lacks of autonomy will not be hard to establish. But independence is by no means an absolute concept; all sorts of gradations may occur. In case of doubt a court may conceivably sometimes turn for help to the national laws of one of the member States. In this connexion particular reference may be made to the regulation of *Konzernrecht* as laid down in the German *Aktiengesetz*[25] (in the other member States this subject has not yet as such been regulated). But for the rest, the courts will have to decide in the light of the existing circumstances and it may be hard to avoid arbitrariness. Therefore the decisions cannot be expected to be entirely free of casuistry on this point. But, however this may be, this drawback cannot be of decisive importance, since adoption of the intra-enterprise conspiracy doctrine would, be it on different points, carry with it similar problems. For instance the difficult problem involved in establishing the borderline between restriction of trade *vis- à- vis* third parties on the one hand and affecting "internal competition" on the other hand (and in connexion with the latter concept: is this a valid concept and what is meant by it?). Furthermore, and much more difficult still, how far does the operation of the intra-enterprise conspiracy doctrine extend in that case? It is inconceivable that the courts would want to include the most paradoxical consequences of this doctrine–e.g. the internal conspiracy within the walls of a *company*–in the rules of competition of the Common Market. In that respect too a borderline would have to be drawn which again can only be done somewhat arbitrarily. In short, we are here faced with an objection which is indeed necessarily inherent to the application of rules of law which refer to concepts of an economic nature and therefore, vaguely defined in law.

As was already mentioned, the rules of competition of the Common Market have been patterned after American antitrust law. More generally still, it can be said that just as the cradle of civil law stood in Rome (about 20 centuries ago), the cradle of the rules of competition may be found in Washington (nineteenth century). Therefore, we Europeans can undoubtedly

25. Aktiengesetz, Drittes Buch: "Verbundene Unternehmen".

learn much from the American example, even when concepts and constructions are involved which would seem extremely unorthodox to jurists in civil law countries. But with regard to the intra-enterprise conspiracy doctrine an exeption should be made: this example can only teach us how *not* to go about it.

Chapter 6

THE JOINTLY-OWNED SUBSIDIARY ("JOINT VENTURE") AND ARTICLE 85 OF THE EEC-TREATY

by *Prof. Mr. M. R. Mok*

1. *Joint ventures, introductory notes*

Since about 1950 the form of cooperation between enterprises, generally called "joint ventures" has become an object of antitrust law interest and from 1960 even one of its highlights.

In 1956 it was observed that "joint ventures, in the antitrust sense, are relatively new phenomena".[1] But since 1956 this phenomenon has shown an enormous development and so did, in many parts of the world, the antitrust laws.

Some authors[2] consider expressions like joint subsidiary, jointly-owned subsidiary, joint undertaking, joint venture, fifty-fifty corporation, business-cooperative and cooperative partnership as interchangeable terms.[3] Originally (in the 19th century) the joint venture represented a type of temporary partnership of firms.[4] At a later stage ("corporate") joint ventures got a more permanent character. According to Pitofsky[5] "joint venture, as the term has been used in the antitrust field, is a vague and protean concept, which, at the extreme, might be taken to include all situations in which two or more persons or independent firms join forces to achieve some common goal". Likewise, Areeda[6] considers joint venture as "an expansive notion without definite meaning or antitrust consequence.......... Several persons join forces to achieve a joint 'legitimate' objective which may have anti-competitive implications".

1. G.E. Hale, "Joint ventures: collaborative subsidiaries and the antitrust laws", 42 Va. L. Rev. 1956, 937.
2. S.E. Boyle, "The joint subsidiary: an economic appraisal", VI The Antitrust Bulletin, 303; P.R. Dixon, "Joint ventures: what is their impact on competition?", VII The Antitrust Bulletin 1962, 398.
3. In French the term mostly used is "*filiale commune*", in German "*Gemeinschafts-unternehmen*".
4. Boyle, *op.cit.* note 2.
5. R. Pitofsky, "Joint ventures under the Antitrust Laws", some reflections on the significance of Penn-Olin, 82 Harv. L. Rev. 1969, 1007.
6. Ph. Areeda, "*Antitrust Analysis*" (Boston/Toronto, 1967), 275.

Rahl[7] limits the discussion of joint venture to those in which a separate corporation is formed to conduct joint operation for two or more enterprises which own the joint venture. For this author the key element is the establishment of a separate enterprise. Kaysen and Turner[8] include by joint venture only joint participation in the creation of a new producing organization. They want to exclude joint purchase of existing assets, which they consider to differ little from the merger question. They probably do not intend to limit the scope of their joint venture-notion to *producing* enterprises in a narrow sense. Pitofsky[9] speaks also of the organization or construction of a *new* producing *or servicing* organization.

I am rather attracted by Boyle's simple definition: "A joint subsidiary is basically a company in which the bulk, if not all, of the stock is owned by two or more parent companies". [10] The essential feature is that the common enterprise is embodied in a separate company, which is jointly owned by two or more other enterprises. It does not make much difference whether the jointly-owned subsidiary is a new-established unit, or was previously an independent firm or perhaps a 100% subsidiary of one of the parents. In the National City Lines case, one of the first joint venture-cases the U.S. authorities dealt with,[11] the parent corporations did not create a new firm; they purchased preferred stock of an existing company. In the European Philips-Siemens practice the two electric equipment manufacturers interchanged stock in their record producing subsidiaries, so that both of them became jointly-owned subsidiaries, later amalgamated into one single joint subsidiary. [12]

Hall[13] gives some examples of joint ventures with more than two parents, but estimates, however, that typically the joint venture has but two parents. I would add that normally the two parents will share the stock of the joint subsidiary on a fifty-fifty base, so that no decision concerning the subsidiary's activity can be taken without the agreement of any of the parent companies. Other distributions, (for instance 49-51%) are also conceivable and the decision-making power regarding the subsidiary may then be different from case to case; the same applies to subsidiaries, jointly owned by three or more parent companies.

7. J.A. Rahl "*The Nature and Extent of Conflict between American Antitrust Law and Laws in the Common Market*" in: J.A. Rahl (editor), "*Common Market and American Antitrust*" (New York, 1970), 181.

8. C. Kaysen and D.F. Turner, "*Antitrust Policy*" (Cambridge Mass. I, 1965), 136.

9. Pitofsky, *op.cit.*, note 5, 1007.

10. Boyle, *op.cit.*, note 2, 303.

11. United States v. National City Lines, 186 F, 2d 562/7th Circuit Court of Appeals, cert. denied, 341 U.S. 916 (1951).

12. See infra p. 130.

13. Hale, *op.cit.*, note 1, 928.

The objection of joint ventures include:

–common production
–common distribution
–common research
–common purchase
–sharing of profits and losses
–patent pools
–common know how.

The motives for the establishment of joint ventures may be:

–raising of capital
–spreading of risks
–developing new sources of raw materials
–combining the availability of raw materials with knowledge as to how to convert them into finished products
–obtaining the economics of scale in production and marketing
–making use of complementary or overlapping techniques including production techniques on one hand and sales techniques on the other
–(internationally) fulfilment of the legal, political or psychological need for a local element in investments abroad
–restriction of competition (seldom outspoken). [14]

From a historical point of view, it may be noted, that according to Boyle [15] the joint subsidiary seems to be a purely American invention, probably first used around 1890. Both Boyle and Hale [16] call the Ethyl Company, formed in 1924 and jointly owned by General Motors and Standard Oil of New Jersey, the first important case about which much information is available. Milton Handler [17] draws attention to the railroad terminal corporations of the late ninenteenth century and the formation in 1923 by the French company La Cellophane and the American firm du Pont de Nemours of a jointly-owned corporation to manufacture cellophane in the United States. [18]

The most famous antitrust proceedings concerning a joint venture was the Pen-Olin case, decided by the Supreme Court of the United States in 1964 and again in 1967.[19] In Europe, the former High Authority of the European

14. See for practical examples where most of these motives played a part: Backman, "Joint Ventures and the Antitrust Laws", 40 New York University Law Review 1965, 652.

15. Boyle, *op.cit.*, note 2, 303.

16. Hale, *op.cit.*, note 1, 928.

17. M. Handler, "Emerging Antitrust Issues: Reciprocity, Diversification and Joint Ventures" 49 Va. L. Rev. 1967, 441.

18. See the Cellophane Case, United States v. E.I. du Pont de Nemours & Co. 351, U.S. 377, 383 (1956).

19. United States v. Penn-Olin Chemical Cooperation, 378 U.S. 158 (1964), 389 U.S. 308 (1967).

Coal and Steel Community dealt several times with the establishment of joint subsidiaries.[20] The most important case was Sidmar, decided in 1962.[21] Jointly-owned subsidiaries have several times played a part in the European Economic Community's antitrust policy. The first time was in the Commission's fertilizer decision of November 6, 1968 where the manufacturers of nitrogenous fertilizers in several countries, notably Belgium and France, had employed common selling offices: Comptoir Belge de l'azote and Comptoir français de l'azote. These sales syndicates were examined on their compatability with Article 85 and received finally a negative clearance because they did not affect interstate commerce.[22] A similar decision was taken in 1970 with regard to another sales syndicate for fertilizers (Supexie).[23] In 1971 a joint subsidiary, created by the U.S. firm Colgate-Palmolive and the German Henkel company, for common research purposes, received an exemption under Article 85, paragraph 3.[24]

2. *Joint ventures and competition*

The relation of joint subsidiaries to their parent companies and that of the parent companies to each other, may vary in character. Focusing first on the parents, their relationship before the establishment of the joint venture might have been:

a. unrelated (it is not difficult to devise examples, such as that of a publishing company and a can manufacturer)

b. vertically complementary (e.g. a manufacturer and a whole-saler of a product, or an iron ore mine and blast furnaces)

c. horizontally complementary

(1) enterprises engaged in complementary activities (e.g. bank and insurance companies, manufacturers of small calculators and of large computers)

20. See H. Matthies, "*Gemeinschaftsunternehmen in der Montan-union*", in "*Wirtschaftsordnung und Rechtsordnung*" *Festschrift zum 70. Geburtstag von Franz Böhm*, (Karlsruhe, 1965), 319-343.

21. Sidérurgie Maritime, see 11th General Report on the Activities of the Community (ECSC) (February 1, 1962-Januari 31, 1963), Nos. 346-351.

22. Comptoir belge de l'azote (Cobelaz): O.J. 1968, L. 276/13-19, rectification in O.J. 1968, L. 291/13; [1968] CMLR, D 45 *et seq* and D 68 *et seq.* Comptoir français de l'azote (C.F.A.): O.J. 1968, L 276/29-33; [1968] CMLR, D 57 *et seq.*

23. Decision of December 23, 1970, O.J., 1971, L 10/12-13; [1971] CMLR, D 1 *et seq.*

24. Decision of December 23, 1971, O.J. 1972, L 14/14-18; See Wertheimer, *infra*, 192.

(2) enterprises engaged in the same activity but in a different geographic area

d. actually competitive.

Of course, there are equivocal and marginal situations. An airline and a shipping line may be actual competitors, but they may also exercise complementary activities. It should be noted that complementary or even unrelated enterprises may be potential competitors.

As regards the relation of joint subsidiaries to their parent companies, just as with mergers, three main types may be distinguished:

a. the horizontal joint venture, in which the subsidiary engages in the same type of activities of the parent corporations.

b. the vertical joint venture, in which the subsidiary operates at a different functional level from the parents

(1) backward: the joint venture furnishes the parents, especially with raw materials,

(2) forward: the joint venture is occupied with the sale of the products manufactured by the parents

c. the conglomerate joint venture, in which the subsidiary operates in a different market from that of either of the parents.

Here too, marginal transition and mixed examples can be constructed. For instance: a paper mill and a publishing company (indirect vertically complementary enterprises) establish a printing business as a joint venture: backward integration for one, forward integration for the other parent.

In the Penn-Olin case, the parent companies, Pennsalt and Olin Matthieson were horizontally complementary firms vertically complementary firms and potential competitors at the same time: Pennsalt was a sodium chlorate manufacturer, whereas Olin produced other chemical products. Olin had served as Pennsalt's sales agent. Technically Olin was certainly capable of producing sodium chlorate. The joint venture agreement, establishing the fifty-fifty corporate subsidiary Penn-Olin in Calvert City, Kentucky, called for Pennsalt to operate the production facilities and Olin to concentrate on sale of the produced sodium chlorate to purchasers in the Southeast of the U.S.A. In this way Penn-Olin was a means of forward integration for Pennsalt and of backward integration for Olin Matthieson.

Looking at the impact on competition by the formation and operation of a jointly-owned subsidiary, it is not the relation between the parents and the subsidiary which is of interest. One cannot expect a subsidiary to follow a competitive attitude towards its own mother company.[25] The same applies in

25. See *e.g.* the decision taken by the Commission of the European Communities in the case Christiani & Nielsen, June, 18, 1969, O.J. 1969, L 165/12-14; judgment of the Court of Justice of the European Communities, July 14, 1972, Case No. 48/69 (ICI-Commission) *Recueil* XVIII, 667 [1972] CMLR, 629; cf. van Oven, *infra*, 105-119.

principle to the relation between a joint subsidiary and its parents. As the Supreme Court expressed in its Penn-Olin judgement: "Realistically, the parents would not compete with their progeny". [26]

What is of most interest, is the relation between the parent companies. Some authors go so far as to consider this the only relevant aspect. Brewster for instance uses the following definition: "By joint enterprise we mean any activity whose direction and management is shared by two or more actual or potential competitors". [27] In my view this definition is too narrow, because in cases where there exists a vertical relationship between the parent companies, the creation of a joint venture may also have an anti-competitive effect: by restraining competition between one of the parents and third enterprises.

Often a distinction is made between the effects on competition resulting from the formation of the joint venture and those resulting from the operation of the joint venture. [28] It is also possible to speak of the direct consequences, *i.e.*, consequences in the field of activity of the joint venture, and of the *indirect* consequences, that is in other fields of activity of the parents.

The simplest form of a direct consequence is when the founding firms have been competing with each other for the same product or service and the same geographic market for which the joint venture is formed. If the founding firms were not actual competitors, there are three different possibilities. [29]

a. all parents would have entered the market separately but for the joint venture;

b. at least one but less than all would have entered;

c. none of the parents would have entered on its own. The existence of the joint venture may in such cases affect potential competition (decreasing probability from a) to c)).

As regards the indirect (horizontal) effect on these parents, Boyle [30] has observed: "A second consequence of the development of joint subsidiaries is the provision of a common corporate meeting ground of the type economists have long objected to. It makes the development of common problems of action a simple matter because they have legitimate reasons for consulting with one another". As Wyzanski [31] pointed out, "it is inconceivable that firms engaged cooperatively in one industrial area would not act the same

26. 378 US at 168 (see note 19).

27. K. Brewster, *Antitrust and American Business Abroad*, (New York, 1958), 200.

28. See *e.g.* Rahl, *op.cit.*, note 7, 7 and Matthies, *op.cit.*, note 20, 334.

29. Cf. Pitofsky, *op.cit.*, note 5, 1030.

30. Boyle, *op.cit.*, note 2, 312.

31. Judge J. Wyzanski in United States v. Minnesota, Mining and Manufacturing Co., 92 F. Supp. 947 (D. Mass. 1950).

way in others. In fact, most of those objections which economists make to the operation of the export associations can be applied to the joint subsidiary". In Dixon's words: "There is justifiable doubt that business strategists can treat one another as belligerents in one market, when they are allies in another". [32]

This common meeting ground effect has been designated by the High Authority of the European Coal and Steel Community as the "group effect". [33]

According to Kaysen and Turner [34] the seriousness of the risks which joint ventures cause for competition depends principally on four considerations:
a. whether the joint venture possesses or threatens to possess substantial market power
b. whether the parent companies, individually or collectively, possess such power
c. whether the parent companies are competitors
d. whether the product of the joint venture is closely related–horizontally or vertically–to those produced by the parent companies.

Inverting those four considerations and keeping in mind that the common meeting ground theory does not play a big part if the parents are not competitors, and no part at all if the parents are completely unrelated, we find joint ventures, which have no anticompetitive effects and thus are irrelevant from the point of view of antitrust law. However, many joint ventures will in practice not fulfil these requirements. Whether antitrust rules may be applied against them, depends of course on the rules concerned. We will see in the following paragraph that in the United States the main provision against anti-competitive joint ventures is Section 7 Clayton Act, a provision that does not have an equivalent in any other legal system.

3. *American antitrust law and joint ventures*

In 1959 the 1000 largest American manufacturing corporations were already engaged in at least 345 joint ventures. [35] That number has most probably increased since. All the same, the number of joint ventures against which antitrust proceedings have been directed is very limited. In 1940 one of the

32. Dixon, *op.cit.*, note 2, 407.

33. French: "*effet de groupe*", Decision "Sidmar", *supra*, note 20; Cf. Matthies, *op.cit.* note 20, 334; Brewster *op.cit.* note 27, 205; Van Ommeslaghe, *Die Anwendung der Art. 85 und 86 der Rom-. Vertrages auf Fusionen Gesellschaftszusammenschlüsse und Gemeinschaftsunternehmen* in: *Beiträge zum EWG-Kartellrecht*, (Köln, 1966), 41-109 at 100.

34. Kaysen and Turner, *op.cit.*, note 8, 138.

35. Tractenberg: "Joint ventures on the domestic front: A study in uncertainty, "VIII Antitrust Bulletin, 1960, 797.

oldest American joint ventures, the Ethyl Corporation, was involved in an antitrust case, but it was not the joint venture as such, which was at stake. [36]

Backman [37] considers the Associated Press-case the first joint venture court decision, but in reality no typical joint venture problem was involved. [38]

Speaking about the periode prior to 1960, Pitofsky points out: " . . . the most striking feature of the pre-1960 cases, all of which were under the Sherman Act, is that there were very few opinions in which the antitrust consequences of joint ventures, in and of themselves were analysed. There were a few cases in which the existence of a joint venture constituted one line of evidence tending to prove price fixing or market allocation agreements between independent corporate parents, but the legality of the joint venture itself was not at issue. When joint ventures have been analysed in their own right, the courts and most antitrust commentators generally have refused to assimilate them into *per se* categories of comparable outright agreements, even where the joint venture entity had considerable market power and a demonstrable affect on market price. Instead the tendency was to focus on potential benefits of the joint ventures, particularly on the fact that such arrangements might make it possible to place a new and more efficient competitor in the market. Almost without exeption the courts did not consider whether one or more of the corporate parents was a potential entrant by means of internal expansion into the market served by the joint venture so that the overall effect of the venture might have been to lessen either actual or potential competition. Also, the courts for the most part attached very little weight to the possibility that cooperation between the joint ventures would spill over into fields unrelated to the operation of the joint venture, or that corporate parents would lead to stifle the development of this jointly owned subsidiaries (..........). As a result, the Government had more defeats than victories in attacking joint ventures under section 1 (of the Sherman Act), even when it challenged arrangements which were little different from outright price fixing or market allocation". [39]

One exception to this trend formed the *National City Lines*- case.[40]

36. Ethyl Gasoline Corp. v. United States, 309 U.S. 436, 435 (1940).

37. Backman, *op.cit.*, note 14, 651.

38. Associated Press v. United States, 326 US I (1945). Associated Press is a news gathering agency to which at the time of the case more than 1.200 newspapers subscribed. The by-laws of the organization prescribed that membership of A.P. was a pre-requisite to obtaining any news supplied either by A.P. itself or by one of its subscribers. The Supreme Court prohibited Associated Press from continuing to operate by-laws, which restricted the admission of newcomers. Even if the agency was organized as a company, with the subscribers as shareholders, in reality the case showed the characteristics of a cartel in the form of an association.

39. See Pitofski, *op.cit.* note 5, 1017-1018.

40. See note 11.

National City Lines, operating bus services in a number of cities, sold preferred stock to manufacturers of buses (notably General Motors) and other furnishers of products used for transportation services (among them Standard Oil of California and Firestone Rubber). This arrangement was condemned as a violation of the Sherman Act, because rival manufacturers of those products were foreclosed from selling to National City Lines. This is, indeed a very clear example of a "vertical" joint venture, restraining competition between each of the parent companies and third enterprises.

A year before, judge Wyzanski of Massachusetts rendered his rather famous judgment in the *Minnesota Mining and Manufacturing Company*-case.[41] Four important American manufacturers of coated adhesives (representing 80% of the domestic output in the U.S.A.) created a joint venture to establish factories abroad. Judge Wyzanski condemned this combination in very strong wording as contrary to Section 1, of the Sherman Act. "Joint foreign factories like joint domestic price-fixing would be invalid *per se* because they eliminate or restrain competition in the American domestic market. That suppression of domestic competition is in each case the fundamental evil, and the good or evil nature of the immediate manifestations of the producers' joint action is a superficial consideration.[42]

Joint subsidiaries were involved in the famous Supreme Court *Timken* judgment[43] condemning U.S., British and French Timken for allocation of markets but the decision was more significant for what it said about restrictions of competition through trademarks than for its comments on joint ventures. On behalf of the majority, Justice Black rejected a joint venture contention advanced as a defence.

Also in 1951 a district court judgement, concerning joint ventures in four Latin American countries between *Imperial Chemical Industries* and du Pont de Nemours condemned these practices.[44] The court held that these joint ventures were designed to eliminate existing, as well as to preclude potential competition. Contrary to Judge Wyzanski a year before, the court concluded: joint ventures may become unlawful by their purpose or effect, but are not unlawful per se.

The same court (Southern District Court of New York) dealt in 1961 with an old joint venture, created in 1929 by *Pan American* World Airways and the Steamship Company W.R. Grace.[45] This case seems to contrast with the

41. See note 31.
42. *Id.*, at 967.
43. Timken Roller Bearing Co. v. United States, U.S. 593, 596 (1951).
44. United States v. Imperial Chemical Industries Ltd., 100 F Supp. 504, 577 (S.D.N.Y. 1951).
45. 193 F. Supp. 18 (S.D.N.Y. 1961). The decision was reversed by the Supreme Court (371 U.S. 296 (1963)), that hold that these matters should be decided by the Federal Aeronautics Board.

Supreme Courts holding, some years later in Penn-Olin, according to which parents would not compete with their own progeny. According to Judge Murphy the international exclusion of a wholly owned subsidiary is lawful, but that of a joint venture varies with the market power of the parent and of the particular relevant market. Pan Am was condemned for monopolization in violation of Section 2 of the Sherman Act, by excluding its joint venture from the market in which Pan Am itself operated.

By far the most important joint venture case until now is *Penn Olin.* [46] The formation in 1960 by Pennsalt and Olin Matthieson of a joint manufacturing and sales subsidiary called Penn-Olin, which commenced production in late 1961, was challenged by the Department of Justice under Section 1 of the Sherman Act and Section 7 of the Clayton Act. It was the first time that a joint venture was examined under Section 7. The District Court ruled that the Government had failed to establish a reasonable probability that both companies would have entered the south eastern sodium chlorate market but for the joint venture, and that the formation of the joint company was not likely to lessen competition substantially in the area.

This ruling, however, was reversed by the Supreme Court. The majority opinion, formulated by Justice Clark held that a finding should have been made by the District Court as to the reasonable probability that either one of the corporations would have entered the market by building a plant, while the other would have remained a substantial potential competitor. The ruling listed a series of criteria for this test.[47] On remand the district court concluded that neither parent company would have entered the market but for the joint venture, and dismissed the Governments complaint again. This time (in 1967) the district court's judgment was affirmed by the Supreme Court.

Already in 1964 Mr. Justice Clark for the majority of the Supreme Court ruled that there was no violation of Section 1 of the Sherman Act. However, on this point Mr. Justice Douglas (with whom Mr. Justice Black agreed) dissented. They remarked that "agreements among competitors to divide markets are per se violations of the Sherman Act (..........). What we have in substance is two major companies who on the eve of competitive projects in the southeastern market join forces. In principle the case is not different from one where Pennsalt and Olin decide to divide the southeastern market.......... Through the "joint venture" they do indeed divide it fifty-fifty. That division through the device of the "joint venture" is as plain and precise as though made in more formal agreements. As we saw in the Timken case, agreements between legally separate persons and companies to suppress competition

46. See, note 19 and *supra*, p. 124.

47. This list is quoted by Pitofsky, *op.cit.*, note 5, 1011 (footnote 12). See also: Areeda, *op.cit.*, note 6, 621-630.

among themselves and others "cannot be justified by labeling the project a 'joint venture'".

Although the Penn-Olin case ended with a complete failure for the Government, it opened perspectives for a future application of Section 7 of the Clayton Act. As regards the dissenting opinion of Justice Douglas even if the majority of his brothers did not share his view, his ideas may turn out to be useful, especially for those legal systems (as that of the European Common Market) which lack a provision such as Section 7, Clayton Act.

In 1964, two months before the (first) Supreme Court decision in the Penn-Olin case, the Department of Justice attacked another joint venture under both the Sherman Act and the Clayton Act. The joint venture in question was *Mobay*, formed in 1954 by two chemical firms. American Monsanto and German Bayer for the manufacturing of chemical products. The Government claimed that Monsanto's abandonment of a plan to enter the market in question made it an especially attractive partner to Bayer. Finally a consent decree forced the sale of Monsanto's interest to Bayer.[48]

The latest joint venture judgment I found is that in the *Northern Natural* Gas-case.[49] Applying the Supreme Court consideration from Penn-Olin, the D.C. Circuit Court reversed an F.T.C. order authorizing American and Canadian firms to engage in a joint venture for the construction and operation of a natural gas pipeline, holding that the Commission "failed to apply proper standards to determine relevant antitrust policy and consequently ignored significant anticompetitive effects of the joint venture".

4. *European joint venture as an example: Philips Siemens*

The 1962 annual report of the Dutch manufacturer of electric and electronic products, Philips, mentioned that on October 1st, 1962, a cooperation with the German Siemens was initiated in the field of the making of sound recording products (especially records). This cooperation was carried through by a reciprocal capital participation. Soon it became clear[50] that this participation was effectuated by the interchange of 50% of the stock of the N.V. Philips Phonographic Industries (previously a wholly owned subsidiary of Philips) against 50% of the stock of the Deutsche Grammophon Gesellschaft GmbH (previously a wholly owned subsidiary of Siemens). Both subsidiaries preserved their "legal indepence"[51] and continued their own activities.

48. March 20, 1967, 1967 Trade Cas. § 72.001.

49. 399 F. 2d-953 (D.C. Cir. 1968); cf. "*Antitrust Developments, 1968-1970*", American Bar Association, (1971).

50. See *e.g.* Vereinigte Wirtschaftsdienste, Feb. 2, 1963, p. 8.

51. According to the Philips Report. Of Course, "legal independance" is a meaningless expression in this context.

It was expected that this cooperation would strenghten the position of both firms on the international market. [52]

Subsequent Philips annual reports continue to mention the satisfactory cooperation with Siemens on the record production field, although they give only details on the activities of P.P.I., obviously considered by Philips as its "true" daughter. This situation changes, however, in the report of 1966, which focuses also on the activities of the stepdaughter D.G.G. The 1967 report speaks of intensification of the "fruitful cooperation with Siemens in the combination PPI/DGG". The combination enlarged its activities, *inter alia* by purchasing several (sheet) music publishers.

The Philips annual report of 1971 mentions a new step, namely the establishment of the "management and holding companies" Polygram B.V. (Netherlands) and Polygram GmbH (Germany). Philips and Siemens participate each for 50% in the capital of the twin-holding companies, which are, thus, at the same time joint ventures, to which the record-producing activities will henceforth belong. A jubilee memorial of Siemens [53] informs us that Polygram has a turnover of 1,2 Billion DM (almost $ 400 million) and a market share of 30% in the Federal Republic of Germany. The same memorial mentions a 100% subsidiary of Polygram, called Polymedia, a company for "audio-visual communication". Obviously the production of so-called video tape and cassettes are here involved and, whatever the formal structure, Polymedia is in fact also a Philips-Siemens joint venture.

It is important that Philips and Siemens are (or could be!) competitors on almost every field of their activity. The cooperation in the joint venture Polygram forms a very clear illustration of the "common meeting ground" theory. And, indeed, newspaper-reports predicted cooperation between the two concerns for the production of computers, stating the cooperation in the record-production: "Philips and Siemens know each other very well and they know also what cooperation means". [54] Both partners, however, have other common meeting places. Siemens for instance participates with AEG and General Electric in the joint subsidiary Osram, the only European incandescent lamp manufacturer of some importance, other than Philips. With Robert Bosch, Siemens has a joint venture for the production of electric domestic appliances. Philips, in its turn participates in the same field in joint ventures with another German firm, Bauknecht and with Italian Indesit.

52. *Id.*, the report does not specify what it means by "both firms": the (henceforth joint) subsidiaries or the parent companies, i.e. Philips and Siemens.

53. F.C. Delius, *Unsere Siemens-Welt, Ein Festschrift zum 125-jährigen Bestehen des Hauses Siemens* (Berlin, 1972), 41. It seems that Siemens-people are not yet fully accustomed to the presence of a foreign stepdaughter: Philips Phonographic Industries is called "Philips Pornographic Industries"!

54. *Het Financiële Dagblad* (Amsterdam), September 24, 1971.

5. *Quasi-merger or quasi-cartel?*

There are joint ventures, which in fact may be considered as a kind of cartel. We met an example in the Associated Press-case.[55] Sales syndicates have always been considered as cartels.[55a] Pools of profits and losses are, whether they have a corporate form or not, cartels as well.

Other joint ventures, on the contrary, are variations of mergers, especially if the parent companies cease to be independently active enterprises, but continue their existence merely as holding companies.

Mostly, however, joint ventures are neither genuine cartels, nor mergers. The question whether they are comparable with cartels or rather with mergers, has much to do with the inadequacy of antitrust laws, which ignore joint ventures as a separate kind of restrictive business practices. Kaysen and Turner[56] say the joint venture may be viewed as a form of quasi-merger. Dixon points out: ". . . . . if two firms, each with a sizeable share of the market for a commodity, pool this business into a joint venture, the effect–for all practical purposes–is similar to that of a merger. It is really the old "trust" technique in a modern dress".[57]

On the other hand we saw that Justice Douglas in his dissenting opinion in the Penn-Olin case considered the joint venture as a means of market allocation, so if not a cartel, at least a quasi-cartel.[58] Pitofsky[59] holds the belief that "when one or both parent firms actively compete in the same product and geographic market as the joint venture, the inevitable coordination of competitive activities between parent and partly-owned subsidiary and the resultant stifling of aggressive behaviour of the joint venture should be treated under typical cartel rules. (..........) Where both parents decide to join forces on the eve of independent entry, it is obvious that the effect of a joint venture on competition is much like that of a simple cartel. For example, if full marketing authority for both firms is delegated to a joint sales agency, competition among sellers as to prices, customers, and markets is eliminated to about the same extent as by a traditional cartel conspiracy". According to

55. See, note 38.

55a. The Commission considered the various national fertilizer syndicates (some examples mentioned in note 22) as restrictions of competition in the sense of Art. 85. The reason that negative clearances were granted was that (at that time) the Commission thought that the interstate commerce was not affected. In its decision of December 23, 1971 concerning the *Nederlandse Cement-Handelmaatschappij* (O.J. 1972, L 22/16) the Commission stated that this syndicate, concluded by German manufacturers for the sale of concrete in the Netherlands, was prohibited under Art. 85.

56. Kaysen and Turner, *op.cit.*, note 6.

57. Dixon, *op.cit.*, note 2, 407.

58. See *supra,* p. 129-130.

59. Pitofsky, *op.cit.*, note 5, 1035, 1036, 1039.

Emmerich[60] a restrictive practice cannot claim a special treatment for the reason of its corporate organization. Fikentscher[61] distinguishes the relations between each of the parents and the subsidiary on one hand, and the relation between the parents themselves on the other. He considers that between parents and subsidiary, because of the corporate relation, something like a cartel is not conceivable. However, it is precisely the relation between the parent firms (or, if the parents are vertically complementary, between one of the parents and third parties), which interests us here.

A point of resemblance with a merger is that whereas most cartels, at least effective cartels, with the exception of specialization agreements embrace a majority of the market participants (in number of turnover) a merger and a joint venture may be entered into by only two out of many enterprises which are active on a certain market. A point of resemblance with cartels is, on the other hand, that the participants maintain their independence. Characteristic of cartels is precisely that it is between *independent* enterprises that competition restraining agreements, conspiracies or practices are made.

Taking the Philips-Siemens case as an example, one could say that PPI and DGG (via an intermediate stage) have melted together into Polygram, in other words have entered into a merger. It is, however, also possible to maintain that P.P.I. and D.G.G. were no real enterprises. The enterprises were Philips and Siemens and they subsisted as independent entities. The combination of the record-producing subsidiaries into (twin) joint ventures may be regarded as equivalent to a sweeping production and sales agreement between the parent companies.

Except in the case of a conglomerate joint venture (conglomerate cartels do not exist unless perhaps for the collective enforcement of resale price maintenance), both conceptions may be defended to a certain extent. The claim of the U.S. Department of Justice in the Penn-Olin and Mobay-cases that both Section 1 of the Sherman Act and Section 7 of the Clayton Act were violated, confirms to this conclusion. It is true that after the Supreme Courts decision concerning Penn-Olin joint venture-case are likely to be examined primarily, if not only, under Section 7.[62] The High Authority of the European Coal and Steel Community also examined joint ventures only under Article 66 of the Treaty.

Under American law the application of only Section 7 of the Clayton Act seems to be rather sufficient to weed out the anticompetitive effects of joint

60. V, Emmerich, "Die Auslegung von Art. 85 Abs. 1. EWG-Vertrag durch die bisherige Praxis der Kommission, 6 Eur 1971, 328.

61. W. Fikentscher, "Kooperation und Gemeinschaftsunternehmen im Licht der Art. 85 und 86 EWGV". Europees Kartelrecht (Louvain, Post-Graduate Course 1967-1968) Antwerpen-Utrecht 1970, 177 *et seq*. esp. 200 *et seq*.

62. Rahl *op.cit.*, note 7: "Section 7 of the Clayton Act is the primary source of legal control for domestic corporate joint ventures".

ventures. Mr. Justice's Clark list of testing criteria [63] presents a complete examination of the impact of a joint venture on competition, its advantages and disadvantages. American antitrust law does not make a clear-cut distinction between contractual restrictions of competition, mergers and effects of a dominant position on the market. European law does. Rightly Matthies rejects the construction that Article 66 of the ECSC-Treaty would be a *lex specialis* in regard to the general rule of Article 65. [64] This author contends that the High Authority should have examined joint ventures also under Article 65. All the same it is at least understandable that the High Authority, in cases where it could have applied both Article 65 and Article 66, preferred to limit itself to the latter. The two provisions aim at the same purposes. Substantially, the application of the first could not have led to another result than that of the second. From the point of view of procedure, Article 66 has some advantages in comparison with Article 65.

In the European Economic Community the legal situation is different from that in the United States and that in the European Coal and Steel Community. Anti-merger regulations are absent, setting aside the possibility of application of Article 86 in a limited number of cases (see the next paragraph). The question of application of Article 85 on the establishment and operation of joint subsidiaries is therefore of much more importance than that of Section 1 of the Sherman Act or of Article 65 of the ECSC-Treaty.

6. *Article 86 of the EEC-Treaty*

Contrary to the ECSC-Treaty, the EEC-Treaty does not contain any special provision on mergers. The Commission, however, in its Memorandum on Concentration of 1965 [65] held that mergers under certain circumstances can come under Article 86 of the Treaty. Concentration of enterprises may be considered as an abuse of a dominant position in cases where this concentration leads to the establishment of a monopoly, thus to the complete elimination of competition.

Until now, the Commission applied Article 86 on a merger in only one case, namely in the Continental Can-case. [66] Although there was no question of a complete monopoly, the Commission there contended that the acquisition of a Dutch manufacturer of the same products, by the Continental Can

63. See note 47.

64. Matthies, *op.cit.*, note 19, 337.

65. EEC Commission, *Memorandum to the Member States on Concentration of Enterprises in the Common Market*, (Studies on competition No. 3, Brussels 1966); CCH COMM. MKT. REP. No. 26, p. 1 (separate print).

66. Decision of December, 9, 1971, O.J. 1972, L 7/25-39; [1972] CMLR, D 11. In principle confirmed by the judgment of the Court of Justice of February 21, 1973, Case No. 6/72, [1973] CMLR, 199-239.

concern, which already held a dominant position for tinplate packing in a substantial part of the Common Market, was a violation of Article 86.

When we consider the formation of a joint venture as a quasi-merger and we take our stand on the Commission's interpretation which was (in principle) upheld by the Court, such a formation can be deemed to be a violation of Article 86 in two types of cases.

a. where the joint venture has a monopoly-position

b. where at least one of the parents had already a dominant position, which was used to effectuate the quasi-merger. Besides, it will be possible that Article 86 will be applied against a joint venture which has, and takes improper advantage of, a dominant position in a substantial part of the Common Market, but then the existence of the joint venture is not at stake.

Cases of the type described in a. and b. may occur, but they are likely to be a small minority of the total number of joint ventures. We saw that, according to a Siemens publication, the Polygram record joint venture has a market share of 30% in Germany. In other parts of the Common Market, this will probably be no more. So Polygram is far from being a monopolist. It seems likewise improbable that either Philips and Siemens had a dominant position on the record market at the moment of establishment of the joint venture, putting aside whether the Continental Can doctrine could be applied against existing joint ventures, or only against the formation of new ones.

It is likewise improbable that any of the American joint ventures described in paragraph 4, would have been considered violating Article 86, either under the 1965 Memorandum conception, or under the Continental Can doctrine. A possible exception is the Associated Press-case where perhaps something like a monopoly was involved. But precisely that case could certainly be prohibited under Article 85, as it was in fact under Section 1 of the Sherman Act. On the other hand, Penn-Olin would most probably not come under Article 86. Penn-Olin's share of the expanded relevant market in 1962 was important, but far from being a monopoly: about 27.6 per cent. No question either of a dominant position of Pennsalt at the moment of formation of the joint venture: 8.9 per cent of the sales in the relevant market, whereas Olin Matthieson, although a powerful enterprise, was on that market not active at all. [67]

The conclusion must be that if there is a need for control of joint ventures in the Common Market, Article 86 will but in exceptional cases be an adequate instrument.

67. Areeda, *op.cit.* note 6, 623.

7. *Article 85 of the EEC-Treaty*

Generally, joint ventures will be established by an agreement between enterprises. This will be valid for mergers as well. In both cases such agreements can restrain or even prevent competition. When they will do so is not easy to determine. This will depend on which effects one wants to consider. For the time being it seems for instance highly improbable that, according to European understanding, conglomerate mergers or conglomerate joint ventures will be accepted as competition restraining practices.

An advisory working group of professors, that prepared for the EEC-Commission the Memorandum on Concentration of 1966 thought that Article 85 could be applied in certain cases of mergers. The Commission, however, did not share this opinion. The Commission argued that Article 85 does not relate to agreements or practices which modify the ownership of enterprises, such as mergers and take-overs. However, this can be different, said the Commission, when after the concentration economically independent enterprises subsist ("for instance at the formation of joint subsidiaries").[68] The Commission saw also economic arguments to apply Article 85 to some joint ventures.

There are indeed several differences between the situation where two or more enterprises enter into a merger and where they establish a joint subsidiary. A merger is fundamentally a non-recurring proceeding. Through the fulfilment of the merger contract, the merging enterprises cease to be enterprises or, in other words, the agreement, as a consequence of its own fulfilment, ceases to be an agreement between enterprises. With joint ventures this is different. The ventures should not only agree about the establishment of the joint subsidiary, but also about its continuous common operation afterwards. This implies that if the parents are competitors (actual as in the Philips-Siemens case, or potential as in the Penn-Olin case), they agree to exclude mutual competition.

A second particularity of joint ventures, that we do not find in mergers, is that the parent-companies in fields other than those covered by the joint subsidiary, can remain, or may become, competitors. In those other fields their relation may be affected by the partial combination.

Also if we accept that Article 85 does not apply to mergers, there are consequently enough reasons to adopt another attitude towards joint ventures. The question is therefore: *when* do joint ventures–or rather: the formation and operation of joint ventures–come under Article 85? In this connection, it is useful to remark, that in the literature many advantages of joint ventures are mentioned.[69] The fact that there are, on the other hand,

68. Memorandum, *note 65*, para. 14.

69. See *e.g.* Kaysen-Turner, *op.cit.*, note 8, 136; Dixon, *op.cit.*, note 2, 399; Van Ommerslaghe, *op.cit.*, note 33, 90.

also disadvantages[70] need not be considered. Unlike Section 1 of the Sherman Act, Article 85 contains the possibility of exemption (paragraph 3) and consequently no rule of reason applies to Article 85 (unless one would conclude that paragraph 3 is a worded rule of reason). Even if a restrictive agreement or practice is very advantageous: this does not matter for the applicability of the prohibition rule of Article 85, paragraph 1. The favourable effects, however, may bring about that an exemption is granted.

It is conceivable that a cartel-agreement could be concluded, which restrains competition primarily, but which has at the same time favourable effects. Article 85, paragraph 3 aims especially on such cases. It is, however, also conceivable that some enterprises conclude a mutual collaborative agreement, not with the purpose to restrain competition, although as a result competition will be restrained, either among the parties, or with third parties (ancillary restraints).

The ACEC-Berliet case[71] could be considered in this class. This research cooperation between vertically complementary enterprises fall, in the opinion of the Commission under the scope of Article 85, paragraph 1, but received an exemption pursuant to paragraph 3. Conceivably ACEC and Berliet could have dressed their collaboration in the joint venture cloth. In my opinion that should not have changed the Commission's decision. Indeed, the same decision was taken in the case Henkel-Golgate,[72] also a research cooperation, but this time between competitive firms and organized as a jointly-owned subsidiary. The Commission concluded that the agreement by which the joint venture was established resulted in a perceptible restraint of competition. The corporate structure of the cooperation did not play a part in the Commission's argument.

The best starting-point for the judgment of joint ventures under Article 85 seems to be: how the case would be treated, if the same cooperation would not have had a corporate form? That was indeed the course the Commission adopted in Henkel-Colgate. From the fact that it even did not say a word about the corporate form in the part of the decision that concerns the applicability of Article 85, paragraph 1, it may be concluded that such a form is in the eyes of the Commission not relevant, or at least not decisive.

It should be remarked that, according to both the Court of Justice and of the Commission of the European Communities, it is not sufficient if an agreement restrains competition, but this restraint must be noticeable.[73] It looks long odds that this additional criterium will turn out to be very

70. See *e.g.* Kaysen-Turner, ibid.; Dixon, *id.* at p. 403, 409; Pitofsky, *op.cit.*, note 5, 1008, 1012

71. Decision of the E.C. Commission of July, 17, 1968, O.J. 1968, L 201/7-11; [1968] CMLR, D 35 *et seq.*

72. See note 24.

73. Judgment of the Court of Justice of July, 9, 1969, Case No. 5/69 (Völk-

important for the judgment whether joint ventures will come under Article 85. If a joint venture is formed between enterprises, who have but a limited share of the market and if a sufficient number of competitors subsist, the fact that competition is precluded between two market participants must not be noticeable for what happens on the market as a whole. A practice is not noticeable, according to the Commission, if the products, covered by that practice form not more than 5 per cent of the relevant market and if the total turnover of the firms concerned is not more than 15-20 million units of account.

Those criteria can only be used in one direction: it is not impossible that a practice will be deemed to be not noticeable, although these limits are exceeded. Particularly for joint ventures in some cases higher limits may be handled. All the same, in the Penn-Olin case, where 27.6 per cent of the relevant market was concerned, the restraint of competition would probably have been deemed to be noticeable, the more so because there was only a very limited number (3) of other competitors.

For the rest it seems impossible to give a definite opinion on concrete cases without a profound knowledge of facts. It must be taken into account that even if the restraint of competition on the market in question is considered to be unnoticeable, it will be necessary to examine what may be the effect on other activities of the venturers, in view of the common meeting ground-theory. In the hypothesis that it is accepted that the cooperation between Philips and Siemens in the domain of records does not noticeably restrain competition, because the significance of the two firms on the record market is too tiny and enough competition subsists on that market, there could be a danger for competition on other markets (for instance that of lamps), where these two enterprises have a larger significance.

The application of the other criteria of Article 85, paragraph 1 (to affect trade between Member States) on joint ventures, will probably not offer any special problem. The circumscriptions, given by the Court of Justice [74] are also valid and useful.

As regards Article 85, paragraph 3, the Commission has pointed out in its Memorandum on Concentration, that this provision has not been formulated and is unworkeable for mergers. [75] Here again, for joint ventures, the situation is quite different. Only one of the so called difficulties would apply on joint ventures as well: the examination of all existing joint ventures.

It would indeed be expedient to concentrate the attention on the

---

Vervaecke), *Recueil*. XVI, 295-307, [1972] CMLR, 273 *et seq*. Notice of May, 27, 1970, C 64/1-2; [1970] CMLR, D 15 *et seq*.

74. See particularly the judgment in the case 56/65 (LTM-MBU) June, 30, 1966, *Recueil* XII, 337-377, at 359; [1966] CMLR, 357-377, at 375.

75. Memorandum, note 65, paras 8-10.

establishment of new joint subsidiaries. What counts in fact is to prevent joint ventures becoming an alternate way to restrict competition, a means of escape because genuine cartels are prohibited. It would be unwise and unreasonable to look too much at the outward appearance of a restrictive practice. That does not mean that all joint ventures in the Common Market, or at least a large part of the new joint ventures should be prohibited. Not only that the non-noticeable joint ventures may be eliminated from the field of application of Article 85. The third paragraph of that article offers adequate possibilities to permit joint ventures that are reasonable. I think the Commission, in its Henkel-Colgate decision, showed the right way: it refused to be deluded by the corporate dress of the collaboration, but it granted an exemption because the agreements made sense.

Chapter 7

VALIDITY AND NULLITY OF RESTRICTIVE BUSINESS AGREEMENTS

by *Mr. J. G. van der Wielen*

The jurisprudence of the Court of Justice of the European Communities with reference to the status at civil law of restrictive business agreements is characterized by the fact that the Court initially granted provisional and full validity both to notifiable existing agreements which have been duly notified and to existing and new non-notifiable agreements which have not been notified, but with its latest judgement in re-Haecht v. Wilkin Jansen completely changed its mind and swallowed for the greater part the validity of restrictive business agreements in favor of the sanction of nullity resulting from the second paragraph of article 85.[1]

The rules laid down in Article 85 of the EEC Treaty and Regulation No. 17 concerning illegality and nullity of those restrictive business agreements which satisfy the conditions of Article 85 section 1 and a possible exemption from the application of section 3 caused a spate of notifications in Brussels. As a result the Commission experienced a serious administrative problem and this led to delay in dispatching the requests. The resulting uncertainty as to their position in law on the part of the parties to the agree-

1. The term "existing agreements "or" old agreements" should be taken to mean agreements which have been concluded before March 13, 1962, the date on which Regulation No. 17 (O.J. 204/62) became enforceable.

The term "new agreements" should be taken to mean agreements which have been concluded after this date. Notifiable agreements were those which must be notified pursuant to Article 4 or Article 5 ,Regulation No. 17 in order to be eligible for exemption;
the agreements belonging to the categories enumerated limitatively in Article 4, section 2 of Regulation No. 17, are non-notifiable.

The Act relating to the conditions of entry in the Common Market by the new members of the European Communities and to the adaptation of the Treaties, adds a new Article 25 to Regulation No. 17. This article provides that regarding agreements, decisions and concerted practices which as a consequence of entry in the Common Market come under Article 85 of the EEC-Treaty, the date of entry applies as the date Regulation No. 17 has become enforceable. This means that agreements concluded before January 1, 1973 are "existing agreements" and agreements concluded after that date are "new agreements" inter alia in view of the status at civil law of the restrictive business agreements concerned.

ments which had been notified, caused the Court proceeding on the line of reasoning followed in the Bosch-judgement to grant in its judgements in the cases Portelange v. Smith Corona, Bilger v. Jehle and Rochas v. Bitsch far reaching effect both to old notifiable agreements which had been notified and to non-notifiable agreements which had not been notified.[2] As a result of these judgements of the Luxemburg Court of Justice the prohibitionary system laid down in Article 85 and Regulation No. 17 was transmitted into a system of misuse which closely resembled the system of the British Restrictive Trade Practices Act of 1956 and its later amendments.[3]

In its first four judgements on validity and nullity of restrictive business agreements the Court pushed the nullity of cartel agreements provided in the second paragraph of Article 85 as far as possible to the background: only after the Commission had tested an agreement to the first and third paragraphs of Article 85 and had concluded that the agreement comes under the prohibition of the first paragraph but does not fullfil the conditions of exemption of the third paragraph would nullity enter. In the Bilger-judgement the Court established that any late nullity resulting from a decision made by the Commission or a national authority only would take effect henceforth. In its (second) Haecht-Wilkin Jansen-judgement of February 6, 1973 the Court puts the sanction of nullity of Article 85 fully in the forefront.[4] The Court, referring to article 1 of Regulation No. 17, ascertained that the nullity of prohibited agreements takes automatically effect without a preceding decision of the Commission. The Court makes some difference between agreements existing on the date Regulation No. 17 has taken effect and agreements concluded after that date. The Court grants a *"terme de grâce"* to existing agreements: the general principle of legal security requires that the judge only declares an existing agreement null and void after the Commission has taken a decision on the basis of Regulation No. 17. Parties to new agreements can only carry out their agreements at their own peril. The judge has the obligation to declare a new agreement null and void at any moment parties concerned invoke the nullity of such an agreement. The judge

2. Judgement of April 6, 1962, case No. 13-61 (De Geus and Uitenbogerd v. Bosch and Van Rijn), *Recueil* VIII, 89 *et seq*; [1962] CMLR, 1 *et seq*;
Judgement of July 9, 1969, case No. 10-69 (Portelange v. Smith Corona Marchant International), *Recueil*, XV, 309-319;
Judgement of March 18, 1970, case No. 43-69 (Bilger v. Jehle), *Recueil* XVI, 127-139; Judgement of June 30, 1970, case No. 1-70 (Rochas v. Bitsch), *Recueil* XVI, 515-526; [1971] CMLR, 104-118.

3. See Ham's article in this book *supra*, 2.

4. The first Haecht-judgement was pronounced December 12, 1967, case No. 23-67 (Brasserie De Haecht v. Oscar Wilkin and Marie Janssen), *Recueil* XIII, 525 *et seq*. [1968] CMLR, 26 *et seq*.
The second Haecht-judgement was pronounced February 6, 1973, case No. 48-72 (Brasserie de Haecht v. Oscar Wilkin and Marie Janssen), [1973] CMLR, 287-309.

however is free to suspend the procedure to give the parties to the agreement the opportunity to inform themselves of the opinion of the Commission as to the applicability of Article 85 to the agreement concerned. The nullity of restrictive business agreements is always retro-active, unless the Commission applies Article 7 of Regulation No. 17.

The consequences of the second Haecht-judgement are that the full validity of existing non-notifiable and notifiable agreements has been reduced to a limited provisional validity whereas new agreements, notifiable or not, are not provisionally valid at all but can only be carried out at their own peril by their parties, that means are "provisionally null". The judgement practically cancels the judgements in the Portelange- and Bilger-cases and finishes the uncertain position of new notifiable notified agreements.

In the following I intend first to summarize the Courts decisions in the cases mentioned above, especially its reasons for granting that both notifiable existing agreements which have been duly notified, and existing and new non-notifiable agreements which have not been notified might be carried out in full until a decision as to their compatibility with Article 85 has been reached and its reasons for withdrawing, in the second Haecht-judgement, practically the validity granted to restrictive business agreements in favor of a more strict application of the prohibition of Article 85, first paragraph, and the sanction of the second paragraph of Article 85.

Next I intend to discuss a few questions raised by the jurisprudence of the Court of Justice, relating to respectively the position of old and new restrictive business agreements before and after the second Haecht-judgement.

The Court's judgements

The Court of Justice of the European Communities used the terms "validity" and "provisional validity" for the first time in 1962 in its considerations preceding the Bosch-judgement. It gave its decision on April 6, 1962 in a preliminary decision on a question put by the court at The Hague pursuant to Article 177 EEC. The Court of Justice was asked in effect whether Article 85 was applicable to restrictive business agreements as from January 1st, 1958 when the Rome Treaty had become effective, and if so, whether an agreement which came under the prohibition of Article 85, section 1 was null and void *ab initio* as a result of the sanction attached to illegality.

The Court answered the first question in the affirmative, the second one in the negative. Although both the authorities in member States and the Commission were competent to apply Article 85 in the period between the date of commencement of the Rome Treaty and the date of commencement of Regulation No. 17, Article 85, section 3 had not been applied in that period. To declare restrictive business agreements which contravene Article 85, null before the tests as meant in Article 85, section 3 could have been applied, was

not considered an acceptable procedure by the Court. It would be contrary to legal security if an agreement which had been null for some time could after exemption become retrospectively valid.

Therefore the Court opted for a transitional arrangement to the effect that agreements and decisions which were in existence at the time Regulation No. 17 became operative, are not null and void merely because they come under Article 85, section 1—such agreements should be considered valid if they come under Article 5, section 1 of Regulation No. 17 and are therefore non-notifiable, and provisionally valid if they are notifiable and have been duly notified to the Commission.

The Court stressed that such validity is not of a definite nature but rather terminates as soon as the Commission reaches a decision as to the eligibility of the agreement concerned for exemption or as soon as the competent national authority decides that the agreement is illegal and null by virtue of Article 85, section 1.

The Bosch-judgement raised the matter of the precise content of provisional validity respectively of trust agreements.

Advocate-General Roemer gave in his conclusion in the Portelange case three possible answers to this question:
The first conception holds that, although the prohibition of Article 85 is paramount, provisional validity implies that in the period between notification and final decision of the Commission an agreement which has been duly notified, is not absolutely null so that the parties to the agreement may carry it out on a voluntary basis. The only tie binding the parties is the obligation that they must do nothing which may prevent exemption at a later date. The Commission adhered to this conception as is apparent from its comments in the Portelange and Bosch cases.

According to the second conception, parties to a provisionally valid agreement may only apply to the court for provisional remedies such as an order to third parties to refrain from certain acts with respect to the parties to the agreement. According to this conception, once again, no action lies for damages and/or performance.

The third conception holds that provisional validity, though not definite, is perfect: parties to a provisionally valid agreement may bring an action for damages and performance. The Advocate-General and the Court adopted the latter conception in the Portelange judgement. This judgement was handed down in reply to a question put by the Brussels Tribunal de Commerce concerning the effects of provisional validity as granted to agreements which have been duly notified to the EEC Commission before the latter had started the procedure mentioned in Regulation No. 17.

This question arose from an action brought by the Belgian Portelange firm against Smith Corona Marchant International Ltd of Lausanne, a Swiss company. The two enterprises had concluded in 1961 an exclusive agency con-

tract concerning typewriters and calculators which had been notified to the Commission pursuant to Article 5 of Regulation No. 17. After March 13, 1962, an additional agreement had been concluded concerning an exclusive agency contract in regard to electro-copying machines. This supplementary contract had not been notified. When Smith Corona unilaterally cancelled the latter agreement, Portelange instituted proceedings before the Tribunal de Commerce in Brussels. SMC alleged that the agreement was illegal and null pursuant to Article 85, section 1 of the EEC Treaty. Portelange maintained that the agreement was provisionally valid. The latter argument caused the Tribunal de Commerce to submit the above questions to the Court of Justice.

According to its comments in the course of the proceedings, the Commission appeared to regard the supplementary agreement as a separate contract which was notifiable but had not been notified and therefore it considered the question put by the Brussels court to lack foundation. This is why the Commission concluded that the application for a preliminary decision should be dismissed.

In its reply to the question put by the Brussels court, the Court of Justice argued largely as it had done in the Bosch-judgement. Nullity of restrictive business agreements only commences when such agreements, having been considered in light of both the first and third section of Article 85, are found to come under section 1 but not under section 3 since they do not satisfy the conditions mentioned in the latter section. The Court held that so long as this has not been established, any duly notified agreement should be considered valid. As to the content of such validity the Court observed that to conclude on the ground of the non-definite nature of the validity that provisionally valid agreements cannot be carried out in full, pending the Commission's decision pursuant to Article 85, section 3, would be contrary to the principles of legal security. Having considered the objections to perfect validity of notified agreements as against the objections attached to the state of legal insecurity in which the parties would find themselves during the waiting period, the Court concluded that legal security carries the greater weight and that therefore notifiable agreements which have been duly notified should have full effect until such time as the Commission shall have reached its decision.

As is apparent from the comment the Commission submitted pursuant to Article 20 of the Statute of the Court of Justice in the course of the proceedings, the Commission thought otherwise; it observed that parties could at best be permitted to carry out their agreement on a voluntary basis and that no action for damages and/or performance should lie. The Court countered these objections by pointing out that in the case of an agreement which infringes the rules of competition of the Treaty the Commission could make a provisional decision pursuant to Article 15, section 6 of Regulation No. 17. By doing so the Commission warns parties to a notified agreement that it considers the agreement concerned to come under Article 85, section 1 while not

satisfying the requirements for exemption laid down in Article 85, section 3. If after such a decision, parties continue to carry out their agreements, they do so at their own peril. In other words, by means of a decision pursuant to Article 15, section 6, the Commission was able to terminate the validity of a notified agreement.

In its third judgement in connection with the problem of the status at civil law of restrictive business agreements, the Court discussed the position of non-notifiable agreements which have not been notified before the Commission has reached a decision. In the Bosch-judgement the Court had already concluded that such agreements are valid without the qualification "provisionally". In its decision of March 18, 1970 in re Bilger v. Jehle the Court further elucidated this concept of "validity".

The case Bilger v. Jehle concerned a complaint lodged by a brewery against a married couple keeping a café who in contravention of an agreement to supply beer concluded between the parties, had sold brands other than the Bilger brand.

The brewery had won its case in the first instance and on appeal, but the decision of the higher court had been set aside by the *Bundesgerichtshof* and the case had been referred back to the *Oberlandesgericht* in Karlsruhe. Before this court, the Jehle couple argued for the first time that the agreement to supply beer was contrary to Article 85 and therefore null and void. The Bilger brewery argued, on the other hand, that the agreement was valid. All this caused the *Oberlandesgericht* in Karlsruhe to submit two preliminary questions to the Court of Justice.

In the first place, the *Oberlandesgericht* asked whether an agreement to supply beer between two enterprises established in the same member State which obliges a café-keeper to buy solely from a certain brewery, concerns inter-state commerce and thus is notifiable pursuant to Article 5, section 2 of Regulation No. 17. The second question concerned the interpretation of Article 85, section 2 EEC in view of the possible retro-active effect of an exemption which the Commission might grant pursuant to Article 85, section 3 EEC and Article 6 of Regulation No. 17 in the case of non-notifiable agreements. Finally the court asked whether a non-notifiable agreement which had not been notified, is valid.

The Court replied to the first question that an agreement to supply beer does not relate to inter-state commerce within the meaning of Article 5, section 2 of Regulation No. 17 and thus is not notifiable. According to the Court, this does not mean, however, that such an agreement cannot affect inter-state commerce.

In reply to the second question, the Court first further defined the competence of the national courts in the member States to apply Article 85, section 1. According to the wording of Article 9 of Regulation No. 17 the authorities in the member States are, pursuant to Article 88 of the Treaty, com-

petent to apply Article 85, sections 1 and 2 so long as the Commission has not started the procedure mentioned in Regulation No. 17. The Court considered that the term "authorities of the member States" includes also the national courts because Article 88 refers to the national rules of law concerning competence and legal proceedings. Neither Article 88 of the Treaty nor Article 9, section 3 of Regulation No. 17 contain rules as to the date of commencement of nullity for the national court to apply. Supposedly, however, existing and new non-notifiable agreements cannot be declared null retro-actively at such later time as they might be found to come under Article 85, sections 1 and 2. The fact that the institutions of the Community may, upon conditions laid down in Article 85, section 3, declare Article 85, section 1 (illegality) and section 2 (sanction of nullity) inapplicable, implies that the said institutions may infer that if agreements which they have exempted from notification, are afterwards found to be null, such nullity can only take effect as from the date of the finding.

Any other solution would seriously endanger legal security. If an agreement is concluded which is exempt from notification because its potential adverse influence on trade is considered slight, the parties to such a non-notifiable agreement may infer that it shall at least have the same effect as an agreement which has been duly notified and concluded before March 13, 1962. The Court concluded that non-notifiable agreements which have not been notified, are perfectly valid whether concluded before or after March 13, 1962, so long as nullity has not been established.

Just as in the Portelange case, the Commission objected to perfect validity of restrictive business agreements–in this case of non-notifiable agreements. This time the Commission argued that it is harder to track down non-notifiable contracts than notifiable agreements whilst the former could also be injurious.[5] Once again the Commission advocated limited validity: parties may carry out their agreement on a voluntary basis but they are bound to refrain from any acts which might prevent exemption from application of Article 85, section 1.

The fourth judgement concerning validity of restrictive business agreements handed down by the Court, the decision in the case Rochas v. Bitsch concerned the question as to whether notification of an (existing) standard agreement may be taken to refer also to exclusive agency contracts concluded after the pattern of the existing standard contract. The Court of Justice answered this question in the affirmative. This means that not only the notified existing standard agreement was valid until a final decision by the Commission has been reached, but also the subsequent identical agreements which have not been notified. In the course of the proceedings, the Commission

5. Baardman is the same opinion: See Baardman, Tien jaren Europees Kartelrecht, 1962-1972, (Zwolle 1972), 21.

observed that the exclusive agency contract in dispute contained an export prohibition. According to the Commission, it was clear that an exclusive agency contract containing such export prohibition infringes Article 85 so that the legal effects of this agreement were never in doubt even if it had been notified. To recognise an export prohibition as legal would mean that the parties concerned could isolate a national market until the Commission has taken a decision. This could not be tolerated, commented the Commission, because both decisions pursuant to Article 85, section 3 and pursuant to Article 15, section 6 take considerable time on account of the procedural guarantees required by Regulation No. 17.

Nevertheless the Commission admitted that even export prohibitions may fall within the purview of Article 85, section 3, for instance when a beneficiary of a concession is obliged to incur abnormally great expense in introducing a certain product on the market. In its conclusion the Commission held that a notified export prohibition between parties should be regarded as provisionally valid although no rights in respect of third parties could be derived therefrom, a minimum which ensued already from the Portelange-judgement.

As observed above, the Court declared exclusive agency contracts provisionally valid, even if they contained an export prohibition. In three considerations only, the Court referred to the Commission's comment: the prohibitionary clause which was at issue in the case concerned, had been imposed on retailers who were permitted to sell only to direct consumers in any case. Without prejudice to the exercise of the powers granted to the Commission pursuant to Article 85 of the EEC Treaty and to Regulation No. 17, a prohibition of this scope cannot alter the provisional validity of a duly notified agreement.

The fifth and most recent judgement by the Court of Justice concerning the problems related to validity and nullity of restrictive business agreements means a complete reversal of the Court's jurisprudence. The second Haecht-judgement of February 6, 1973, concerned just like the Bilger-case a number preliminary questions on the applicability of the EEC competition rules to so called brewery-agreements. After a long legal fight before the Liège Tribunal de Commerce, resulting from the non-fulfillment of its contractual obligations by a married couple keeping a café which was financed by the Haecht-brewery, and which had already led to a preliminary ruling by the Court of Justice in 1967, the Haecht brewery argued that the brewery agreements between the Wilkin-Jansens and Haecht were provisionally valid, and the Wilkin-Jansens that the agreements were contrary to Article 85 and therefore null and void. The result was that the Liège Tribunal de Commerce submitted the following preliminary questions to the Court of Justice of the European Communities:

1. Should the proceedings as meant in Article 2, 3 and 6 Regulation No. 17 be considered as begun by the Commission as from the day on which the latter acknowledge receipt of an application for negative clearance or of a notification for the purpose of obtaining exemption pursuant to Article 85, section 3, of the Treaty?
2. May notification of a standard agreement pursuant to legal measures taken in 1968 also be taken as a notification of a similar agreement concluded in the course of 1963?
3. Is nullity of non-notifiable agreements regarded as effective as from the day on which one of the parties to the agreement invoked such nullity or only as from the day of the decision by the Court or the decision by the Commission in which it was established?

Before the Court answered the preliminary questions, it devoted a number of general considerations to the problem of the scope and effects of the sanction of nullity of the second paragraph of Article 85.

The Court considered that Article 85, paragraph 2 strikes out from the date the EEC-Treaty took effect all agreements which come under the prohibition of the first paragraph with nullity. The prohibition contained in Article 85, section 1 is softened by the possibility of exemption provided in the third section of the same Article, but the Treaty doesn't contain any transitional arrangement, concerning the effects of the sanction of nullity to agreements existing on the date Regulation No. 17 took effect. Whereas Regulation No. 17 enables the Commission to act with a certain flexibility applying the sections 1 and 3 of Article 85, and to consider the particularities of each agreement or other restrictive business practices, section 2 of Article 85 doesn't leave any scope to the judge to act with the same flexibility enforcing the sanction of nullity provided in this section. If the Regulation No. 17 enables the Commission to consider the general principle of legal security, the Regulation doesn't soften the effects of section 2 of Article 85: its first Article affirms that restrictive business agreements, decisions and concerted practices falling under Article 85, section 1 are prohibited and automatically void without a preceding decision by the Commission being necessary.

The judge may appreciate whether and how he considers, applying Article 85, section 2, the general principle of legal security. When applying Article 85, section 2 a clear distinction must be made between agreements existing on the date Regulation No. 17 has taken effect and agreements which have been concluded after that date.

Legal security requires, in particular if the agreement has been notified, that the judge declares existing agreements null and void only after the Commission has taken a decision on the basis of Regulation No. 17. On the contrary new agreements can only be executed by their parties at their own peril in the period preceding a decision by the Commission whereas notifica-

tion doesn't have an adjourning effect. The Court acknowledged that the judge has to reckon with the long delays in the procedure of the Commission when applying Article 85. But this doesn't discharge him of the duty to declare new restrictive business agreements null and void at any request of the parties concerned. The judge may suspend the procedure, if he deems it necessary that the parties know the view of the Commission on the applicability of Article 85 to their agreement. The competence or obligation of the judge to ask the Luxemburg Court of Justice preliminary questions remains untouched. The judge doesn't need to suspend the procedure if it is clear from the beginning that the agreement concerned does not come under the prohibition of Article 85 because it has not perceptible effects on competition within the Common Market nor affects the interstate commerce or if on the other hand it is clear that the procedure concerns a forbidden agreement under Article 85, section 1.

The Court finished its general considerations with the observation that although the abovementioned considerations in the first place concern notifiable agreements they apply as well to non notifiable agreements because the exemption from the duty to notify an agreement is a general but not decisive indication that non-notifiable agreements are generally speaking less harmful than notifiable agreements.

The Court answered the third question of the Liège Commercial Court starting from its general considerations:

The second section of Article 85 strikes agreements prohibited by Article 85, section 1 automatically with nullity. This nullity can affect future and past legal effects of the agreement. The nullity mentioned in Article 85, section 2, is retro-active.

Answering the first question of the Liège judge the Court considered that the Commission begins the procedure according to Article 9 of Regulation No. 17 by an official act, which shows clearly the Commission's will to prepare a decision. The acknowledgement of receipt of an application for negative clearance or of a notification for the purpose of obtaining exemption pursuant to Article 85, section 3 of the Treaty cannot be considered as an official act. The Court answered the second question with the observation that notification of a standard agreement must be taken as a notification of all agreements concluded by the same enterprise following the example of the standard agreement.

Consequences of the Haecht II-judgement

The Haecht II-judgement has far-reaching consequences for the status at civil law of restrictive business agreements falling under Article 85. The full validity which the Court had granted to old notifiable notified agreements and to old and new non-notifiable agreements in its Portelange and Bilger-

judgements has been annulled for the greater part by the Court. Moreover the Court ascertained that new notifiable agreements (as well as new non-notifiable) cannot claim any provisional validity in the period before a final decision by the Commission.

It is striking that the Court considered in the Haecht II-judgement just like it had done in the Bilger- and Portelange-judgements the interests of legal security as against the interest of an effective application of the prohibition of the first section of Article 85, but has come te reverse conclusions: the sanction of nullity of the second section of Article 85 prevails, but can be suspended for a limited period as far as old agreements are concerned. New agreements must be declared void by the judge, whenever a party concerned asks for it.

In the following, I intend to discuss respectively the status at civil law of the new and existing agreements before and after the second Haecht-judgement. At the same time I shall try to answer the question whether the Court's refusal to grant provisional validity to new agreements is justified by the fact that parties to such agreements are able to know when agreement comes under the prohibition of Article 85 or not. The second question I intend to discuss is whether the criticism provoked by the Portelange-judgement and especially by the Bilger-judgement justifies the withdrawal by the Court of the validity granted to other restrictive business agreements than new notifiable agreements.

The position of new agreements

Before the Haecht II-judgement the position of new notifiable agreements was not clarified.[6] The Bosch-judgement dealt with existing notifiable and non-notifiable agreements. Commentators on the judgement were split as to whether the Court's pronouncement in this judgement could be correspondingly applied to new agreements.[7] The wording of the Portelange-judgement did not make it clear whether new notifiable agreements were also valid until the Commission shall have reached a decision. On the other hand the Court had assumed that the supplementary agreement between Portelange and Smith Corona concluded after Regulation No. 17 had become effective, should be considered as part of the existing exclusive agency contract and that therefore the question put to the Court referred to an existing agree-

6. See Van Gerven's exhaustive article on this question: Heeft het begrip "voorlopige geldigheid" door het Portelange-arrest definitief afgedaan? SEW, 1970, p. 7-36.

7. See inter alia Baardman, De buitentoepassingverklaring, de groepsgewijze ontheffing, Europees Kartelrecht (Europese Monografieën nr. 2, Deventer 1965) 108-112 and Samkalden, Het Bosch-arrest en de nieuwe kartelafspraken, SEW 1964, 257-262.

ment. In its judgement in re Bilger v. Jehle the Court indicated how to resolve the problem as to whether the Court's judgement in re Portelange may also apply to new notifiable agreements. The Court considered inter alia that "having concluded an agreement which in view of the slight risk that it will affect commerce between member States was exempt from notification parties could reasonably expect the agreement in this respect at least to be allowed to produce the same effect as notified agreements which had been concluded before March 13, 1962.[8]

As to non-notifiable agreements the Court declared in its Bilger-judgement both existing and non-notifiable agreements valid.

Side by side with the Court's judgements there was an argument against extension of the provisional validity of existing notifiable restrictive business agreements, which was advanced by Van Gerven who held that the Court in the Bosch-judgement explicitly provided a transitional arrangement for existing agreements, because Regulation No. 17 is silent on the position at civil law of agreements which have been concluded before Regulation No. 17 became effective while the Commission has not yet reached a decision as to the applicability of Article 85, section 1 and 3 to those agreements.[9] This transitional arrangement was further elaborated in the Portelange-judgement though not extended to new agreements.

Another argument, and in my opinion the most important one, against extending the validity of existing notifiable agreements which have been duly notified to new agreements holds that, owing to the refinement of anti-trust law by the institutions of the European Communities, parties now entering into an agreement which restricts competition are less uncertain as to the fate of their contract, when tested by the Commission to the rules on competition of the EEC-Treaty.[10] If this argument is accepted, the Court's consideration that new notifiable agreements can only be executed at their own risk of the parties to the cartel during the period preceding a decision by the Commission and can be annulled at any time by the judge at the request of any party concerned seems to be justifiable. It is therefore interesting to know whether there is some insecurity left concerning the applicability of the Articles 85 and 86 to restrictive business arrangements.

Since 1962 the Commission has given approximately fifty decisions in individual cases.[11] These decisions relate to various types of agreements the

8. *Recueil*, XVI, 137-138;

9. Van Gerven, op cit., note 6, 23.

10. *Id.* at. 26.

11. See the exhaustive essays by Baardman, De beschikkingspraktijk in kartelzaken van de Europese Commissie in de jaren 1968 tot en met 1970, SEW 1971, 119-139 and SEW 1972, 59-81 in which the practice of the Commission relating to decisions in the years 1968-1971 is discussed and his inaugural address mentioned in note 4.

greatest group consisting of exclusive agency contracts which in view of their number and because they often contain clauses which restrict import and export between member States have been and still are considered by the Commission as injurious to the realisation of the common market. This is why the Commission in the first years after the entry into force of Regulation No. 17 paid much attention to this type of agreement. The Commission has given in addition individual decisions in connection with co-operation agreements, among which specialisation and rationalisation agreements, and licensing agreements. Up till now the latter has been the subject of only four recent individual decisions. Recently a shift is perceptible in the cartel-policy of the Commission in the direction of decisions in which different types of agreements have been prohibited and in which in a few cases heavy fines have been imposed. These decisions related to horizontal price-cartels, price-discrimination and fencing off of parts of the Common Market. By decision of January 2, 1973 the Commission imposed e.g. heavy fines on sugar-enterprises because of protection of different national sugar-markets: against unchecked imports of competing sugar from other markets within the EEC-territory.[12] In addition to the Commission's individual decisions the Council laid down two regulations empowering the Commission to grant exemption to exclusive agency contracts, licensing agreements regarding the application of norms and types, research and development of products or processes up to the stage of industrial application.[13] In 1967 the Commission issued a regulation in which defined the requirements for category-exemption of exclusive agency contracts and in December 1972 the Commission published a regulation regarding category-exemption with respect to specialisation agreements.[14]

Over the years the Commission has published apart from regulations and decisions, a number of Notices which are not legally binding, the most recent

12. Decision of the Commission of January 2, 1973 European Sugar Industry. O.J. 1973 Nr. L 141/17.

13. Regulation No. 19/65 by the Council of March 2, 1965 relating to the application of Article 85, section 3 of the Treaty to certain agreements and concerted practices, O.J., 533/65;
Regulation No. 2821/71 by the Council of December 20, 1971 relating to the application of Article 85, section 3 of the Treaty to certain agreements, decisions and concerted practices, O.J. 1971, L 285/46, [1972] CMLR, D4.

14. Regulation No. 67/67 by the Commission of March 22, 1967 relating the application of Article 85, section 3, of the Treaty to certain exclusive agency agreements, O.J. 849/67.
Regulation No. 2598/72 by the Commission of December 8, 1972, modifying Regulation nr. 67/67 (renewal until December 31, 1982), O.J. 1972, L 276/15.
Regulation No. 2779/72 by the Commission of December 21, 1972 relating the application of Article 85, section 3 of the Treaty to certain specialization agreements, O.J. 1972, L 292/23; [1973] CMLR, D 12.

concern co-operation agreements and so-called "Bagatellfälle".[15] The last named are agreements which in view of the small share in the market and the small turnover of the parties concerned, have no palpable effect on the competition on the relevant part of the Common Market. It cannot be denied that as a result of the refinement of European anti-trust policy, very briefly described above, by the institutions of the Communities—the contribution of the Court in this field has been and still is considerable—the matter of the agreements which come under Article 85, section 1 and are eligible for exemption (individually or as a category) has been gradually clarified. On the other hand the Court decided in its first Haecht-judgement that when considering a restrictive business agreement in light of the rules of competition of the Rome Treaty and the implementing regulations not only the content of the agreement should be noted but also its effect on the market concerned. The system laid down in Article 85 makes it imperative to observe also any cumulative material effects in the economic and legal context which they may have in combination with other arrangements, decisions and practices with reference to competition specifically on the market on which such effects are felt.[16] This approach by the Court implies that in fact each agreement has to be reconsidered before a definite opinion to its compatibility with Article 85 can be given. The Courts consideration in the Bilger judgement that agreements, which do not concern inter-state commerce and are exempted from the duty of notification, can affect interstate commerce indicates that the effects of an agreement to competition within the Common Market are more important for its review on the basis of Article 85 than its material contents. The same is true for the Courts consideration in its judgement in re 8/72, Vereniging van Cementhandelaren v. Commission.[17] The VCH alleged that the restrictive business arrangements in question did not fall within the competence of the Communities, because the agreements and decisions had an exclusively national character, were restricted to Dutch territory and did not concern inter-state commerce, which meant that inter-state commerce within the Common Market could not be affected. The Court answered that an agreement between enterprises which completely covers the territory of a member-State, naturally leads to a consolidation of the division of the Common Market in national markets, which means an obstacle to the

15. The Commissions Notice concerning agreements, decisions and concerted practices with regard to co-operation between enterprises, O.J. 1968, C 75/3 as amended in O.J. 1968, C 84/14.
The Commissions Notice of May 27, 1970 concerning agreements, decisions and concerted practices of little importance which do not come under Article 85 section 1 of the EEC-treaty, O.J. 1970 C 64/1; [1970] CMLR, D 15.

16. Judgement of December 12, 1967, case No. 23/67 (Brasserie De Haecht v. Wilkin and Janssen) *Receuil* XIII, 525 *et seq*; [1968] CMLR, 26 *et seq*.

17. Judgement of October, 17 1972, case No. 8/72. (Vereniging van Cementhandelaren v. Commission) *Receuil* XVIII, 977-1004; [1973] CMLR, 7-23.

economic interpenetration aimed at by the Rome Treaty and which protects the national production.

The Notice by the Commission concerning so-called Bagatellfälle indicates that the Commission also considers the effects of a restrictive business agreement as more important than its contents.

In conclusion it can be said that owing to the recent refinements of European anti-trust law by the Community institutions parties to a new agreement have a fairly clear notion of the agreements which can and cannot pass the muster of Article 85, section 3. A number of restrictive business agreements can be said to be illegal "per se", such as horizontal price fixing contracts, exclusive agency contracts containing absolute territorial protection and other agreements which may lead to partitioning of the Common Market. On the other hand, besides the fact that the Commission has dealt with a restricted number of types of agreements (with exclusive agency contracts and cooperation agreements for example but much less with licensing contracts), the Court and the Commission stress both that a given agreement needs to be judged within its economic and legal context and that its effects on competition are decisive for the applicability of Article 85. This means that parties to an agreement cannot be always sure whether their agreement comes under the prohibition of the first section of Article 85 and can be exempted on the condition of Article 85, section 3. In other words a certain measure of uncertainty will always be present. Therefore it is justified to grant new agreements a degree of validity in the period between notification and the final decision. This provisional validity ought to imply that the parties concerned can only apply to the civil court for an order for provisional remedies but cannot sue for damages and for performance.

The Haecht II-judgement however does not leave any scope for such a limited provisional validity of new agreements. The Court considers that parties to new notifiable and non-notifiable agreements as long as the Commission did not take a decision can only carry out their agreement at their own peril. In the Portelange-judgement the Court answered the Commissions objection to grant to notifiable agreements some provisional validity that the Commission always was competent to address a provisional decision pursuant to Article 15, section 6 of Regulation No. 17 to parties to a restrictive business agreement, in which the Commission informs parties that their agreement comes under the prohibition of the first section of Article 85 and that exemption cannot possibly be given. The Court considered that after such an announcement by the Commission parties to the agreement could only carry out their agreement at their own peril. In other words, by means of a decision pursuant to Article 15, section 6 the Commission was able to terminate the validity of a notified agreement. Probably the Court meant to say that parties after a decision pursuant to Article 15, section 6 could not apply to the civil court for an order for provisional remedies, but that "to carry out at their

own peril" means that the agreement is null and void pursuant to Article 85, section 2.

In the Haecht II-judgement the Luxemburg Court considered that the judge is obliged to declare new agreements null at the request of any party concerned. This means that if one party to a new agreement which comes under Article 85, section 1 applies to the judge for an order for provisional remedies, but the other party claims the nullity of the agreement pursuant to Article 85, section 2, the judge is obliged to meet the wishes of the party last-mentioned. It is conceivable that the judge grants provisional remedies before suspending the procedure, but even for this the Haecht II-judgement does not give any room: the nullity of restrictive business agreements coming under Article 85 prevails and in particular the nullity of new agreements is pushed by the Court to the forefront, without any scope for provisional validity.

The position of old agreements

Before the Haecht II-judgement old notifiable and old and new non-notifiable agreements had the same status at civil law: they were perfectly valid before the Commission had taken a decision. Moreover non-notifiable agreements could only be declared null with effect from the decision of the competent authorities.

The Haecht II-judgement has fundamentally changed this situation. The difference between notifiable and non-notifiable agreements as far as their status at civil law is concerned has disappeared: new non-notifiable agreements have got the same position as new notifiable agreements: they are automatically null and can only be carried out by the parties concerned at their own peril.

The Court has maintained some, provisional, validity for old agreements: the judge does not declare these agreements null before the Commission has taken a decision. This nullity is retroactive. This does not necessarily mean that parties to an old agreement cannot sue for damages and or performance but the fact that nullity impends over the parties like the sword of Damocles will induce the judge to grant only provisional remedies. The Court has considerably weakened the status at civil law of old agreements, in view of a more strict application of the sanction of nullity pursuant to Article 85 and Regulation No. 17, which had been pushed to the background in the Bosch-, Portelange- and Bilger-judgements.

Both the Portelange- and Bilger-judgements have provoked severe criticism: because the prohibitionary system laid down in Article 85 and Regulation No. 17 was transmuted into a system of misuse which closely resembles the system of the British Restrictive Trade Practices Act 1956 and its later amendments, and because the Court collided–particularly in the

Bilger-judgement—with a number of provisions of Regulation No. 17:[18] with Article 1—agreements coming under Article 85, section 1, are automatically prohibited without a preceding decision by the Commission—with Article 6—the Commission is competent to fix the date from which a decision of exemption pursuant to Article 85, section 1, will take effect—with Article 7 —competence of the Commission to cover the bad past of old agreements.[19]

The criticism relating to the Court's judgement on provisional validity of restrictive business agreements was mainly earned by the Bilger-judgement and particularly by the considerations that the fact that the institutions of the Community may upon conditions laid down in Article 85, section 3 declare Article 85, section 1 (illegality) and section 2 (sanction of nullity) inapplicable, implies that the said institutions may infer that if agreements which they have exempted from notification are afterwards found to be null *such nullity can only take effect as from the date of the decision by the Commission or other competent authorities.* Any other solution would seriously endanger legal security.

This limitation of the effect of the sanction of nullity as far as non-notifiable agreements are concerned has provoked much opposition because of the collision with Regulation No. 17 and because the Court granted non-notifiable agreements a kind of category-exemption during the period before the final decision by the Commission and before the Commission had the opportunity to judge whether the agreement comes under Article 85 section 1 and fulfills the conditions of individual exemption. The criticism was strengthened by the fact that the wordings of the judgement made it possible to apply the limitation of the sanction of nullity even to old notifiable, notified agreements.

As a matter of fact the abovementioned considerations—even if limited to non-notifiable agreements—were at cross purposes with the policy of the Council and the Commission in relation to the determination of the agreements which shall be non-notifiable and which shall be eligible for category-exemption. This is the more apparent now that in December 1971 the Council extended in two regulations the non-notifiable agreements mentioned in Article 4, section 2, so as to include specialization agreements on the one hand, and enlarged the Commission's power to grant category-exemption in

18. See inter alia Steindorff, Volle Wirksamkeit angemeldeten Wettbewerbsbeschränkungen in den Europaischen Wirtschaftsgemeinschaft, Der Betriebsberater 1969, 980-982 and Ulmer, Europäisches Kartellrecht auf neuen Wegen? A.W.D. 1970, 193-195. The latter is fiercely opposed to the system of provisional validity and full effectiveness as evaluated by the Court of Justice of the European Communities. Baardman, *op cit.* note 4, 20-21 and Van Gerven *op. cit.* note 5 and in Over voorlopige geldigheid en over nietigheid van kartelafspraken SEW 1970, 271-302 on the other hand are more moderate. See also Megret, Louis, Vignes, Waelbroeck, *Le droit de la Communauté Européenne*, vol. IV, concurrence, 168.

19. See note 18.

respect of agreements concerning the application of norm and types, research and the development of products or processes and finally specialization agreements on the other hand.[20]

As to the latter category the Commission published in December 1972 a regulation enumerating the requirements which parties to a specialization agreement must satisfy so that their contract may be eligible for category-exemption.[21]

These requirements are concerned with the content of the agreement on the one hand and the maximum share of the relevant market the parties may supply and the maximum turnover of the parties, allowable for purposes of eligibility for category-exemption on the other hand. The requirements for the purposes of category-exemption of specialization agreements are more exacting than those which have to be satisfied in order to escape compulsory notification. After the Bilger-judgement such a difference did not make sense any more, since owing to the fact that subsequent nullity was no longer retroactive, non-notifiable agreements found themselves, in any case until they would have been declared null, in the same situation as agreements which had been granted category-exemption.

The critics to the Bilger-judgements concentrated themselves on the limitation of the effect of the sanction of nullity of the second section of Arcticle 85. The most important statement of the Court in the Haecht II-judgement is that nullity of restrictive business agreements resulting from a prohibition pursuant to Article 85, section 1 is always retroactive. The Court meets in this way the wishes of its critics. The Court makes however another step backward: the Court drops the difference between notifiable and non-notifiable agreements as far as the status at civil law of restrictive business agreements is concerned.[22] Old and new restrictive business agreements are automatically null. The judge however does not declare old agreements null before the Commission has taken a decision.

Old agreements have therefore maintained some provisional validity, but the meaning of this provisional validity is uncertain. It is not inconceivable that they are still perfectly valid but the fact that nullity of an old agreement can enter retroactively after a decision by the Commission means that the judge will probably only grant provisional remedies at a request by one of the

20. Regulation No. 2821/71 by the Council of December 20, 1971 relating to the application of Article 85, section 3 of the Treaty to certain agreements, decisions and concerted practices, O.J. 1971, L 285/46; [1972] CMLR, D 4.
Regulation No. 2822/71 by the Council of December 20, 1971 supplementing Regulation No. 17 concerning the application of Articles 85 and 86 of the Treaty, O.J. 1971, L 285/49; [1972] CMLR, D 8.

21. Regulation No. 2779/72 by the Commission of December 21, 1972 concerning the application of Article 85, section 3 of the Treaty to groups of specialization agreements, O.J. 1972, L 292/23; [1973] CMLR, D 12.

22. See Baardman, *op cit.*, note 4, 21.

parties concerned but will refuse to honour a suit for damages and/or performance. Because the Court considered that in this Haecht II-judgement the nullity of restrictive business agreements must prevail it curtailed the perfect validity of old agreements to a restricted provisional validity and has in fact revoked its judgements in the Portelange- and Bilger-cases.

Conclusion

1. The second Haecht-judgement of the Court of Justice of the European Communities signifies a complete reversal of the jurisprudence of the Court concerning the status at civil law of restrictive business agreements before the Commission has decided whether an agreement comes under the prohibition of Article 85, section 1 and fulfilled the conditions.

2. Before the second Haecht-judgement the status at civil law of restrictive business agreements was as follows:

– notifiable and notified agreements, existing before the coming into force, March 13, 1962, of Regulation No. 17 were perfectly valid before the Commission had taken a decision pursuant to Article 85, section 3.

– existing and new non-notifiable, non-notified agreements were perfectly valid as long as they were not declared null by the competent national authorities or by the Commission. Nullity which would enter later on could only have effect henceforth from the decision of the competent authorities. An extensive interpretation of the Bilger-judgement meant that this consideration by the Court could also be applied to old notifiable agreements.

– the status of new notifiable agreements was not clear at all. The Portelange-judgement only concerned old agreements.

3. After the Haecht II-judgement the situation has completely been changed.

– The Court dropped as far as the status at civil law of restrictive business agreements was concerned the distinction between notifiable and non-notifiable agreements.

– The Court maintained the distinction between existing and new agreements. Both categories are automatically null and void coming under Article 85, section 1, without a preceding decision by the Commission being necessary (Article 1, Regulation No. 17).

– Because of the legal security the Court considered that the judge will not declare *existing agreements* null before the Commission has decided that the agreement comes under Article 85 and does not fulfil the conditions of exemption of Article 85, section 3.

– Parties to a new agreement can only carry out their agreement at their own peril. The judge has the duty to declare these agreements null at any request of parties concerned, his right to suspend the procedure being reserved. New agreements are therefore "provisionally null". The Commission has the power to lay down pursuant to Article 6 of Regulation No. 17 an exemption decision with retroactive effect. This means that the nullity of restrictive

business agreements can retro-actively be changed into validity.

4. The provisional validity of old agreements possibly signifies that the parties concerned can sue for damages and for fulfillment. However the fact that the nullity of this category of agreement can enter retroactively after a decision by the Commission, will induce the judge to grant provisional remedies only.

The criticism provoked by the Bilger-judgement in particular has caused the Court to push the sanction of nullity again to the forefront. This means that the perfect validity granted to old agreements in the Portelange and Bilger-judgements has been curtailed. The judgement of the Court is understandable in view of the conflict with Regulation No. 17 provoked by the Bilger-judgement, but it provokes serious difficulties for parties to agreements who after the Portelange- and Bilger-judgements reckoned with the perfect validity of their agreement.

5. The Commission has clarified the matter of applicability of Article 85 to restrictive business agreements by his decisions in individual cases, its regulations granting category-exemption to some categories of agreements and its Notices. Moreover the Luxemburg Court has clarified a number of legal problems related to the application of the EEC-competition rules.

The Commission and the Court, however, have in later years stressed the necessity to judge the effect of an agreement to the competition within the Common Market and to the inter-state commerce, rather than the contents of restrictive business agreements. This means that almost each agreement must in itself be judged before the Commission can decide whether it comes under Article 85. Moreover the Commission has concentrated its effort on a restricted number of types of agreement and neglected until a short time ago other types e.g. licensing agreements. This means that parties to new restrictive business agreements cannot always be completely sure whether their agreement comes under the prohibition of Article 85, except in the case of some per se prohibited agreements.

Legal security requires therefore that new agreements will be granted a kind of provisional validity, which implies that parties can apply provisional remedies.

The Haecht-judgement stressing the sanction of nullity of Article 85 section 2 does not leave any scope to provisional validity of new agreements. New agreements can only be carried out at the own peril of the parties concerned and the judge is obliged to declare a new agreement null at any request of parties concerned.

Granting provisional validity to new agreements would mean that old and new agreements would have the same status at civil law whereas the Court has stressed the difference between these two categories of restrictive business agreements. It is therefore not probable that the Court will change its mind again about the status at civil law of restrictive business agreements.

Chapter 8

INDUSTRIAL PROPERTY AND THE LAW OF THE EUROPEAN COMMUNITIES

by *Mr. H. W. Wertheimer*

I. *Introduction*

The dissemination of technology plays a predominant role in the development of the Common Market. This is underlined by Article 2 of the Treaty which sets out as the aims of the Community the promotion of a harmonious development of economic activities and an accelerated raising of the standard of living. To achieve these goals the transfer of knowledge embodied in industrial property constitutes an indispensable vehicle.

On the other hand the Treaty equally provides in its Article 3(f) that the activities of the European Community shall include the establishment of a system ensuring that competition shall not be distorted within the Common Market.

Although industrial property and competition both aim at the same ultimate goal viz. the raising of the standard of living in our society their underlying philosophies differ profoundly. While the laws on industrial property confer upon its owner a legal monopoly, competition law strives at doing away with all kinds of inequalities between competitors. The monopoly of the industrial property–so the reasoning holds–should provide an incentive to its owner to take the risks involved when making the necessary investments to exploit his right and thus contribute to technological progress. Competition philosophy at the other hand contends that monopoly breeds laziness and self-sufficiency while at the same time the monopolist charges the public with excessive prices. Inevitably in all legal systems where both industrial property legislation and competition laws exist some clashes are bound to occur. In the European Economic Community there is a special dimension to this problem since industrial property rights are still based on domestic legislation of the member States while the EEC-competition law is community legislation.

Quite a few attempts have been made to delineate a clear borderline between both bodies of law. Thus it was held that the "normal use" of industrial property should not come under the EEC-competition rules. "Normal use" has been said to mean all practices which were permitted under domestic law

according to traditional commercial practice. This viewpoint is now more or less abandoned since such a statement would imply that the domain of industrial property would be totally excluded from the impact of the EEC-rules of competition. This contention cannot be upheld for the simple reason that since the Treaty came into force domestic law itself has changed, particularly in that Community Law has become part of the national systems of law of the member States. This implies that the EEC-competition rules—being provisions of a self-executing nature—now form part of the national system of law. Therefore they determine together with intrinsic national law the tenor of domestic law and consequently what should be a "normal use". For that reason, the "normal use" theory amounts to a chain of circular reasoning.

Another group of experts taking a less ambitious view accept that competition rules may have an impact on the exercise of industrial property rights even on those hitherto permitted by domestic law. They argue, however, that all those restrictions which are inherent in the exclusive rights of industrial property, as delineated by domestic law, should be immune from interference by the competition rules of the EEC. They hold that property rights created and guaranteed by domestic law cannot be curtailed by Community Law. They assert that their view is supported by the treaty-provisions themselves, in particular by the Articles 36 and 222, that will be discussed later on. This view is widespread among experts in the Common Market countries, especially in Germany. But can it be upheld?

Industrial property rights originate in national rules of law, generally embodied in national statutes. The various statutes of the member States of the EEC differ markedly between themselves. Thus the scope of industrial property rights being governed by these various systems of national law varies accordingly.

If the EEC-rules of competition should not impinge on the inherent rights of industrial property, this view would amount to a different application of Community Law according to the national industrial property rights it would be confronted with. For, the scope of the industrial property right involved would determine the extent of the applicability of the rules of competition. Such way of application of Community Law has however been repeatedly rejected by the Court of Justice of the European Communities that is entrusted with the task of ensuring uniform interpretation of Community Law throughout the whole European Community.

Especially with reference to competition law in the EEC and its relationship to national law the Court rendered the following opinion:[1]

> "However such parallel application of the national system should only be allowed in so far as it does not impinge upon the uniform application, throughout the Common Market, of the Community rules on restrictive business agreements and of the full effect of the acts decreed in application of those rules."

Furthermore the Court held that

> "Any other solution would be incompatible with the objectives of the Treaty and with the character of its rules on competition".

Therefore, the theory according to which the EEC rules of competition should not impinge upon the inherent rights of industrial property as outlined by domestic law cannot be upheld. One should accept the idea that in principle inroads into these rights cannot be discounted.

Since the global theories mentioned above are not capable of laying down a clear demarcation line between industrial property and the EEC-rules of competition an analysis should be made as to how the European authorities have tried to solve this problem. Since the EEC-rules of competition themselves do not refer to the subject matter, the European authorities have clarified their position by issuing regulations and general notices on the one hand and decisions and publications on individual cases on the other hand.

II. *Acts of a general character referring to the relationship between Industrial Property and EEC-competition law.*

In chronological order the regulations and general notices will be discussed that deal with the question as to how to ascertain whether restrictions imposed by the exercise of an industrial property right are prohibited or permitted by the EEC-rules of competition.

1. *Council Regulation No. 17/62 of February 6, 1962*[2]

Although this Regulation concerns only indirectly the question of this interrelationship it is yet important to see in what way the Council dealt with licensing agreements. In principle all agreements which have as their object or result the restriction of competition and which are likely to affect trade between the member States are held to be prohibited under Article 85(1). In order to obtain an exemption under Article 85(3) they have to be notified to

1. Judgment of February 13, 1969, case No. 14-68 (Wilhelm et. al. v. Bundeskartellamt), *Recueil* XV, 14, [1969] CMLR, 118.
2. p. 204/62. The Regulation became effective on March 13, 1962.

the Commission of the European Communities. Some kinds of agreements even when falling under Article 85(1) are not subject to such obligation. They are specified in Article 4(2) of the Regulation No. 17. Among those are the agreements mentioned in Article 4(2) (2b) i.e. agreements whereto only two undertakings are party and the sole object of these agreements is to impose restrictions on the exercise of rights of any person assigning or using industrial property rights or know-how. The reason why the Council felt it could free these agreements–if they come under Article 85(1)–from the obligation of a notification to the Commission is explained in the preamble to the Regulation. There it was held that they entail special features which may make them less dangerous to the development of the common market.

Since the provisions in the Regulation lifting the obligation for a notification to obtain an exemption is of a purely formal character, it gives no guidance on the issue of substance as to which kind of licensing agreements comes under the ban of Article 85(1) and which one does not. This view is confirmed by the preamble to the Regulation which states that this flexible system for certain categories of agreements does not prejudge the question of their validity under Article 85. There is no doubt that agreements exist embodying restrictions on the exercise of industrial property rights which escape the ambit of Article 85(1), but on the other hand there certainly will be agreements of that description which come under its prohibition. Otherwise Article 4(2) (2b) of Regulation No. 17/62 could have no sense at all.[3]

Up to February 1973 it was generally held that the preferential status of this kind of licensing agreements when coming under Article 85(1) entailed a consequence of a substantial character. Agreements falling under Article 85(1) and subject to a compulsory notification are considered null and void as long as this notification was not submitted to the Commission. Agreements under Article 85(1) exempted from this obligation were lawful right from the moment they had been concluded. To that effect was the judgment of the Court in the Bosch-case[4] where it held that agreements not subject to a compulsory notification and not notified must be considered valid. In the Bilger v. Jehle case[5] the Court explained its position more fully by stating that an agreement exempted from a compulsory notification and not notified, was fully valid until its nullity had been declared. The Court gave no indication on the issue as to by which authority this nullity should be established. But one could safely assume that it was implied that all the competent authorities–in this case the Commission or the national author-

3. The same reasoning was adopted in the case No. 32/65 (Italian Republic v. EEC-Council and EEC-Commission), *Recueil* XII, 590, [1969] CMLR, 61.

4. Judgment of April 6, 1962, case No. 13/61 (De Geus & Uitdenbogerd v. Bosch), *Recueil* VIII, 89 *et seq* (esp. p. 108), [1962] CMLR, 1 *et seq*.

5. Judgment of March 18, 1970, case No. 43/69, *Recueil* XVI, 138. Annotation Maas and Van der Wielen, 8 CMLRev. 1971, 244-247.

ities designated by their domestic legislation to apply competition law—were meant.[6]

For this kind of agreements the Court in its judgment gave also a general protection against a retroactive effect of the nullity resulting from a possible prohibition. It has been argued that this opinion applied equally to all these competent authorities. This view was not shared by the Commission.[7] It held that the Court did not say that a decision of the Commission finding an infringement of Article 85 could only have effect for the future. To its mind the Court only addressed itself to the national judiciary for that purpose.

This whole system has been suddenly changed by the Haecht II-judgment[7a] of the Court of Justice. In reversing completely its position the Court now held, that all agreements subject to a compulsory notification and notified should be considered as lacking any legal validity, so long as the Commission has not rendered a decision in their behalf. Exactly this same system applies to those agreements that are exempted from compulsory notification, so that any advantage as to their legal validity has now disappeared. For all practical purposes there hardly seems left any difference at all. One may insist on the privilege of not having to notify one's agreement but so long as the Commission has no knowledge of its existence it cannot render a decision in its behalf, and so long this agreement is held to be invalid. So whoever wants to obtain a decision from the Commission will be well advised to notify his agreement as soon as possible whether he is under compulsion to notify or not.

Originally Article 4(2) (3b) of the Regulation mentioned as exempted from compulsory notification those agreements coming under Article 85(1) where the sole object is joint research to improve techniques, provided that the result is accessible to all parties and that each of them can exploit it.

By Council Regulation No. 2822/71 of December 20, 1971[8] this paragraph was changed. The compulsory notification is now lifted for agreements where the sole object is joint research and joint development. In its Explanatory Memorandum to the European Parliament[9] the Commission states that it deleted the part of the sentence beginning with the word "provided" because according to now prevailing views agreements on the exploitation of the results of joint research and development on conditions as alluded to in

6. Also Judgment of April 4, 1970, *Bundesgerichtshof*, AWD 1970, 416-417.

7. Answer to written question No. 4/71 of Mr. Springorum, O.J. 1971, C 57/6.

7a. Judgment of February 6, 1973, case No. 48-72 (S.A. Brasserie de Haecht v. Wilkin-Janssen), [1973] CMLR, 287-308. Cf. Van der Wielen, *supra*, 140-159.

8. O.J. 1971, L 285/49, [1972] CMLR, D 8.

9. Doc. Nr. 71/70 of July 19, 1970.

the old Article 4(2) (3b) are not considered to contain any restriction of competition at all.

2. *Manual to Articles 85 and 86*

In September 1962 when the day approached that all agreements falling under Article 85(1) existing at the date of the coming into effect of Regulation No. 17–March 13, 1962–had to be notified[10] to the Commission–but for those mentioned in Article 4(2) of the Regulation–the Commission issued a Manual[11] in order to give some guidance to the enterprises concerned on the one hand, but also to stem as far as possible the forthcoming tidalwave of notifications it anticipated.

Where Article 4(2) (2b) is discussed the Manual states that this provision only concerns limitation imposed on the licensee and does not cover restrictions accepted by the licensor nor restrictions embodied in agreements for the joint exploitation of patents.

Article 4(2) (2b) only concerns restrictions imposed on the licensee in the exercise of industrial property rights. Restrictions which are not directly related to such exercise do not come under Article 4(2) and should be notified when falling under Article 85(1). These restrictions may exist where the licensee

– assumes commitments extending beyond the period of validity of the industrial property right.
– may not deal in any competing product.
– undertakes not to export to an other member State.
– undertakes to impose competitive restrictions on his customers.

Undoubtedly the Commission is of an opinion that in all those cases Article 85(1) clearly applies and a notification should be made.

What in point of fact the Commission did understand by the rather ambiguous phrase "restrictions on the exercise of industrial property rights and know-how" has never been made clear. It can be assumed, taking into consideration the Commission's views expressed in the official Notice of December 24, 1962–to be dealt with hereafter–that it may cover restrictions imposed on the licensee as to the selling price of the products manufactured under the licence, or the tie-in clause obliging the licensee to buy products not covered by the exclusive right from the licensor or any other person designated by

10. Notification day for existing agreements was November 1, 1962, but for bilateral agreements, which had to be notified, February 1, 1963.

11. Manual published by the Information Services of the European Communities, Doc. Nr. 8062/4/IX/1962/5, 25 pages + 4 annexes.

him provided these products are essential for meeting the standards of quality prescribed by the licensor.

Where know-how agreements are involved it may be assumed that those restrictions which according to that Notice would fall beyond the scope of Article 85(1) when they are embodied in patent licensing agreements, would come under Article 4(2) (2b) if they were inserted in know-how agreements.

3. *Notice on Patent Licensing Agreements*

In order to clarify more specifically its position on patent licensing agreements—and only this kind of agreements—the Commission took another step. On December 24, 1962 the Commission issued its Notice on Patent Licensing Agreements[12] —afterwards commonly referred to as the Christmas Message— in which it made known which clauses in patent licensing agreements—to its mind—dit not fall under the prohibition ex Article 85(1). The purpose of this Notice, the Commission stated, was to give enterprises some information as to the line of conduct the Commission would follow when applying Article 85 (1). The obligations imposed on the licensee mentioned in this Notice cover obligations as to the restrictions on the methods of exploitation (manufacture, use, distribution) on the field of use, on the quantity to be manufactured, on the utilization as to time, area and power to dispose of the licence. To the mind of the Commission these obligations did not fall under Article 85(1) because they involve exclusively the partial retention of the right of prohibition embodied in the exclusive right of the patentee.

Furthermore the Notice covers obligations as to standards of quality the licensee should meet. In this connection obligations may be imposed on the licensee to take delivery of certain materials not protected by the patent insofar as the quality cannot be ascertained according to objective criteria. To the mind of the Commission these obligations cannot restrict the competition eligible for protection insofar as they are indispensable for a technically proper exploitation of the patent.

It was obvious that this Notice which deals with patent licensing agreements only, was moulded along the lines of Article 20 of the German Law against Restrictions of Competition concerning the same subject. But when comparing both texts one perceives that the clause on export prohibition and the one on pricefixing as well as the non-attack clause are manifestly lacking in the Notice of the Commission. It is submitted that this discrepancy cannot be attributed to sheer coincidence.

The Notice furthermore states that the exclusive licensing agreement im-

12. O.J. p. 2922/62.

plying the licensor's undertaking not to utilize the invention himself so closely approaches an assignment of rights that it does not seem to give rise to any objection.

The Notice is not applicable to agreements on patent pools, reciprocal licensing and multiple parallel licensing.

Although this Notice had no legal binding force, it reflected the official view of the Commission at that moment. Therefore it was be anticipated that the enterprises would rely heavily on the views expressed in this document. It came therefore more or less as a surprise when indications became apparent pointing to the fact that the Commission did no longer stick altogether to the views embodied in the Notice.[13]

As it was, the views laid down in this Notice do not coincide any more with those implied in the subsequent Regulation No. 67/67[14] providing for category-exemptions for exclusive distributorship contracts. According to the Notice exclusive selling licences of patented goods do not fall under the ambit of Article 85(1) since the Notice equally declared permissible to combine all the restictions mentioned in the Notice that, taken separately, would not come under Article 85(1). According to Article 3 of Regulation No. 67/67 the category-exemption for exclusive distributorship contracts shall not apply when the contracting parties exercise industrial property rights–i.e. patent rights–to prevent third parties from obtaining the products under contract in other areas of the Common Market of from selling them in the contract territory. But when an exemption can be withdrawn from certain groups of agreements it presupposes that in principe they do fall first under the scope of Article 85(1). Since said agreements, economically speaking, comprise all the elements of exclusive licensing agreements for selling patented goods a certain contradiction exists in comparison with what has been declared before in the Notice of December 24, 1962. It seems warranted to assume that since then the Commission has changed its mind in this respect.

But also more in general, doubts can be cast on the Notice in question. It specifically focusses its attention on the legal contents of the patent licensing agreements and declares them to fall beyond the reach of Article 85(1) for that reason only.

13. Alexander, "*Article 85 of the EEC-Treaty and the exclusive licence to sell patented products*", 5 CMLRev. 1967-8, 465-475, was the first one to point to this change in mind.

14. Regulation No. 67/67 of the Commission on the application of Article 85(3) of the Treaty to groups of exclusive distributorship contracts, O.J. p. 849/67, [1967] CMLR., D 1.

However, on various occasions the Court of Justice[15] ruled that agreements should not be evaluated on the merits of their juridical nature alone; rather a predominant consideration should be given to the economic context in which they occur. Article 85(1) is said to rest on an assessment of the repercussions of the agreement from two aspects, i.e. "trade between member States" and "competition", requiring an economic evaluation. Thus the effects of the agreements on the market place are determinant for the question whether or not the conditions of Article 85(1) are fulfilled.

Since the Commission has held in the Burroughs-Delplanque decision[16] as well as in the Burroughs-Geha Werke decision[17] that the exclusive patent licensing agreement for manufacturing may come under the prohibition laid down in Article 85(1) it became once more manifest that the Commission no longer adheres in all respects to its Notice of December 24, 1962. For the sake of legal security it seems indicated that time has come for the Commission to spell out clearly to what extent it still supports its views set out in this Notice.

4. *Council Regulation No. 19/65 on the application of Article 85(3) of the Treaty to groups of agreements and concerted practices.*

In order to enable the Commission to cope with the many ten thousands of notifications it had received and to simplify its task, the Council of Ministers issued Regulation No. 19/65[18] by which the Commission was authorized to declare the ban of Article 85(1) not applicable to certain groups of agreements. In doing so the Council implemented the possibility to exempt groups of agreements from the prohibition of Article 85(1) as was provided for in Article 85(3).

Contrary to the proposals of the Commission[19] to the Council the Council Regulation did not grant a general authority for category-exemption but only singled out two groups of agreements. These were bilateral exclusive

15. Judgment of June 30, 1966, case No. 56/65 (Soc. Techn. Minière v. Maschinenbau Ulm), *Recueil* XII, 359. [1966] CMLR, 375.
Judgment of March 15, 1967 Cons. Cases Nos. 8-11/66 (Noordwijks Cement Akkoord), *Recueil* XIII, 117, [1967] CMLR, 103.
Judgment of December 12, 1967, case No. 23/67 (Brasserie de Haecht v. Wilkin and Janssen), *Recueil* XIII, 537, [1968] CMLR, 40.
Judgment of May 6, 1971, case No. 1/71 (Cadillon v. Höss), *Recueil* XVII, 356; [1971] CMLR, 429.

16. O.J. 1972, L 13/50, [1972] CMLR, D 67.

17. O.J. 1972, L 13/53, [1972] CMLR, D 72.

18. O.J. p. 533/65.

19. Doc. IV/COM (64) 62 def., of February 26, 1964; Eur. Parliament 1964-1965, Doc. 5 of March 3, 1964.

distributorship contracts and bilateral agreements involving limitations imposed in connection with the acquisition or use of industrial property rights–therefore not only patents–and know-how. It can be assumed that under this last broad definition come obligations imposed on the licensor, as well as all restrictions that could reasonably be imposed on the licensee. Although the Commission did not obtain all it wanted, for all practical purposes this Regulation met with the Commission's immediate needs since the overwhelming majority of the notifications presented dealt with these two kinds of agreements.

It could be anticipated that the Commission would now use the power it had received under Regulation No. 19/65 which defined the outline of the Commission's terms of reference, and that it would issue a regulation on a category-exemption for certain classes of licensing agreements to dispose of the thousands of notifications it had received. However, so far it has not adopted this course. It seems that the licensing agreements were so varied in nature that the Commission has not yet seen its way to solve the problem by means of category-exemptions. That some real difficulties exist may be borne out by the fact that the Commission announced in 1964[20] that it had started proceedings on 10 cases in the difficult field of licensing agreements, but that is was not before December 1971 that the first official decisions[21] on licensing agreements were taken.

5. *Regulation No. 67/67 on the application of Article 85(3) to groups of exclusive distributorship contracts*

Pursuant to Council Regulation No. 19/65 the Commission issued Regulation No. 67/67[22] concerning category-exemptions for exclusive distributorship contracts. In an indirect way the Commission gave here some insight in its views on the issue of the exercise of industrial property rights in the Common Market. In Article 3 of this regulation the Commission made it clear that it would withdraw a category-exemption from exclusive distributorship contracts whenever industrial property rights were exercised to prevent to third parties the importation of the products under contract which were lawfully marketed in another part of the Common Market. In its preamble to

20. Eighth General Report on the activities of the Community (EEC) (April 1, 1964-March 31, 1965), No. 57, p. 63.

21. Burroughs/Geha Werke and Burroughs/Delplanque, Commission's Decisions of December 22, 1971, O.J. 1972, L 13/50, [1972] CMLR, D 67 and D 72.

22. O.J. p. 849/67, [1967] CMLR, D 1. For a detailed outline of the Regulation, see Champaud, "*The group exemptions of EEC-Regulation 67/67*", 5 CMLRev. 1967-68, 23-34. The validity of this regulation is being extended till 1982 without any further substantive amendment being made, O.J. 1972, L 276/15.

the regulation the Commission denounced such exercise of industrial property rights as a misuse. At the same time the preamble contended that the regulation does not prejudice the relationship between the EEC-rules of competition and industrial property rights since only the conditions for applying the regulation on category-exemptions were spelled out therein and no position was taken on individual applications for an exemption. However, it seems apparent from the term "misuse" that in principe the Commission will not allow an exclusive licensee to invoke industrial property rights for stopping imports by third parties. Therefore, not only the benefit of the category-exemption is being withdrawn according to the wording of Regulation No. 67/67, but it can also be taken for granted that an application for an individual decision for exemption under Article 85(3) will be refused by the Commission when the exercise of such exclusive right serves only to fence in national markets against parallel imports, but for some exceptional cases. In fact, the Commission did not exclude that a temporary approval of an absolute territorial protection for an exclusive distributorship contract could be considered if it serves to enable a new manufacturer to penetrate into the relevant national market.[23] Moreover the Court of Justice made it clear that an exclusive distributorship contract even though it provided for an absolute territorial protection was apt to escape the purview of the rules of competition on account of the weak position of the parties for the products covered by the agreements.[24]

6. *Commission's Notice on agreements, decisions and concerted practices concerning cooperation beween enterprises.*

More and more the Commission became convinced that cooperation especially between small and medium-sized enterprises should be facilitated to enable them to adapt their operations to the new dimensions of the Common Market thereby increasing their productivity and competitiveness. Such cooperation would especially be welcomed if it would be set up between enterprises located in different member States. In order to encourage such cooperation the Commission issued in 1968 a "Notice on agreements, decisions and concerted practices concerning cooperation between enterprises"[25] outlining which kind of agreements do not, to the mind of the Commission, come under the prohibition of Article 85(1) since purportedly these agreements would not restrict competition. This Notice although having no legal binding force can be construed as a general negative clearance for the

23. First General Report on the activities of the Communities (1967), Nr. 44, p. 60.

24. Judgment of May 6, 1971, case No. 1-71, (S.A. Cadillon v. Höss Maschinenbau K.G.), *Recueil* XVII, 356, [1971] CMLR, 429; cf. Snijders, *supra,* 63-76.

25. O.J. 1968, C 75/3, [1968] CMLR, D 5.

groups of agreements mentioned therein. Its enumeration, however, is not exhaustive. Other kinds of cooperation-agreements can also qualify for not coming under the ban of Article 85(1). On the other hand some forms of cooperation-agreements between enterprises may fall under the ambit of rules of competition but then can be exempted under Article 85(3) EEC or authorized under Article 65(2) ECSC.

Although the Notice quite explicitly is designed to foster cooperation between small and medium-seized enterprises it applies to all enterprises, irrespective of their size.

Among the cooperation-agreements mentioned in this Notice are ranged agreements having as their sole object

a. the joint carrying out of research and development projects

b. the joint placing of research and development orders

c. the assignment of research and development projects among the participating parties.

All these agreements[26] do not affect the competitive position of the participants insofar as they do not include the stage of production. If, however, the enterprises undertake commitments that entail restrictions on their own research and development activity, this obligation can constitute an infringement on the rules of competition of the Treaties.

A restriction of competion may exist when agreements are concluded on the practical exploitation of joint research and development operations, in particular if the participating enterprises commit themselves to manufacture only products or types of products developed jointly or to split up future production among themselves. The nature of joint research requires that its results be exploited by the participating enterprises in proportion to their participation. If certain participating enterprises are entirely excluded from the exploitation of the results or to an extent not commensurate with their participation there may be a restriction of competition.

If the granting of licences to third parties is explicitly or tacitly excluded a restriction of competition may exist. The fact that research has been carried out on a joint basis justifies, however, the commitment to grant licenses to third parties only by a unanimity vote or by a majority decision.

The Notice also holds as not restrictive of competition those agreements having as their sole objective the use of a collective quality trademark to designate goods complying with certain standards of quality, under the

26. A more detailed account on joint research and development agreements is given by Schmitt, "*Cooperation et dimension en matière de recherche et de développement au regard de la législation Européenne*", contribution to the International Colloquium on "*R. and D. and competition in the European Communities*" organised by the University of Grenoble in April 1970, p. 126.

condition that every competitor meeting the quality requirements shall also have access to the collective trademark on the same conditions as everybody else. Obligations to accept quality control for the products that carry the trademark do not constitute a restriction of competition.

There may be a restriction of competition if the right to use the collective trademark is tied up with obligations as to production, sale and prices or when participating enterprises are under the obligation to manufacture or sell the products of the guaranteed quality only.

7. *Commission's Notice on agreements, decisions and concerted practices of minor importance not coming under Article 85(1).*

In order to promote the cooperation between small and medium-sized enterprises the Commission took a further step by stating in an official Notice [27] that agreements that affect trade between member States and competition only in a minor way do not come under the prohibition of Article 85(1). In its Cooperation-Notice of 1968 the Commission had already made an allusion to this effect where it held that other types of cooperation than those mentioned in the Notice could equally escape the ambit of Article 85(1) in cases where the combined market-position of the cooperating enterprises is too weak for their agreement to restrict competition in the Common Market and to affect interstate commerce in a perceptible manner.

In a way this position was already adopted before by the Commission itself as far back as in its first decisions on individual cases[28] where the perceptibility-test was applied to the restriction of competition criterion. The Court of Justice applied the same standard when it ruled that the impact of the agreement on competition should be perceptible.[29] This perceptibility-test would be determined by a number of criteria. Among them the Court mentioned the size and the shares of the parties to the agreement on the relevant market. [30]

In the Völk v. Vervaecke case[31] the Court made its position even clearer when it held

27. Commission's Notice of May 27, 1970, O.J 1970, C 64/1, [1970] CMLR, D 15.

28. Grosfillex-Fillistorf-decision of March 11, 1964, O.J. p. 915/64, [1964] CMLR, 237, and implicitely in the Nicolas Frères/Vitapro-decision of July 30, 1964, O.J. p. 2287/64, [1964] CMLR, 505.

29. Judgment of June 30, 1966 case No. 56/65 (Société Technique Minière v. Maschinenbau Ulm), *Recueil* XII, 359-360, [1966] CMLR, 375.

30. In the judgment of November 25, 1971, case No. 22/71 (Béguelin Import Co. v. G.L. Import-Export), *Recueil* XVII, 960, [1972] CMLR, 96, the Court mentioning the same criteria applied the perceptibility-test to the restriction of competition as well as to the effects on interstate commerce.

31. Judgment of July 9, 1969, case No. 5/69, *Recueil* XV, 259 *et seq.* [1969] CMLR, 273 *et seq.* In the judgment of May 6, 1971, case No. 1/71 (Cadillon-Höss),

> "that an agreement escapes the prohibition of Article 85(1) when it only affects the market insignificantly account being taken of the weak position held by the parties on the market in the products in question."[32]

On the basis of these findings the Commission could safely hold in its Notice that those agreements that exert no perceptible influence on the market-position of third parties would not be held prohibited. In the present Notice the Commission has given a quantitative definition of the concept of "perceptibility" so that the enterprises can ascertain for themselves which one of the agreements concluded by them do not come under Article 85(1) because of their minor importance. The limits fixed are the following:
(1) The share of the products under contract should not amount to more than 5% of the relevant market, and in addition
(2) the aggregate annual turnover of the parties to the agreement taken together, as well as of the firms economically associated with them, do not exceed 15 million units of account or, where agreements among trading companies are concerned, 20 million units of account.

The total turnover is obtained by taking the turnover in all goods and services for the last fiscal year.

The Notice states that it applies to agreements between enterprises engaged in the manufacture or distribution of goods. One must infer therefrom, equally taking into consideration the formula adopted for assessing the total turnover, that the Notice does not refer to industry engaged in services alone.

The question can be raised whether this Notice applies to licensing and know-how agreements. Strictly speaking some doubts can be expressed on the issue whether this is so, since industrial property rights and know-how can hardly be construed to represent "products" as mentioned under condition 1). Moreover, if a consultants agency is involved that supplies its customers with know-how, it concerns an enterprise operating exclusively in a service industry.

Fortunately the Notice declares that the standards it lays down for the perceptibility test are not exhaustive. One may therefore not run too high a risk if one assumes that in the manufacturing and trading industry the Notice would be applicable by analogy to licensing agreements if the exclusive rights involved in the contract refer to products covering no more than a 5 percent share of the relevant market and the turnover criteria are met. For the service industry the amount of turnover mentioned in the Notice is rather high.

Recueil XVII, 356, [1971] CMLR, 420, the weak market position was related to the absence of a perceptible impact on interstate commerce.

32. *Recueil* XVII, 302, [1969] CMLR, 232.

Some caution in applying the Notice by analogy to this industry seems recommendable.

Actually the Notice represents more or less a general negative clearance. This does not take away that under special circumstances the Commission may hold that agreements even qualifying for the conditions laid down in this Notice could yet fall within the prohibition of Article 85(1). The Notice in fact declares that it does not prejudge a judgment of the Court of Justice. And rightly so since the Court held in the Brasserie de Haecht case[33]

> "To judge whether it is hit by Article 85 (1) a contract can thus not be isolated from that context . . . With regards to that objective, the existence of similar contracts of that type as a whole are such as to restrict the freedom of trade."

In point of fact this holding implies that for ascertaining the legal position of an agreement, consideration should be given not only to other similar agreements concerning the same product that one of the contracting parties has concluded with third parties, but also to similar agreements concerning competing products that third parties in the same industry have concluded among themselves.

Thus the position taken by the Commission in the present Notice represents only a partial reflection of the Court's opinion. No absolute guarantee exists that agreements qualifying for the requirements laid down by the Notice escape the ambit of Article 85(1).

On the other hand the Notice is right in stating that in an individual case agreements that exceed the quantitative limits set out in the Notice may under certain conditions impair interstate trade and competition only in a negligible way and therefore would not come under Article 85(1).

8. *Council Regulation No. 2821/71 referring to the application of Article 85(3) of the Treaty on groups of agreements, decisions and concerted practices.*

The Council after proposals made by the Commission to that effect issued a regulation[34] enabling the Commission to lift the ban of Article 85(1) on certain groups of agreements whenever they relate to

33. Judgment of December 12, 1967, case No. 23/67 (Brasserie de Haecht v. Wilkin and Janssen), *Recueil* XIII, 537, [1968] CMLR, 40. Comments by Mailänder "Restrictive patterns by multiple agreements", 6 CMLRev. 1968-69, 353-367.

34. Council Regulation No. 2821/71 of December 20, 1971, O.J. 1971, L 285/46, [1972] CMLR, D 4.

a. the application of norms and types,
b. research and development of products or processing up to the stage of its industrial application, as well as the exploitation of the results including conditions concerning industrial property rights and secret technical know-how.
c. specialization, including the agreements indispensable to its realisation.

By adopting this "enabling regulation" the Council would make it possible for the Commission to adopt in its turn regulations exempting from the prohibition of Article 85(1) classes of agreements of the abovementioned types. In the preamble to the enabling regulation the Council explained that agreements on the cooperation between enterprises enabling them to work more efficiently and to adapt their productivity and competitiveness to the dimensions of the Common Market should be encouraged, because they are economically desirable. In particular the Council held in respect of the cooperation in the field of research and development as well as in respect of the exploitation of its results that they contribute to bridging the currently existing technological gap in Europe in comparison with conditions elsewhere.

It is undeniable that because of its global wording a certain overlap exists between the contents of the present enabling regulation and the Notice of 1968 where the Commission declared that certain agreements on joint research and development as well as certain modalities of their exploitation do not fall under Article 85(1) at all. The Commission's implementing regulation should make it clear where the boundary line between both domains lies.

A certain overlap also exists with the Council Regulation No. 2822/71, mentioned before, where the compulsion on prior notification was lifted for joint research and development agreements. This duplication, however, was explicitly recognized in the Commission's explanatory memorandum submitting its proposals to the Council where it was stated that this legislative measure was aimed at encouraging cooperation agreements of these types even before the category-exemption regulation of the Commission would enter into force.[35]

It seems indeed that the issuance of a Commission's implementing regulation on joint research and development agreements cannot be anticipated before long and that the Commission is not contemplating to grant an overall exemption to all possible agreements of this type.[36]

35. Doc. COM(70) 535 def. of May 27, 1970, embodied in Doc. No. 71/70 of July 10, 1970, of the European Parliament.
36. Information contained in W.u.W. 1972, 144.

III. *Decisions and Announcements on individual cases concerning licensing agreements.*

Apart from acts of a general nature concerning licensing agreements outlined in the preceding part of this paper acts of the Commission referring to individual cases dealing with licensing agreements will be discussed. These acts can be divided into various classes.

First come the decisions pronounced by the Commission which conclude the proceedings in an individual case.

Second come the announcements the Commission has to publish pursuant to Article 19(3) of Regulation No. 17/62 before rendering a decision on a negative clearance or an exemption on Article 85(3). By means of this publication containing a summary of the relevant application or notification, interested third parties are invited to submit their observations.

Third comes the information about the informal competition policy of the Commission appearing in the monthly Bulletins of the European Communities and the annual General Reports on the activities of the European Communities. Here the Commission gives an account about the conclusion of cases that do not reach the official stage because the enterprises concerned have given in to the "counts of objections" formulated by the Commission. The greater majority of all cases are settled in this way. Before, however, dealing with these acts of the Commission some factual information should be given.

1. *Some figures about the number of notifications concerning licensing agreements received by the European Commission.*

At the end of March 1963 the Commission had received about 34,700 notifications, about ninety percent of which (31,250) concerning so called old agreements, i.e. those existing on the date Regulation No. 17/62 entered into force (March 13, 1962).[37]

At the end of March 1964 the number had increased to some 37,000 notifications. About 81% thereof–some 30,000–dealt with exclusive distributorship agreements and about 16%–some 5,900–with licensing agreements.[38] In the following year this number did not change materially, nor the proportional ratio of the kind of contracts involved.

At the end of March 1966 the number of cases in the files of the Commission had reached the peak of about 38,300, some 38,000 of them because

37. Sixth General Report on the activities of the Community (EEC), (April 1, 1962-March 31, 1963), point 43, p. 63.

38. Seventh General Report on the activities of the Community (EEC) (April 1, 1963-March 31, 1964), point 65, p. 66.

of notifications submitted by the enterprises themselves.[39] In the course of the year 1965-1966 some 1400 cases were liquidated because the contracting parties had terminated their agreements. At the end of March 1967[40] about 31,400 of the total of some 37,000 notifications, concerned exclusive distributorship contracts. At the end of the year 1967 the total number of cases had decreased to some 23,400. This spectacular result had been achieved by the removal from the files of some 13,000 cases through the application of Regulation No. 67/67 concerning the category-exemption for exclusive distributorship contracts. The General Report stated equally that some 4,700 notifications dealing with licensing agreements were on the Commission's files.[41] The next year the situation did not change very much but in 1969 the Commission took again an important step[42] by removing from its dossiers some 11,700 notifications concerning exclusive distributorship contracts not containing export-prohibition clauses and some 1,100 notifications relating to exclusive distributorship contracts for the export to countries outside the European Community after a test-decision in this field.[43] As a result thereof, together with the withdrawal of a 1,000 cases mainly because the agreements involved had voluntarily been terminated by the enterprises involved, some 9,400 cases remained in the files of the Commission. Thus it had disposed of what was called the mass-problem in respect of the notifications on exclusive distributorship contracts.

In 1970 another 2,100 cases could be removed from the files because of the Commission's Notice of May 27, 1970 on the agreements of minor importance. Of the remaining 7,340 dossiers at the end of 1970 the major part–about 3,500–consisted of licensing agreements.[44] Thus the mass problem had shifted to the group of licensing agreements. The difference of 1,200 in comparison with the number of 4,700 mentioned in 1967 can mainly be attributed to the fact that a number of notifications submitted claiming to be concerned with licensing agreements in reality dealt with exclusive distributorship contracts, no industrial property rights being involved.

In 1971 the total number of cases pending had decreased to 4,556. About

39. Ninth General Report on the activities of the Community (EEC) (April 1, 1965-March 31, 1966), point 45, p. 61.

40. Tenth General Report on the activities of the Community (EEC) (April 1, 1966-March 31, 1967), point 43, p. 84.

41. First General Report on the activities of the Communities (April 1, 1967-December 31, 1967), point 43, p. 56.

42. Third General Report on the activities of the Communities (January 1, 1969-December 31, 1969), point 30.

43. Rieckermann-AEG/Elotherm case, Decision of November 6, 1968, O.J. 1968, L276/25, [1968] CMLR, D 78.

44. Fourth General Report on the activities of the Communities (January 1, 1970-December 31, 1970), point 23.

2,800 cases could be disposed of without a decision, partly because the agreements had been adjusted in conformity with the rules of competition, partly because the agreements were terminated or did not exist any more. Of the remaining 4,556 cases, 2,000 were dealing with licensing contracts,[45] more than half of which being notified by enterprises located outside the Common Market.[46] The difference of 1,500 compared with the 3,500 of the preceding year is mainly explained by the fact that the Commission after enquiry among the contracting parties was informed that in the meantime the agreements in question had ceased to exist or were terminated. In view of the limited legal lifespan of patents this decrease in numbers was not so surprising. Hence somehow the mass problem seems to evaporate because of the lapse of time involved.

In 1972 the total number of cases pending had decreased further to 2,873 the greater part thereof consisting of licensing agreements.[46a] Therefore the number of licensing agreements still in the files of the Commission may amount to some 1,200 to 1,300. The difference with the preceding year can again be attributed to the fact that a number of contracts were terminated or cancelled because the legal lifespan of the patents in question had lapsed.

Nevertheless what remains surprising anyway is the great number of licensing agreements that had been notified in the course of the years because of the precaution taken by the Council in Regulation No. 17/62 to exclude from compulsory notification all bilateral licensing agreements that impose on the licensee restrictions in the exercise of the exclusive rights.

2. *Commission's decisions on individual cases of licensing agreements.*

The Commission announced in 1964 that it had started ten new proceedings on licensing agreements by making enquiries in this difficult domain.[47] In 1966 the Commission stated that by decisions on test cases in the field of licensing agreements it had to develop a certain established practice in this domain. Several cases of patent-, trademark- and know-how licensing agreements were being investigated. Restrictive clauses frequently being found in licensing agreements were under study. Test-decisions on agreements between small and medium-sized enterprises in the field of research that could favour-

45. Fifth General Report on the activities of the Communities (January 1, 1971-December 31, 1971), point 135, p. 95.

46. Schlieder in "*Panel discussion on the dissemination of technology*", Annual Meeting of the American Bar Association, July 1971, 40 Antitrust Law Journal 1972, 946.

46a. Sixth General Report on the activities of the Community (EEC) (January 1, 1972-December 31,1972), point 86.

47. Eight General Report on the activities of the Community (EEC) (April 1, 1964-March 31, 1965), point 57, p. 63.

ably be decided upon, were being prepared.[48] In 1969 the Commission announced that standard-decisions on licensing agreements were in preparation with the object of studying the possibility of category-exemptions.[49] In 1970 the Commission declared that the first decisions laying down standards for licensing agreements could be anticipated in the near future.[50]

After all these declarations of good intentions it comes somewhat as a disappointment that the first official decisions on licensing agreements were not rendered before the end of December 1971. It concerned two licensing agreements on patents and the supply of technical information related thereto, of Burroughs (USA) as a licensor with Geha Werke (Germany) respectively Delplanque (France) as licensees.[51] Both licensees received non-exclusive manufacturing licences on some patents and exclusive manufacturing licences on others confined to a certain member State only. There were however no territorial restrictions on sales. The licensed products are sold by the licensor and the licensees all over the Common Market on a nonexclusive basis, although under different trademarks. The Commission issued a negative clearance.

The lawful owner of a patent, so the Commission held, may confer the use of the rights embodied in his patent to third parties by granting licences for a certain territory covered by the patent. However, an exclusive manufacturing licence may entail a restriction of competition if the holder undertakes to restrict the exercise of his exclusive right in a certain territory to a single enterprise and confers upon that one enterprise alone all the rights to exploit his invention. As a corollary thereof he prevents other enterprises from using it, while at the same time he has lost the capability to enter into agreements with other applicants for licences. In the present case the restriction was however not perceptible, because of the small market-share of the products under contract while moreover all licensees and licensor were free to sell the products in the whole Common Market. This opinion of the Commission constitutes virtually a departure from its position reflected in its Christmas Message of 1962, where it left open the question whether such exclusive arrangement restricted competition or not.

Apparently to give some guidance to industry the Commission emphasized that in case of a non-exclusive licence on patents and know-how no restrictions of competition were involved

48. Tenth General Report on the activities of the Community (EEC) (April 1, 1966-March 31, 1967), points 40 and 45, pp. 83 and 84.

49. Third General Report on the activities of the Communities (1969), point 30.

50. Fourth General Report on the activities of the Communities (1970), point 23.

51. Decisions of December 22, 1971, O.J. 1972, L 13/50 and L 13/53, [1972] CMLR, D 67 + D 72.

(1) when the licensee was prohibited to grant sublicences except to wholly dependent companies,
(2) when the assignee of the know-how was pledged to secrecy on the technical knowledge obtained, even for a period of ten years after termination of the contract. Since the essence of know-how is its secrecy, mandatory secrecy was held to be an indispensable condition for the owner to deal in this knowledge with other enterprises. One can detect here an allusion to the argument of the Court of Justice–discussed later on–that the EEC rules of competition should respect the essence of the exclusive rights. In passing the Commission gave its definition of the concept of technical know-how by stating that it constitutes a complex of industrial processes not protected by legal provisions on industrial property.
(3) when the obligation is imposed on the licensee not to use the know-how after the termination of the agreement.
(4) when the obligation is stipulated that the licensed products should be produced in sufficient quantities and the technical instructions of the licensor should be followed. This condition serves the sole purpose of permitting a sufficient and technically adequate exploitation of the rights that these patents confer on their holder.
(5) when a non-exclusive licence is granted to use the trademarks of the licensor, and the licensee is under the obligation to indicate that the product was manufactured under licence of the licensor. This obligation has no other purpose than to identify the products in order to facilitate the control on the quality and on the quantity of the products under contract by the licensor. This condition carries no restriction of competition in particular since the licensee may also affix other trademarks to the products under contract.
(6) when the stipulation has been made to settle disputes by arbitration.

These first decisions are the issue of an analysis of the contents of some 500 notified licensing agreements.[52] This analysis was carried out in order to determine the clauses which most frequently occur in those contracts, and the restrictions imposed in connection with the exercise of industrial property rights and the transfer of know-how which are covered either by the protection inherent in the patent rights or are necessary to maintain the secrecy of know-how, or do not restrict competition even though they do not arise essentially from the rights given by the patent or know-how.

The next two decisions pertaining to licensing agreements were issued in June 1972.

The first one concerned a ten year licensing agreement between a German

52. First Report on Competition Policy, belonging to the Fifth General Report on the activities of the Communities (1972), point 80.

subsidiary of the French company, Raymond, Grenoble, and a Japanese company, Nagoya Rubber Company, on patents, know-how, utility models and trademarks.[53] Under this licensing agreement Nagoya is granted the exclusive right to manufacture only in Japan plastic fasteners mainly for the automobile industry. Exportation of the fasteners to the Common Market countries is prohibited. However, if the fasteners are built into parts of Japanese automobiles they may be exported all over the world. Nagoya may not in any case challenge the validity of any of Raymond's rights during the term of the agreement. Nagoya must make every effort that his products come up to the European standards of Raymond. To ensure that those standards are met Nagoya has to allow certain quality controls by Raymond. The partners agree to keep each other informed of all the improvements they make in the Raymond-techniques. If Raymond should obtain patents for any improvement, it must offer an exclusive licence for Japan to Nagoya first, who can refuse. Any improvements of the Raymond-techniques developed by Nagoya are to become property of Raymond as far as non-patentable innovations are involved. In case of patentable innovations Nagoya is to grant a non-exclusive licence to Raymond. For inventions in the field of fasteners patented by Nagoya lying outside the scope of the Raymond-techniques Nagoya has to grant Raymond a non-exclusive licence for the patents obtained outside Japan. In an earlier version of the licensing agreement Nagoya was under the obligation to transfer to Raymond the ownership of any improvement Nagoya had developed in the Raymond-techniques and to grant exclusive licences for the patents Nagoya obtained on inventions in the field of fasteners outside the Raymond-techniques. On the Commission's recommendation the parties modified their agreement in the way as detailed above. Nagoya is prohibited from granting sublicences. The economic details are that Raymond is the largest producer of plastic fasteners in the Common Market. The automobile manufacturer Toyota holds a majority interest in Nagoya.

It has taken the Commission quite a while to come to its decision since it was back in 1970 that it published its intention to take a favorable decision in the licensing agreement in question.[54] Although it had not been explicitely stated in the announcement it was to be anticipated at that time that a negative clearance was most likely to be issued because of the close resemblance this case showed to the Rieckermann-AEG/Elotherm negative clearance decision,[55] which dealt with an exclusive distributorship contract for

53. Raymond/Nagoya-decision of June 9, 1972, O.J. 1972, L 143/39; [1972] CMLR, D 45.

54. Raymond/Nagoya-announcement, O.J. 1970, C 144/8.

55. Rieckermann-AEG/Elotherm-decision, *supra*, note 43.

Japan coupled with an export-prohibition clause to other countries. Because of the only minor–if any–effects of this clause on competition within the Common Market a negative clearance was issued.

This expectation came true since in fact a negative clearance was issued. On the exclusivity of the licence the reasoning follows the same lines the Commission adopted in the Burroughs' decisions. The owner of an industrial property right can by granting a licence transfer for a particular territory the use of the rights flowing from the industrial property. The exclusivity of the licence implies however that the owner loses the right to make agreements with others while they on their part are prevented from obtaining a right to exploit the industrial property as well. Under certain circumstances an exclusive licence may therefore restrict competition coming under Article 85 (1). In the present case however the competitive situation within the Common Market is not affected.

The export-prohibition imposed on Nagoya has no perceptible impact on competition in the Common Market either. The prohibition applies only to the fasteners as such which are highly specialized products designed for a specific model and are produced only on special order. The production of fasteners is carried out in close cooperation with the automobile manufacturers while the pre-production stage can extend up to two years. Under these conditions it is hardly conceivable that a European manufacturer would be prepared to undertake such cooperation with Nagoya since he could obtain the same products from Raymond. Because of the special nature of the product, therefore, the export-prohibition clause has no perceptible effect on competition within the Common Market.

For the first time the Commission directed its attention explicitly to the non-attack clause. It found that in principle this kind of stipulation involves a restriction of the licensee's freedom which does not belong to the essential characteristics of the industrial property right–a holding reminiscent of the judgment of the Court of Justice in the DGG/Metro-case.[56] This clause deprives the licensee of the capability to contest the validity of the right so as to have the royalty fees reduced and certain restrictions removed which would improve his competitive position and that of interested third enterprises, as well as eventually of the consumer.

However, by challenging Raymond's industrial property rights in Japan Nagoya could only strengthen its competitive position in the Far East since exports to Europe were ruled out. Therefore any repercussion within the Common Market is lacking. Because of its ties to Toyota it is highly

56. Judgment of June 8, 1971, case No. 78-70, *Recueil* XVII, 487 *et seq.*; [1971] CMLR, 631 *et seq.*; see *infra*, 215-223.

improbable that Nagoya would start production in Europe. Only then Nagoya would be interested in contesting the European rights of Raymond.

Nagoya's obligation to permit certain quality controls by Raymond are held indispensable for the proper exploitation of the invention and the know-how, and are to that extent permissible.

The exchange of information is designed to ensure the transmission of experience in the implementation of patents, know-how, and utility models, and hence constitutes part of their contractual exploitation. It does not entail a restriction of competition. Nagoya's obligations to grant a non-exclusive licence to Raymond for the patents, if any, Nagoya owns outside Japan on improvements in and outside Raymond's techniques would not prevent Nagoya from equally granting licences to other enterprises within the Common Market. In the earlier version of the agreement this was not the case.

The negative clearance was issued because the Commission could not assume that the licensing agreement was having the object or effect of restricting competition in the Common Market without it being necessary to examine whether the agreement was restricting trade between member States.

Although generally the negative clearance decisions are somewhat succint in their reasoning it should be noted that this time the Commission went out of its way to explain in detail what it had in mind. Especially its finding on the non-attack clause will have to be noted as a new element in the further exploration of the nature of the clauses frequently appearing in licensing agreements.

The second case on licensing agreements that was issued in June 1972 concerned the Davidson-decision.[57] This one basically revolved round the issue of the legality of exclusive licensing agreements on patents and know-how connected with these patents, under Article 85(1).

The facts were that Davidson holds patents in Europe pertaining to a manufacturing process, and to equipment used in this process, for armrests and upholstered seats for automobiles. Besides Davidson has developed a body of know-how to apply the patented process more economically. In order to promote the utilization of its processes in Europe, Davidson established a network of licensees. Thus Davidson granted exclusive licences to three enterprises established in Germany, France, and Italy respectively for

57. Davidson Rubber Company-decision of June 9, 1972, O.J. 1972, L 143/31; [1972] CMLR, D 52.

the utilization of his patents and know-how in their assigned territories. The parties agreed to exchange all the information that could be of use in implementing the patented processes. In fact Davidson designated the German licensee to pass on to the others the know-how he had received from Davidson. To that end the licensees had entered into know-how licensing agreements among themselves. Each licensee agreed to keep secret all the information received and to grant Davidson and his fellow licensees for their respective territories a non-exclusive licence for any patent on improvements which he had invented himself. The licensees may grant sublicences but only with Davidson's consent.

On the suggestion of the Commission the non-attack clause was removed from the licensing contracts, while at the same time a stipulation was inserted to the effect that no clause of the agreements could be invoked to prevent the sale of the products under contract from one member State to the other. As a result thereof the clause was deleted under which each party agreed not to export the products under contract to the other's territory which condition was formerly embodied in the know-how contracts concluded between the licensees.

However, as a rule each licensee delivers only to automobile manufacturers whose main establishment is located in the territory allotted to him by the exclusive manufacturing licence. All the licensing contracts were concluded for the duration of Davidson's patents. Any disputes between parties arising out of the contracts should be submitted to arbitration.

In evaluating the compatibility of these contracts with the EEC rules of competition the Commission held that although the owner of a patent is fully entitled to grant licences for the use of a patent for a specified territory, an exclusive licence may restrict competition and be prohibited under Article 85(1). While in the Burroughs and Nagoya-decisions the actual fact-situation did not warrant a virtual restriction of competition to arise within the Common Market, the Commission found in this case that in fact this was so because the Davidson process was the most important process for the manufacture of the products in question, while moreover the number of competing processes and of manufacturers using them was limited, while the Davidson licensees cover a substantial part of the market. It may be true that their exclusive position is mitigated by the stipulation that the contract articles could be sold freely to other member States, the exclusivity granted by Davidson, nevertheless, was not only hampering Davidson's freedom of action but also did it perceptibly alter the position of third parties, in particular the manufacturers of automobile interior fittings, that might wish to apply the patented process. Thus the existence of a perceptible restriction of competition within the Common Market was established.

As to the impact on interstate commerce the Commission held that by

withholding from third parties the opportunity to use the patents and know-how, they were by the same token possibly prevented from effecting exports to the other parts of the Common Market. Therefore–so the Commission held–the exclusivity clause can be assumed to adversely affect, directly or indirectly, trade between member States and thus jeopardize the realisation of the objective to bring about a single market between member States.

By way of comment it should be noted that here the Commission did not apply the perceptibility test. Apparently it construed Article 85(1) in such a way that once the perceptibility test was applied to one parameter of this provision it became superfluous to do so again with the other. This view was in conflict with the opinion of the Court of Justice in the Béguelin-case [57a] according to which the perceptibility test should be applied to both criteria. In the Haecht-II-case [57b] the Court of Justice however changed its mind and held that it was sufficient for the applicability of Article 85(1) when the perceptibility could be shown for one of the parameters. Thus the Commission had anticipated with some good fortune on the position the Court would take.

After having found that the exclusivity clause fell within the purview of Article 85(1) the Commission went on to examine whether it could be exempted under Article 85(3). Hence the test was applied whether the conditions contained in this paragraph were fulfilled. It was not difficult to show for the Commission that the licensing agreement promoted economic progress–the exploitation of a modern process was made possible in the EEC–and technical progress and the improvement of production, since the licensing agreements permit a rational adaption of the Davidson's techniques to the requirements of the European market by entrusting the exploitation of the processes to European enterprises. A fair share of the benefits resulting therefrom accrues to the users, i.e. the automobile manufacturers, because of the availability to them of products adapted to their individual needs, and because most of them can now rely on a more regular and dependable supply.

The exclusive rights granted to the licensees can be regarded as indispensable since at the outset Davidson would not have succeeded in finding third parties willing to apply his techniques in Europe without his agreeing to limit the number of enterprises and his giving assurances that they would not be exposed to competition by new licensees later on. Moreover, without the guarantee of obtaining exclusive rights the licensees would not have agreed to make the necessary investments to develop the process and to adapt them to the requirements of the European market. In passing it can be observed that

57a. See note 30.
57b. See note 7a.

implicitly this holding demonstrates that the Commission would apparently not even oppose an absolute territorial protection for a limited period to a new manufacturer when he is entering the market, a view the Commission had expressed also on other occasions.[58]

Finally the Commission found no excessive restriction of competition since other competing processes exist which are implemented by a number of enterprises in the Common Market. Furthermore the automobile manufacturers themselves produce one third of their own requirements, while the licensees are free to export their products to other parts of the Common Market. In view of all these considerations the Commission concluded that the conditions of Article 85(3) are fulfilled so that an exemption from the prohibition under Article 85(1) could be granted to the exclusive licensing agreements.

Although the non-attack clause was deleted from the agreements nevertheless the Commission gave its opinion on this stipulation. It held that this clause not to challenge the validity of the patents prevented the licensees from making use of the opportunities they had under domestic law to release them from their contractual commitments, possibly by a claim of nullity. Hence this stipulation represents a restriction of their actual and potential competitive ability while–in view of Article 85(3)–the Commission could not see why it was indispensable for the achievement of the beneficial objectives of the agreements.

As to the know-how licensing agreements the licensees had concluded among themselves the Commission found that the original export-prohibition clauses constituted a perceptible restriction of competition that could not be considered indispensable for the achievement of the beneficial objectives of the agreements. Now that these conditions were deleted the Commission was willing to apply Article 85(3) to these know-how agreements. The term of validity of this grant for an exemption will coincide with the term of validity of the Davidson patents to which the know-how is closely connected.

Finally the Commission did not hold the following clauses to be covered by Article 85(1) since they did not perceptibly restrict competition.

a. The grant-back obligation of the licensees to license Davidson and the other licensees for any patented improvement of the Davidson process, since this obligation is not exclusive and hence each licensee remains free to convey his experience to third parties.

b. The obligation of the licensee to grant sublicences only with Davidson's approval since this obligation is covered by the licensor's right at the one

58. First Report on Competition Policy (1972), point 49.

hand and is justified at the other hand by the licensor's interest not to have his know-how divulged without his consent to enterprises other than those authorized to utilize it.

c. The obligation to submit all disputes to arbitration since the nature of this obligation nor the text of the agreements do give rise to arbitral awards that could change the evaluation of this case.

In this decision the Commission for the first time held an exclusive licensing agreement to be falling within the purview of Article 85.

This opinion constitutes a clear-cut and significant departure from its position taken in the Christmas-Notice of 1962 where the Commission had held that an exclusive licence in itself would not come under the definition of Article 85(1). It argued at that time that apart from the question whether or not such exclusive agreement restricts competition it is not in view of the situation in which the Community now stands, likely to affect trade between member States. The Commission held also that the exclusive licence approached so closely an assignment of rights that it does not give rise to any objection. Apart from the fact that this last argument already fell to pieces in the Grundig/Consten-case and later in the Sirena/Eda-case where the Court of Justice held that an assignment of rights could be caught by the rules of competition, the statement that interstate commerce is not affected was flatly contradicted in the present decision. The Davidson-decision will be remembered for this "volte face" of the Commission.

However apart from that aspect this decision might open up unexpected avenues because of the lighthearted way in which the Commission accepted the existence of the possibility that trade between member States could be affected in an indirect way, once it had ascertained that competition within the Common Market was perceptibly restricted. This leads to a widening of the scope of the field of applicability of the European rules of competition to the detriment of the field of application of national law of the member States in this domain and hence to an expansion of the competence of the Commission superseding the national authorities. It implies however also that the rules of competition may apply to situations where external trade of the Common Market as a whole is affected. Actually any restriction of external trade of the Common Market as such, or of one of the member States with third countries, is liable to have an indirect impact on trade between member States. In point of fact in the Notice on agreements of selfrestraint on Japanese exports to the Community[59] the warning was given that suchlike agreements even between the Japanese themselves may come under the EC's competition rules. In this vein it should not be held as totally excluded that a

59. O.J. 1972, C 111/13.

special situation–unlike the one in the Nagoya-decision–can present itself in which an exclusive licensing agreement concluded within third countries may be affected by Article 85(1).

For all the reasons explained above it can be argued that this decision was not void of some major importance.

A number of other decisions exists in which licensing or assignment agreements on industrial property played a supplementary or a secondary role. Quite a few of them are of minor importance to the subject dealt with in this paper because these agreements in themselves did not interfere with the functioning of the common market.[60] On the other hand the agreement on the registration of a trademark in the Grundig/Consten-decision, that will be discussed in connection with the Courts decision in this case,[61] though being of a supplementary character, was of paramount importance to the subject matter.

Further mention should be made of the Nicholas Frères-Vitapro decision[62]. where the French enterprise Nicholas sold its foreign assets outside the Common Market–including trademarks, patents and designs–to Vitapro (U.K.) with the provision that for an indefinite period Vitapro was enjoined from using the transferred trademarks within the Common Market. Nevertheless the Commission issued a negative clearance because the agreement did not split up the Common Market into various zones while moreover a sharp competition existed already in the sector of the products under contract. For that matter competition was not perceptibly restricted within the Common Market. After the entry of the United Kingdom into the EEC this decision may come up for review[63] even though the agreement in question preceded the date of U.K.'s entry.

A number of decisions dealt among other things with the use of collective trademarks within the Common Market to guarantee a certain standard of quality[64] and with an association for upholding orderly market conditions

60. Mertens en Straet/Bendix Corp.-decision of June 1, 1964, O.J. 1426/64; [1964] CMLR, 416. Alliance de Constructeurs français de Machines-Outils-decision of July 17, 1968, O.J. 1968, L 201/1; [1968] CMLR, D 23.
Jaz Peter decision of July 22, 1969, O.J. 1969, L 195/5; [1970] CMLR, 129.
FN-CF decision of May 28, 1971, O.J. 1971, L 134/6. Continental Can Company-decision of December 9, 1971, O.J. 1972, L 7/25; [1972] CMLR, D 11.

61. Decision of September 23, 1964, O.J. 2545/64; [1964] CMLR, 489; see *infra*, 204-208

62. Decision of July 30, 1964, O.J. 2287/64; [1964] CMLR, 505.

63. Alexander, "Industrial property rights and the establishment of the EEC", 9 CMLRev. 1972, 43, is right in raising this point.

64. Transocean Marine Paint Association-decision of June 27, 1967, O.J. 1967,

and consequently with the task of opposing infringements on the trademark rights of its members.[65] It transpires from all these decisions that to the mind of the Commission a restriction of competition exists whenever obligations in respect of production and sale are attached to the right to use a collective trademark. Thus the freedom of the trademark-users to set their own prices and to produce and sell other goods than those of the guaranteed quality may not be curtailed. The Commission had already voiced such an opinion in its Cooperation-Notice of 1968. Moreover the Commission will not allow trademark rights to be exercised when the only reason is to protect the domestic market against non-authorized imports of lawfully marked goods from other member States.

Besides the issue of the collective trademark the Transocean decision[66] granting an exemption under Article 85(3), also broached the issue of patent licences. The agreement concluded between the members of the Association stipulated among other things that those members who owned patents for products that may further the sales of Transocean Marine paints are under the obligation, when granting licences, to give other members priority. The Commission held this obligation to constitute a restriction of competition since it restricted the freedom of the patent-owner, when granting licences, as well as the possibility of non-members to obtain such licences.

It is recalled that in this instance no actual patent licensing agreement was involved but a multilateral agreement on an obligation of the patent holder if and when he is going to grant licences. Nevertheless one cannot get away from the feeling that in comparison with the Official Notice of December 1962 the Commission assumed much less readily in the Transocean-decision that a restrictive clause in a patent-licence is covered by the patent itself.[67] It provides another example for the submission made before that in subsequent years the Commission no longer adhered fully to its views expressed in 1962.

In the GEMA-decision[68] entailing the application of Article 86 EEC combatting the abuse of dominant market positions the Commission qualified as an abuse the conduct of GEMA to extend licensing agreements on copyrights to unprotected works by claiming a remuneration for their use by the licensees,

---

163/10 [1967] CMLR, D 9. VVVF-decision of June 25, 1969, O.J. 1969, L 168/22; [1970] CMLR, D 1. Association pour la promotion du tube d'acier soude électrique-ment-decision of June 29, 1970, O.J. 1970, L 153/14; [1970] CMLR, D 31.

65. ASPA-decision of June 30, 1970, O.J. 1970, L 148/9; [1970] CMLR, D 25.

66. See note 64.

67. See also: Mok, "The cartel policy of the EEC Commission, 1962-1967", 6 CMLRev. 1968-69, 84.

68. GEMA-decision of June 2, 1971, O.J. 1971, L 134/15 (esp. 25); [1971] CMLR, D 35.

the recording manufacturers. This practice was applied to records designed for exports as well so that it had a direct unfavourable impact on interstate trade because of this unjustified price-increase.

The Commission also qualified as an abuse GEMA's practices to levy the total royalty-amount on records imported at the trading level irrespective of the fact whether some royalty on these records had already been paid abroad. Hence these records were charged twice which in itself constituted a discrimination to the detriment of the importing dealers because the imports of manufacturers were not charged.

The SAFCO-decision [69] concerns a joint export sales agency the bylaws of which stipulate that on termination of their membership the participants had to transfer without compensation their trademarks SAFCO had used for exports. The Commission conceded that this obligation in itself might constitute a restriction of competition. Since in the present case, however, the members were not capable of exporting on their own, the trademarks of SAFCO's members existed and had value for exports only because of SAFCO's activity and efforts. Hence the assignment of these trademarks represents only a recognition of this fact.

The Commission also dealt with a number of agreements where in some way joint research and development projects were involved, and which were of minor importance to the issues dealt with in this paper because these joint efforts were not concerned with the exploitation of the results flowing therefrom involving matters of industrial property rights. [70]

More important is the ACEC/Berliet decision [71] where for the first time the Commission came to grips with an agreement on technical cooperation coupled with a joint research and development effort and on the exploitation of the results arising therefrom. Within the framework of the collaboration and the division of labour the partners granted each other a reciprocal exclusivity in one member State while ACEC's outlets in the other member States were restricted to one customer in each of them. This set-up, to the mind of the Commission, entailed a restriction of competition because the agreement curtailed especially the relationship of the partners with third parties. On the other hand ACEC's obligation to secrecy about information

69. SAFCO-decision of December 16, 1971, O.J. 1972, L 13/44; [1972] CMLR, D 83.

70. Eurogypsum-decision of February 26, 1968, O.J. 1968, L 257/9; [1968] CMLR, D 1.
FN-CF-decision of May 28, 1971, O.J. 1971, L 134/6. SOPELEM-Langen-decision of December 20, 1971, O.J. 1972, L 13/47; [1972] CMLR, D 77.

71. ACEC-Berliet-decision of July 17, 1968, O.J. 1968, L 201/7; [1968] CMLR, D 35.

on technical knowledge obtained from the joint research effort was held not to constitute a restriction of competition. One could in all fairness not expect Berliet to supply its knowledge and means to a joint project if competitors would profit from its results without being bound by the same strings attached to this cooperation as Berliet was, so the Commission explained. In doing so it introduced, perhaps unwillingly, a kind of rule of reason when applying Article 85(1).

The Commission found that the conditions laid down in Article 85(3) were fulfilled for the following reasons:

The specialization and division of labour in research as well as in production enabled each partner to concentrate on the tasks most suited to it. In the case of agreements that have not yet produced their effects the appreciation of its beneficial impact for the user can only be based on the evaluation of the probabilities involved. In the Commission's view a sufficient probability existed that the expected results could be achieved more quickly because of the joint research. One could not reasonably expect one of the parties to take the trouble to develop a new technique in collaboration with the other partner and then allow the latter to exploit the results of the former's contributions with a third party. This same kind of reasoning was already developed as to Article 85(1) in connection with the secrecy clause concerning know-how. Here the argument of equity served in relation to Article 85(3) as a justification that the reciprocal exclusivity commitments were essential to achieve favorable results from the agreement. For these and other reasons pertaining to the benefits of joint research and development agreements the Commission was disposed to render a favorable decision by granting an exemption under Article 85(3).

In the MAN/SAVIEM-decision [72] on a specialization and rationalization agreement involving equally the fields of research and development the Commission gave a complementary view as to the secrecy clause for technical know-how. It now held that the secrecy obligations are not independent of the joint research and the restrictions of competition going with the joint development. Therefore these restrictions have neither the object nor the effect to restrict competition in a perceptible way. Thus the Commission has refrained from explaining away the secrecy obligations out of considerations of reasonableness as was done in the ACEC-Berliet-decision. Apparently the Commission did not want to create the impression that it would resort to a kind of rule of reason when applying Article 85(1). As has been ascertained in the decisions on the Burroughs' licensing agreements the Commission has developed its argument in accepting the secrecy clause another stage further by holding that secrecy constituted an essential condition for the existence of

72. MAN/SAVIEM-decision of January 17, 1972, O.J. 1972, L 31/29.

know-how. For that reason any obligation imposed on the licensee to observe secrecy on know-how should be held valid.

According to the Commission no restriction of competition existed where the agreement contained the obligation to carry out joint research to be determined on a case-by-case basis, because this obligation was neither coupled with a specialization commitment in research nor with an obligation of the partners to abstain from individual research in this domain. If as a result from the joint research patent and jointly owned know-how are obtained, the spirit and purpose of the agreement imply, so the Commission held, that each party has the right to use them without paying a compensation to its partner.

Of paramount importance to the subject matter is the Henkel-Colgate-decision [73] of the Commission where it clearly dealt with a test-case on agreements involving joint research efforts especially because two major enterprises were involved acting on an oligopolistic market of homogeneous goods where entry of outsiders was made difficult because of the particularly intensive and costly advertising in this industry. Consequently the Commission paid also due attention to the exploitation of the results flowing from this joint undertaking. Under the agreement a joint research-company for the improvement of detergents was established in Switzerland both partners taking part on equal shares. They agreed to contribute to their joint subsidiary all present and future knowledge in the field of the joint research the subsidiary is engaged in, and if necessary to grant it licences. Each of the contracting parties has the right to obtain a nonexclusive licence from the research-company for a royalty of no more than two percent. The research-company may grant non-exclusive licences to third parties. The royalties to be paid for patent-licences must be calculated on each patent—no package licensing being permitted—and may not be claimed for a period exceeding the duration of the patent. Fees for non-patented knowledge must be paid for a fixed number of years not stretching beyond the duration of the protection laid down by the patent-law of the country concerned.

The Commission holds Article 85(1) applicable to the setting up of the joint venture company—in itself a feature to be noted—and to the relationship between the partners pertaining thereto. Though according to the agreement both parties are free to continue their individual research efforts in the fields covered by the agreement, the results of the agreement for all practical purposes—because of the high costs involved, the previous individual failures to succeed in this domain and the fact that the parties have undertaken to impart all their—present and future—knowledge to the joint company—almost

73. Henkel-Colgate/Palmolive-decision of December 23, 1971, O.J. 1972, L 14/14; cf. Mok, *supra*, 120-139.

with certainty will be that all efforts will exclusively be carried out by the joint research-company. The agreement therefore has actually the effect of restricting competition between the parties in the field of research.

This holding of the Commission is most important in that this way of construction of agreements exceeds by far the implications of the present case. It will have its repercussions on a much wider range of decisions to be rendered by the Commission. As it was, in the appraisal of the agreement under review an overriding importance was attributed to its apparently predictable effects over its wording–i.e. the object of the agreement–which pointed in a different direction. Thus in case of an assumed discrepancy between both, the object and the effect of an agreement, its obvious effects are deemed to prevail over its expressed objects.

Because research operations in themselves do not constitute a market-conduct the Commission went out of its way to explain why competition in the field of research is particularly important for the market-conduct on an oligopolistic market of homogeneous goods. Through costly advertising all the market parties try to differentiate their products in the eyes of the consumer by pointing to differences in quality and modes of application. The envisaged joint research cooperation may give the partners a lead over their competitors in quality-competition but between them this kind of competition is stifled. Thus the causal relationship was established between research-operation and market-conduct.

Article 85(3) is deemed applicable because the joint research gives rise to expectations of better results. The contracting partners have not limited the licensing arrangement as to either time or territory. The obligation to pay royalties to the joint company will end even for non-patentable know-how no later than the end of the duration of the patent-protection in the country in question. Thus the period of protection is not unduly prolonged. Under the agreement the partners have the right to obtain licences from the research-company under the same conditions for all countries. It is not excluded that parties will make use of this right in such a way that they allocate markets. Hence the Commission must be informed about all licensing agreements on patents and know-how concluded by the research-company and on the manner these licensing contracts are being applied in the Common Market.

The Commission must see to it that the freedom of production and distribution on which the agreement is silent, is not impaired in such a way that effective competition on this oligopolistic market is becoming compromised. The danger exists that through the acquisition of interests or an interlocking of personnel going beyond the domain of joint research concerted market practices are achieved. Hence the Commission shall be forthwith informed by the contracting partners about all acquisitions and interlocking of personnel occurring between both groups in the sector of the

detergents. The upshot of this condition is that enterprises possessing a major–but not a dominant–position on an oligopolistic market for homogeneous goods may be allowed to cooperate with each other in one functional sector of their activities, but that such cooperation may entail the obligation to allow stricter control on other functional activities that may be affected by that cooperation.

The present decision constitutes undoubtedly a leading precedent in the field of research and development agreements. It will certainly be of major importance to the tenor of the forthcoming Commission's regulation on category-exemptions in this domain.

3. *Official Announcements of the Commission on individual cases of licensing agreements.*

In a number of cases the Commission has initiated proceedings but has not progressed beyond the stage of publication of an announcement declaring its intention to grant an exemption under Article 85(3) or to issue a negative clearance for an agreement, while interested third parties are invited to come forward to present their observations on the agreement concerned within a month. Such publication occurs in the Official Journal and is mandatory by virtue of Article 19(3) of Regulation No. 17/62. It contains the major features of the agreement in question but the Commission has to see to it that justified business secrets are not being divulged. Hitherto in one case only the Commission has made mention of the fact that someone actually had come forward to make his comments. [74]

In a number of cases these announcements concerned licensing agreements. Especially when their date of publication is not too recent, one may wonder whether they will ever reach the final stage of a Commission's decision. An obvious example thereof is the Harbison-Walker-announcement [75] which dates from February 1967. According to this announcement Harbison Walker undertakes for fifteen years to put at the disposal of Basref, a Dutch manufacturer, all its present and future knowledge and know-how concerning the manufacture and the installation of basic fire-proof products. Harbison Walker grants a licence to Basref to manufacture in the Netherlands the products covered by this technical knowledge and know-how for the duration of the contract, and undertakes not to confer on any other manufacturer in the Netherlands a similar licence. The sale of the products covered by the licence is not subject to any territorial or other restriction. All knowl-

74. Association pour la promotion du tube d'acier soude électriquement-decision, note 64.

75. Harbison Walker Refractories Company-announcement, O.J. 418/67.

edge conveyed to Basref must be kept secret. After termination of the contract Basref must cease to use the knowledge it had received. Although this know-how agreement contained some restrictive elements the Commission gave no indication as to whether it wanted to grant an exemption under Article 85(3) or to issue a negative clearance, the latter being more plausible.

Another announcement that may not arrive at the final stage of the proceedings is the Scott-Paper-announcement [76] of 1968. Here Scott Paper Corporation, an American company, had granted to its wholly owned subsidiary, Scott Continental, established in Brussels, a trademark- and know-how licence for the manufacture and sale of paper products throughout the whole Common Market, with the exception of Italy. Besides, Scott Paper Corporation concluded a similar contract with its 50% owned subsidiary Burgo Scott S.p.A., established in Turin, and Cartier Burgo S.p.A. the other 50% parent company of Burgo Scott, with the restriction that here the Benelux-countries were excluded from the territorial scope of the licence. Since no licences were granted to other enterprises only Scott Continental and Burgo Scott were both authorized to use the Scott Paper trademarks in France and Germany. In the Benelux countries the products could only be manufactured and brought on the market at the manufacturer's level by Scott Continental, and in Italy the same held true for Burgo Scott. Both the enterprises had to give assurances to the Commission that they would not prevent the sale of Scott products originating from the other licensee and imported at the trading level, not even by invoking their rights resulting from the trademark legislation. Under these conditions the Commission declared its willingness to take a favourable decision. However, it did not give any indication as to whether it would be a negative clearance or a grant for an exemption, the latter alternative being more probable.

One can infer from the wording of this announcement that the Commission would not object to a trademark-right being used to prohibit the imports of products being effected directly by the other licensee-manufacturer. It may be that this can be explained by the fact that Scott Continental and Burgo Scott belonged to the same concern and the Commission in the Christiani & Nielsen-decision [77] had pronounced the opinion that intra-concern relations are not affected by the competition rules. When however the imports are being performed at the trading level they may not be interfered with, not even by invoking a trademark right.

76. Scott Paper Company-announcement, O.J. 1968, C 110/2.

77. Christiani & Nielsen-decision of June 18, 1969, O.J. 1969, L 165/12; [1969] CMLR, D 36; Cf. Van Oven, *supra*, 109-119.

The SPAR-announcement[78] dealt with a voluntary chain of foodstuff distributors the Commission wants to approve of. When terminating its adherence to this organisation it is agreed that the member has to relinquish the collective SPAR-trademark. It is hardly conceivable that such obligation would entail a restriction of competition.

4. *Unofficial notices reflecting the Commission's policy on licensing agreements*

Besides its official policy the Commission conducts an unofficial competition policy by which it tries to persuade the enterprises to adapt their agreements in accordance with the rules of competition or to cancel them before an official decision is being taken. During the stage of enquiry as well as after instituting proceedings the Commission and the contracting partners are in contact with each other. In the course of those periods the Commission will pass on its remarks, which will eventually be laid down in the "counts of objections", that are officially submitted to the contracting parties. Even thereafter the contracting partners can still readjust voluntarily their agreements to the rules of competition. This unofficial competition policy is quite effective. Although from 1962 to 1971 the Commission had to prohibit only five agreements, 36 agreements were voluntarily dissolved while 589 had to be modified to obtain the Commission's approval.[79] Sometimes these amendments had to be made to obtain the willingness of the Commission to issue a negative clearance or an exemption under Article 85(3) which occured in 29 cases over that same period. But in all the other cases adjustments were being made before or in the course of the official proceedings, whereupon the Commission dropped the case before the stage of the final decision was reached.

A comparatively small number of these cases where the parties had adjusted their agreements or had them voluntarily terminated after intervention of the Commission were published through notices appearing in the monthly Bulletins of the European Communities–as a rule preceded by a press release–and in a very concise form in the annual General Reports. In the majority of these cases the names of the enterprises concerned are not revealed. These notices cannot of course be construed as constituting precedents for the policy adopted by the Commission. On the other hand, however, they provide a certain insight in the position the Commission is taking on a

78. Spar-announcement, O.J. 1972, C 35/28.

79. Borschette, Proceedings of the European Parliament of June 7, 1971, Annex No. 139 to the O.J., June 1971, 22.
Repeated in Weekly Bulletin on Industry, Research and Technology, No. 122 of November 30, 1971.

number of issues that have mostly not been decided upon before. A number of these notices dealt with licensing agreements.

The first notice on licensing agreements [80] concerned a situation in which a German and a French enterprise each holder of a patent on a process for the application of a synthetic product had cross-licensed each other on a royalty-free basis. In addition they had empowered each other to grant sublicences under the reservation that if for the application of the patented processes the sublicensees would buy material not covered by the patents from one of the sublicensors, the sublicensees would obtain special advantageous royalty-conditions. This material, however, was not indispensable for the technically perfect application of the processing. This tie-in clause, so the Commission held, constituted an inadmissible extension of the patent monopoly by which the sales-potentialities of third suppliers on the relevant market were limited in an unwarranted way. Before a decision was taken the enterprises informed the Commission that they had cancelled the sublicences containing the tie-in clause and undertook to allow in future the processing to be applied without imposing these restrictions.

The conclusion seems warranted that a tie-in clause of the kind as described in the present case will not be permitted by the Commission to be included in a licensing contract insofar as it restricts in a perceptible way the possibilities for the licensees to obtain non-patented goods from third suppliers being located in an other member State, or vice versa the possibilities of these suppliers to sell such goods to the licensees.

The second notice dealt with the so-called Remington-case [81] where the American company Sperry Rand Corporation had assigned to its wholly owned manufacturing subsidiary Sperry Rand Italia the trademark "Remington" for electric shavers. When an Italian wholesaler imported original German Remington shavers on the Italian market he was summoned before the Milan court by Sperry Rand Italia for violation of the latter's trademark right. The defendant filed a complaint with the Commission whereupon the Milan court suspended its proceedings until the Commission had handed down a decision. The Commission informed the enterprises concerned that the assignment agreement as it was construed and applied gave rise to reservations as to its compatibility with Article 85 of the Treaty. The use here made of the trademark was not designed to combat its fraudulent use but to

80. Bulletin of the EEC of May 1966, Chapter II, point 10, p. 11, Press-release of March 3, 1966, No. IP 30. Ninth General Report on the activities of the Community (EEC) (April 1, 1965-March 31, 1966), point 53, sub g, p. 70.

81. Bulletin of the EEC of August 1969, Chapter V, No. 5, Press-release of June 11, 1969, No. IP (69) 98.

prevent the importation of authentic shavers from other member States. By seeking objectives–i.e. the isolation of the national market–which are unconnected with the true function of the trademark–i.e. the indication of origin–the assignment-agreement provided Remington Rand Italia with an absolute territorial protection. After the intervention of the Commission the enterprises concerned gave the assurance not to use any longer their trademark to prevent parallel–i.e. not authorized by the holder of the trademark–imports. The proceedings before the Milan court were closed and the dispute was settled by a compromise.

In the present case the Commission had slightly deviated from the position the Court had taken in the preceding Grundig/Consten-case–to be discussed later on [82]–in two respects.

In the first place, the Court had held that it objected against the abuse of a trademark designed to frustrate the effective application of Community Law, while the Commission laid the emphasis on the fact that it was forbidden to seek objectives unconnected with the real function of the trademark, which seemingly slight difference in formulation would come into the open as a major difference of opinion in the Sirena/Eda judgment [83] of the Court of Justice, that will be discussed later on. Whether at that time this difference in approach was material in the eyes of the Commission remains to be seen since when reference was made to this case in the annual General Report of 1969 [84] it was quoted in a stenographic way as "a case involving abusive use of trademark rights".

In the second place the Commission broadened the field for the application of the rules of competition. In the Grundig/Consten-case an independent exclusive distributor, who only performed a distribution function, was denied the use of a trademark right against parallel imports. In the Remington-case, however, the Commission withheld the right to invoke a trademark to an enterprise that was also an exclusive distributor and manufacturer as well.

In addition Remington Rand Italia was a wholly owned subsidiary of the assignor of the trademark. This brings to the fore another feature of this case that equally should be noted. Although the Commission had held in the Christiani & Nielsen-decision [85] that intra-concern agreements escape the ambit of the rules of competition, it now made the distinction in that intra-concern agreements were indeed susceptible to fall under the competition rules insofar as these intra-concern agreements affect materially the

82. *Infra*, 204-208.

83. Judgment of February 18, 1971, (case No. 40-70), *Recueil* XVII, 69 *et seq.*; [1971] CMLR, 260 *et seq.*; see *infra*, 210-215.

84. Third General Report on the activities of the Communities (1969), No. 37, p. 66.

85. See note 77.

competitive position of third parties on the relevant market, as in the Remington-case became apparent.

In this connection the Scott Paper announcement [86] should be recalled in that the Commission would allow a trademark right to be invoked against imports if directly performed by the manufacturer himself belonging to the same concern. Thus it can be assumed that in the Remington-case the Commission would not have stepped in when the imports had been effected by the German manufacturer of the Remington razors himself.

A third notice concerned a number of agreements and concerted practices existing in the flat glass industry the Commission started proceedings against ex officio. [87] On this oligopolistic market of homogeneous goods competition was seriously restricted and interstate trade kept at a low level. Under one of these agreements, a glass-enterprise established in a third country licensed two manufacturers located in different member States to make and sell a special kind of glass. As a result thereof both licensees had agreed to harmonize their merchandising policy on the common contract-territory, part of which was situated within the Common Market. In addition one of the licensing agreements with the producer from the third country stipulated that the restrictions on production and sale would continue even after termination of the licensing agreement or the expiration of the term of validity of the patent involved. Upon objections of the Commission the licensees rescinded the agreements among themselves while the clauses in the licensing agreement that were contrary to Community Law were cancelled. Thereafter the Commission terminated the proceedings without rendering a decision.

It may be of interest to recall in this connection that under Regulation No. 67/67 [88] which provides for a grant of exemption to groups of exclusive distributorship contracts pursuant to Article 85(3) EEC, Article 2(1)(a) provides that it is allowed to impose on the exclusive distributor the obligation not to manufacture or distribute for one year following the termination of the contract, products competing with the products under contract. Thus the Commission's regulation is more lenient towards exclusive distributorship contracts in this respect than the Commission itself was to patent-licensing agreements. Apparently it did not want to extend obligations deriving from the patent monopoly beyond the lifespan of the exclusive right while in the field of exclusive distributorship it acknowledged the possibility that an exclusive distributor could, by taking an unfair advantage of the merchandising knowledge he had acquired from his former principal or by competing

86. *Supra*, 195.

87. Bulletin of the EEC of August 1970, 62-63; Fourth General Report on the activities of the Communities (1970), point 28, p. 24.

88. Regulation No. 67/67 of the Commission of March 22, 1967, O.J. 849/67; [1967] CMLR, D 1; see *supra*, 169.

with competing goods against his former principal, deny to the latter any possibility to penetrate again into this market either by his own efforts or by appointing a new exclusive distributor. Hence, a patent-holder who wants to secure some breathing space after termination of the relationship would be well advised to conclude with his partner a licensing agreement together with an exclusive distributorship contract.

The fourth and hitherto the most important notice in this field concerned an agreement on joint research and licensing,[89] which showed a striking resemblance to the situation dealt with in the Henkel-Colgate/Palmolive-decision.[90] The case in question concerned the setting-up of a joint subsidiary with the purpose of engaging in research activities. This was effected by two important companies that were of about equal size in a market of an oligopolistic structure and that were originating from different member States. In the capital and management of the subsidiary both parent companies participated with equal shares. The joint company should carry on research activities the parent companies had engaged in before without success, while it was empowered to decide whether or not to apply for patents on the results of the joint research and to grant licences or conclude know-how agreements. Each partner had the right to obtain a royalty-free non-exclusive ten year licence for its home market while the other partner had to pay a fee of no more than 2%. For all other countries both partners had equally the right to obtain a non-exclusive licence at the maximum tariff of 2%. The partners held the view that this joint venture met with the requirements outlined in the Commission's Cooperation Notice of 1968[91] and applied for a negative clearance.

In its "counts of objections" the Commission, however, retorted that the way the results flowing from the research activities were exploited did not comply with the rules of competition. It held that cooperation in the field of research should not constitute a device to divide or fence in national markets. This result was achieved, it contended, by conferring an unwarranted territorial preferential position vis à vis the contracting partner through the differential setting of the royalty-amounts. Because of the well-entrenched position on their home market, the oligopolistic structure of the market and the fact that the contracting partners had not ventured hitherto on each other's market, a natural advantage existed already. An artificial preferential position should not be added which weighed more heavily since new developed products were at stake that should replace traditional ones.

89. Bulletin of the EEC of May 1971, 39-42 and Bulletin of the EEC of February 1972, 57-58.

90. See *supra*, 192-194.

91. See *supra*, 170-172.

Besides these arguments that could readily be advanced against the actual contents of the cooperation agreement the Commission went much further by speculating about the possible results that could ensue. It started from the otherwise probable assumption that each partner would take out a royalty-free licence in his home country and that the other one would abstain from applying for it, while in the other countries only one of the partners would take out a licence. As a result of these practices always only one of the partners would remain to exploit in the respective national markets the results of the joint research venture. Thus all direct competition between them would be excluded. But they could exclude all indirect competition as well through the influence they could exert on the conduct of the joint company. For, if parallel imports at the distribution level should occur, it would be up to the owner of the patent, i.e. the joint research company, to decide whether it would sue the parallel importer for infringement of the patent. Because both the parent companies had a decisive influence on the management of the joint company the decision of the latter whether legal proceedings should be instituted depended on the consent of the two parent companies who had to consult each other on the course to be taken. If the research company was actually bringing action for patent infringement against parallel imports this act–in the view of the Commission–would be caught by the ban of Article 85(1) because the exercise of the exclusive right resulted from an agreement or a concerted practice. Such interference against parallel imports constituted according to the Commission a "disguised restricting of interstate trade" in the sense of Article 36(2) EEC and was therefore contrary to the objectives of the Treaty. The Commission wanted to make it clear "once and for all", as it stated emphatically, that such use of the rights flowing from the patent within the Common Market is incompatible with Article 85. In case the results of the joint research were not embodied in patents but in know-how, the same principles as to its exploitation would apply in regard of the rules of competition.

After having heard these "counts of objections" of the Commission the parties suspended the application of the agreement and withdrew their notification.

It is interesting to see how the Commission expressed itself against the use of the rights attached to the patent in order to separate markets because it did not apply here the test–as it did with regard to the trademark–whether or not the industrial property was used in conformity with the objectives for which it was created by the legislator.

A second significant feature of this notice is that the Commission made its view known about the potential impact of Article 85 on the acts of the joint venture. For that matter interference of Article 85 on a number of aspects of the joint venture can be ascertained.

First it has been made clear that the Articles of Association of a joint venture can be contrary to Article 85 which means that the creation of the joint venture itself may be subject to the rules of competition.[92]

Second it now transpires from the present notice that the very acts of the joint venture in as far as they depend on some concertation of the parent companies may come under Article 85(1).

Third, as also is brought out by the present notice—and not so surprising as the former aspect but anyway noticeable, since German Law takes an other view in this respect—the agreements and concerted practices between the joint company and the parent companies as well as between the parent companies themselves to split up by way of specialization and rationalization the fields of activity between them and to abstain from intruding into each others' spheres of activity may come under Article 85(1).[93]

Fourth—which is quite understandable—all agreements of the joint corporation with third parties may be subject to Article 85(1) if they contain restrictions of competition and interfere with interstate commerce.

We now come to that information of the Commission on licensing agreements that was not referred to in the monthly Bulletins in a more or less elaborated way, but that was mentioned, often somewhat succintly, in the yearly General Reports alone. Such information does not pretend to give a clue about the policy adopted by the Commission since the reasons for its interventions were not explained, but rather provides an insight in the issues that were tackled.

First comes an association extending its activities over two member State. which granted licences on a collective trademark to its members when they used material meeting the required standard of quality.[94] The grant of the licence was however always coupled with the obligation for the members to respect certain minimum prices. After objections of the Commission the association discontinued this practice.

92. Alliance de constructeurs français de machines-outils-decision, note 60.
Electrically welded steel tubes association-decision, note 64.
SAFCO-decision of December 16, 1971, note 69.
Henkel-Colgate/Palmolive-decision of December 23, 1971, note 73.
Cf. Mok, 120-139.

93. Specialization and rationalization agreements come under Article 85(1), as is shown in the following decisions:
Clima Chappée-Buderus-decision of July 22, 1969, O.J. 1969, L 195/1; [1970] CMLR, D 7.
Jaz-Peter-decision of July 22, 1969, note 60.

94. Fifth General Report on the activities of the Community (EEC) (May 1, 1961-April 30, 1962), point 48, p. 78, and Sixth General Report on the activities of the Community (EEC) (May 1, 1962-March 31, 1963), point 44, p. 63.

Next comes an agreement on the assignment of a secret chemical process for the manufacture of dye-stuff material that was rescinded because it contained an export-prohibition.[95]

Furthermore the Commission makes mention of the fact that through its intervention adjustments could be obtained in four licensing and exclusive distributorship contracts on beauty care products between a manufacturer and his exclusive distributors operating in other member States.[96] The clauses on the prohibition of sales to wholesalers and retailers by the exclusive distributors, on the prohibition of re-exportation and on the joint setting of selling prices were repealed.

Finally the Commission referred to exclusive licensing agreements on several trademarks granted by a manufacturer in the textile industry to three trade associations of weavers that bought their raw material from the former.[97] The weavers had to comply with very strict norms of manufacture and had to respect a system of minimum prices. In addition the textile manufacturer had created a subvention fund to support the exports of the weavers. After intervention of the Commission the price system and the subvention of exports to the member States were discontinued.

The above mentioned enumeration of the cases in which licensing agreements played a role and that were mentioned in the General Reports alone, is made solely for completeness sake. No specific conclusions can be drawn from them.

IV. *The judgments of the Court of Justice on issues related to industrial and intellectual property.*

The Court of Justice is entrusted with the task to interpret and where necessary to apply the EEC-Treaty. Since its decisions are final the interpretation of the treaty-provisions by the Court is decisive for all the national judicial and administrative bodies in the member States as well as for all the institutions created by the EEC-Treaty itself, the Commission and the Council included, that have to apply Community Law. For that matter the Court guarantees the unity and equality of the administration of justice throughout the Community for all the individuals subject to its jurisdiction. Its judgments are of the highest importance to all issues pertaining to the contents of Community Law and its further development. It is undeniable

95. Ninth General Report on the activities of the Community (EEC) (April 1, 1965-March 31,1966), point 53, p. 69.

96. Tenth General Report on the activities of the Community (EEC) (April 1, 1965-March 31, 1966), point 52, p. 89.

97. First General Report on the activities of the Communities (1967), point 56, p. 67.

that the Court has made–sometimes in a rather unexpected and surprising way–a substantial contribution to a closer integration within the Community. Quite a few of its judgments deal with the interpretation of the EEC-rules of competition. Four of them concern the relationship between the rules of competition and industrial property. They are not the least important among the judgments the Court has delivered. In their domain each of them can even be considered as leading cases denoting sometimes a landmark in the development of Community Law. An analysis of these cases will demonstrate which are the aspects that made them so important.

1. *The Grundig/Consten-case*

The first one is the Grundig/Consten-case,[98] which above all aroused so much interest because of the fact that the Court on appeal by the plaintiffs, Grundig and Consten, sustained the Commission's contention that exclusive resale contracts should not be conducive to a splitting up of the Common Market in separate national segments by conferring upon the exclusive distributor an absolute territorial protection through practising export prohibition clauses. Under these conditions they were therefore prohibited under Article 85(1).

The second issue which made this case so well-known were its implications for the relationship between the EEC-rules of competition and trademark law.

As it was, in order to confer upon his French exclusive distributor, Consten, an exclusive territorial protection, the German manufacturer, Grundig, in addition to resorting to export prohibition clauses being built into his distribution system throughout the whole Common Market, had also created a second line of defence by calling in the help of the trademark. Through its territorial effect, so Grundig reasoned, the trademark could also stem imports of goods that were not authorized by the owner of the exclusive right. To that end an ingenious device was applied. Apart from his original trademark GRUNDIG, Grundig created a second trademark GINT (Grundig International). The first trademark was retained by Grundig everywhere in the Common Market, the second one was parceled out among his respective exclusive distributors in the various countries abroad. The trademarks GRUNDIG as well as GINT were affixed by Grundig himself to the Grundig products in Germany where he had preserved both the trademarks for himself. When Consten brought action against the parallel importers UNEF and later Leissner before the French courts for unfair competition and infringe-

98. Judgment of July 13, 1966 cons. cases Nos. 56 & 58-64), *Recueil*, XII, 429 *et seq.*; [1966] CMLR, 418 *et seq.* 4 CMLRev., 1966-7, 209-220; Annotation by Deringer, 4 CMLRev., 1966-7, 220-232.

ment of the trademark GINT, UNEF filed a complaint with the Commission claiming that the agreements between Consten and its principal, Grundig, conferring upon the former an exclusive distributorship with an absolute territorial protection, were contrary to the EEC-rules of competition. Thereupon the Commission instituted proceedings against both companies while the French courts suspended proceedings until the Commission should have rendered its decision.

The way Consten had obtained the trademark GINT depended on some concertation with Grundig who had effected—as is learned from the findings of the Court—international registration of its GINT trademark. Grundig allowed Consten to file its own registration in France and thus to obtain seemingly an originally acquired trademark. This concertation together with the understanding that after termination of the exclusive contract the trademark GINT would be reassigned to Grundig and the registration in France cancelled, as well as the undertaking of Consten to use the GINT trademark for Grundig articles only, was qualified by the Commission and later by the Court as a supplementary agreement. In its decision of September 23, 1964,[99] the Commission held that the GINT trademark was not required to show the origin of the goods since the GRUNDIG trademark performed that function already, and that the exclusive distributorship contract together with the supplementary agreement were intended to protect Consten against competition by parallel importers of Grundig products and for isolation of national markets. Therefore, the Commission ruled that the agreement on exclusive distributorship and the supplementary agreement on the registration and use of the GINT trademark constituted a violation of Article 85 EEC. Consequently, Grundig and Consten were ordered to cease and desist from any act to hinder or impede the imports of Grundig articles into France by third parties.

The Court[100] which upheld in this respect all the Commission's contentions argued that the purpose of Consten's right to be the sole user of the GINT trademark was to make it possible to control and prevent parallel imports. For that reason the agreement whereby Grundig, as owner of that trademark, by virtue of an international registration, authorized Consten to register the trademark in France in its own name was designed to restrict competition. Consten had become the original holder of the rights arising from registering the GINT trademark, but this was only made possible because of the supplementary agreement with Grundig, Therefore this agreement was subject to the prohibition of Article 85(1). Such prohibition would be ineffective if Consten could continue to avail itself of the trademark for

99. O.J., 2545/64; [1964] CMLR, 489, see also 2 CMLRev., 1964-65, 352-353.
100. *Recueil,* XII, 499-500; [1966] CMLR, 475-476; 4 CMLRev. 1966-67, 215.

the same purpose as that covered by the agreement that was held to be illegal. The Commission's order to refrain from using the trademark to prevent parallel imports is based on Article 3 of Council Regulation No. 17/62,[101] which is compatible with the Community's system of competition, embodying rules which produce a direct effect and are binding upon individuals. The nature and purpose of such a system do not permit the abuse of a trademark, originating from any national legislation, for purposes contrary to the Community's rules of competition.

The term "abuse" has created a lot of misunderstanding. Frequently the view has been advanced that the Court meant to penalize only the abusive use of national property rights conceived either as an abuse pursuant to domestic law or as a use with the sole purpose to jeopardize the Community Laws.[102] Construed in this way the importance of the Court's decision would be very limited indeed. Such interpretation appears unwarranted, for the Court seems to have intended a much broader meaning. The exercise of a national industrial property right may well be intended for a legitimate purpose within the context of national industrial property law taken in isolation and yet by virtue of its effects violate Article 85.[103] The Court's subsequent judgment in the Sirena/Eda-case[104] confirmed this view.

There is a second significant issue that was broached in the pleadings and that would turn out to have a major impact on the whole problem of the relationship between industrial property rights and the EEC-rules of competition in subsequent judgments of the Court. As it was, the plaintiffs presented the argument that the Articles 36 and 222 of the EEC-Treaty embodied the explicit guarantee of the Treaty that its provisions would not impinge upon the legal protection afforded by industrial property as instituted and provided for by the legislation of the member States. Article 36 appears in the context of exempting certain measures of the member States from the general obligations imposed by Articles 30-34 to abolish quantitative restrictions and all measures of equivalent effect on interstate trade. Among the grounds which are expressly exempted from these general prohibitive obligations are mentioned those measures that are "justified for the protection of industrial and commercial property". Article 36 contained however a concluding caveat providing that such measures shall not constitute either a

101. O.J. 204/62.

102. Among others: Jeantet, "*Le principe de territorialité du droit des marques dans le Marché Commun après l'arrêt Grundig*" in "*Brevets et marques au regard du droit de la concurrence en Europe et aux Etats-Unis*", (Brussels, 1968), 71-79, at 75; 4 CMLRev. 1966-67, 490-491.

103. Also Ebb, "*Patent and Trademark License Agreements in the Common Market and Antitrust Law*" in Rahl ed., "*Common Market and American Antitrust, Overlap and Conflict*", (New York 1970),244-311, at 256-257.

104. *Infra*, 210-215.

means of arbitrary discrimination or a disguised restriction on interstate trade. This proviso makes it clear that governmental protective measures may be invalidated if "they turn out to be only colourable exercises of the exempted powers for illegitimate ends".[105] The Court refuted the plaintiff's pleas in this respect by contending without further explanation that Article 36 limits the application of the Articles 30-34, but does not limit the application of Article 85. In its subsequent judgments it would have to refine somewhat its sweeping statement in this respect. As to Article 222, which merely says that the Treaty shall in no way prejudice the property system in the member States, the Court contended that the Commission's injunction left the essence of industrial property rights untouched but only limited their exercise insofar as necessary to enforce the prohibition embodied in Article 85(1). This distinction would be emphasized and repeated time and again by the Court in its subsequent judgments. It is submitted that this seemingly clear distinction is bound to become blurred in its practical application since situations may arise–as is shown in the Parke Davis-case to be discussed later on[106] –that an exclusive and absolute right may be exercised exactly for the purpose of maintaining the essence of that right, or expressed in other words that the prohibition of certain modes of exercise of a right may entail the undermining of the essence of that right.

The comments on this case should not be concluded before having pointed to a slight difference in approach of the issue by Commission and Court.[107] The Commission in its decision placed full emphasis on the fact that the trademark GINT did not perform its essential function as an indicator of origin, and asserted its competence to interfere with the exercise of the trademark right because of the improper way it was used. The Court however did not go into the merits of the character of the GINT trademark and placed the full emphasis on the effectiveness of the application of the EEC-rules of competition that should not be frustrated by the use of a trademark right. Because the Court took this broad position as its framework of reference it can be contented that this case signalled a major development in the relationship between the EEC-rules of competition and the exercise of trademark rights, and industrial property rights in general.

Whatever their differences in approach as to the merits of the nature of the GINT trademark may be, the Commission nor the Court ever contested

105. Ebb, *op. cit.*, note 103, 250.
106. *Infra*, 208-210.
107. Wertheimer, "National trademark law and the Common Market rules of competition", 4 CMLRev. 1966-7, 308-325 and 399-418 (esp. 415) pointed to this difference, not knowing at that time that it would develop into a major difference of view in the Sirena/Eda-case.

Consten's right to challenge real forgery or imitation of the GINT trademark whether it was perpetrated in France or abroad.

2. *The Parke Davis-case*

The Parke Davis-case concerned an owner of process patents on a pharmaceutical product, Parke Davis & Company, who in order to protect his Dutch licensee's interest sued several Dutch distributors for patent infringement, because they had imported the patented drugs from Italy where under Article 14 of the Italian Patents Act no patents may be issued for pharmaceuticals. The parallel importers contended that this way of using the patent was contrary to Article 85(1) since the drugs were lawfully produced in Italy, one of the member States, and had already been brought into free circulation on the Common Market. Therefore their free entry into the Dutch market could not be prevented by interposing a patent right. The Hague Court of Appeal felt that the issue of the interpretation of Community Law was here at stake and by its judgment of June 30, 1967[108] submitted to the Court of Justice of the European Communities two questions for a preliminary decision. These questions were to the effect whether the enforcement of a patent infringement claim against imports from patent-free member States would contravene Article 85 or 86 and whether this question would be affected by the fact that the products protected by the patent were marketed at higher prices than those not so protected.

In its judgment the Court[109] sustained flatly Parke Davis' position by holding that Article 85(1) could not be held applicable to the exercise of a patent right independent of any agreement of which it may be the subject. A patent in itself results from a legal status granted by a State to products meeting certain criteria and thus lacks the elements of agreement or concert required by Article 85. As long as the national rules on the protection of industrial property have not yet been the subject of unification within the Communty, the national character of the protection of industrial property and the discrepancies between the various legislations are liable to create obstacles both to the free circulation of patented goods and to competition within the Common Market.

As to the applicability of Article 86 the Court contended that although a patent confers upon its holder a special protection within a State, this does not imply that the three elements required for that applicability, i.e. the existence of a dominant position, its abusive use and the possibility that interstate trade may be affected by it, can be found. With regard to the

108. 5 CMLRev. 1967-68, 322-323.

109. Judgment of February, 29, 1968, case No. 24-67 (Parke Davis *v.* Probel *et al.*), *Recueil*, XIV, 81-108; [1968] CMLR, 47-61; 6 CMLRev. 1968-69, 129-132: Annotation by Koch in: 6 CMLRev. 1968-69, 217-222,

second question the Court held that the higher price level of the patented products as compared with that of a non-patented product does not necessarily constitute an abuse. This finding is quite understandable since the Treaty itself holds that only inequitable prices would entail an abuse. But this allegation was not made in the proceedings.

Parke Davis advanced the plea–just as was also done in the Grundig-Consten-case–that the Articles 36 and 222 of the Treaty contained an institutional guarantee not to impinge upon the protection the patent was affording according to national law, and that consequently the normal exercise of patent law could not be incompatible with the rules of competition. If the most normal exercise of the right were to be denied–so Parke Davis held–the right itself would be extinguished and, actually, be "expropriated".

The Court upheld this argument. In the field of the provisions relating to the free circulation of products–thus was its opinion–the restriction of importation justified for reasons of the protection of industrial property were allowed by Article 36. For similar reasons the exercise of the rights pertaining to a patent granted under the laws of a member State does not, of itself, involve a breach of the EEC-rules of competition. If the utilization of the patent should, however, degenerate into an improper use of the protection there would be an abuse. In a comparable field, Article 36 does not permit either that the restriction justified by reasons of industrial property shall "amount to a means of arbitrary discrimination or to a disguised restriction on trade between member States". Thus Article 36 was applied in an analogous way to outline the implications of the rules of competition.

Without mentioning Article 222 by name–which is noteworthy because the questions of the Hague Court of Appeal referred to this treaty-provision explicitly–the Court held that the patent rights granted by a member State to its holder are not affected in their essence by the EEC-rules of competition. On the other hand the exercise of those rights of itself would not fall under the Articles 85 and 86 as long as the elements indispensable for the application of these provisions are lacking.

All those involved in this lawsuit–with the exception of the parallel importers–concurred with the Court. The Commission–which was entitled to submit its comments to the Court pursuant to Article 20 of the Statute of the Court–noted that the Dutch patent was being used to serve its main purpose which is to guarantee that the patentholder can exploit its monopoly. Patent-protection was not being used as part of a plan to share out and partition the markets, where patent-protection already exists. Here again the Commission pointed to the fact that the use made of the patent should be in accordance with its main function.

It is manifest that the Court could not have handed down any other

judgment. Should it have done so, then denying to Parke Davis its action would indeed be tantamount to depriving the patent of its essential function. All imports from patent-free territory of goods manufactured there could then invade with impunity territories where patent-protection exists.

In the present case no decision was taken on two important questions since the facts did not allow these issues to crop up.

The first of them was the question whether an owner could prohibit parallel imports if the goods were manufactured abroad under his parallel patent. The Commission tried to elicit from the Court an *obiter dictum* on this score, but in vain. The Commission contended that such use of the patent was not warranted if the owner of a patent had already been able to receive a proper reward for his invention from parallel patents on the imported goods in other member States. Leaving aside the merits of these arguments, it is submitted, however, that this contention can never be determining for the application of the rules of competition, as long as the Commission could not point to the existence of either an agreement or a dominant position.

The second issue which remained undecided was the question what would have been the outcome of this lawsuit if the Dutch patent owner had concluded an agreement with the Italian manufacturer for instance for process know-how to produce the drugs, so that, anyway, these drugs were put on the Italian market, be it without patent-protection, but with the approval of the Dutch patent owner. During the proceeding before the Court an allusion was made as to the existence of such an agreement but the Court dismissed the assumption of its existence. Thus it could not be ascertained what impact an agreement concluded between a patent-owner and a manufacturer in a patent-free area would have had on the issue, viz. whether the patent-owner would still have the right to impede imports in a patent-protected area.

3. *The Sirena/Eda-case*

Here again—as in the Grundig-Consten-case [110]—the aid of a trademark was called in by its owner to stem parallel imports of goods bearing the same trademark and sold at a cheaper price that previously were lawfully put into circulation in an other member State. However, this time the Italian trademark-owner, Sirena, which invoked this right had acquired it by way of an assignment agreement with an American company, Mark Allen, that equally had licensed its trademark in Germany to a manufacturer having produced the parallel imported products, a shaving cream.

The Court of Justice [111] confronted with this situation by a request for a

110. See *supra*, 204-208.

111. Judgment of February 18, 1971, case No. 40-70 (Sirena v. Eda *et al.*), *Recueil*,

preliminary decision from the Milan Court held, that Article 85 applies where in reliance on trademark rights, imports are prevented of products originating in other member States, bearing the same trademark, if their owners have acquired this trademark with one another or with third parties. As to the applicability of Article 86 the Court found that the owner of a trademark does not hold a dominant position merely because he is in a position to prohibit third parties from marketing products bearing the same trademark, in the territory of a member State. The concept of a dominant position was construed to the effect that the holder thereof should have the capability to hamper the maintenance of effective competition on a significant part of the relevant product market within a substantial part of the Common Market, taking into account, in particular, the possible existence and the position of producers or distributors who market similar or substitute products. A higher price-level of a product was not held to reveal necessarily the existence of an improper use of a dominant position but can nevertheless constitute a conclusive indication thereof if such level cannot be justified on any objective grounds.

The Court again referred to Article 36 in contending that although it forms part of a different chapter of the Treaty the principles underlying this provision may also apply to the field of the competition rules, in the sense that, though the essence of the industrial and commercial property rights granted by the national legislation is not affected by the Articles 85 and 86, their exercise may nevertheless come within the prohibitions laid down in these provisions.

The implications of this judgement are rather sweeping indeed. For one thing, because the Court held that the exercise of a trademark may come under the prohibition of the Treaty if it is the object, the means or the result of an agreement thus indicating for the first time which broad relationship between an agreement and industrial property was deemed to suffice for coming under the competition rules.

For another, because of its general statement that the parallel transfers to several concessionairies of national trademark rights protecting the same product, if it has the effect of re-erecting impenetrable frontiers between member States, may affect interstate trade and distort competition in the Common Market. As it is, this opinion applies to a situation in which the Italian owner of a trademark could not uphold his exclusive and absolute

---

XVII, 69-93; [1971] CMLR, 260 *et seq.* Commentary by Alexander, "Industrial property rights and the establishment of the European Common Market", CMLRev. 1972, 35-52.

right against the parallel imports of goods originating from the German user of a trademark with whom the former had not the slightest direct legal, economic or organizational relationship. Only because both derived their trademark right form the same original owner, Mark Allen, Sirena was penalized. This is the more noteworthy because the assignment agreement between Sirena and Mark Allen dated from 1937, thus some 20 years before the incipiency of the Common Market Treaty. One may even wonder whether under these conditions the essence of the trademark has not been affected to some extent.

Anyhow, this judgement went too far to the mind of the Commission which held in its submissions to the Court that the mere transfer of ownership of a trademark does not belong to those effects of an assignment agreement that could come within the scope of Articles 85 and 86, since the Court had held that they have no bearing on the ownership of such a right. As to the exercise of industrial property rights which according to the Court could only be affected by these provisions, the Court itself had ruled that merely the improper use of the rights flowing from national trademark law should be prevented. Hence the definite transfer of a trademark could only be caught by these provisions if, be it indirectly, this trademark would be used for purposes foreign to the agreement or if it is used to achieve a result similar to what a prohibited agreement was aiming at. This case was not comparable to the Grundig-Consten-case. The issue in the present case, on the contrary, concerns merely the simple transfer of an intangible asset carried out prior to the entry into force of the Treaty.

We see here the clash between the views of the Commission and the Court simmering right from the start, now coming into the open. It is clear that the Commission's views were of a less sweeping nature than those of the Court.

Taking stock of the holdings of the Court one can deduce therefrom the following implications as to constraints put on the trademark user in regard to the exercise of his right against parallel imports from other member States.

Apart from the cases where the impact on interstate trade or on the restriction of competition is of minor importance the Sirena-case demonstrates that the users of a trademark–be it the owner or a licensee–are no more entitled to prevent the parallel imports of goods bearing the same trademark if they and the users abroad–be it a trademark-owner or a licensee–derive their title through assignment- or licensing agreements from the same owner who had originally established that right within the various Common Market countries. In cases a licensee is confronted with parallel imports originating from a licensee abroad obtaining his title from the same trademark-owner, domestic legislation in some countries already does not permit such exercise of a national trademark so that the issue from a

Community Law point of view cannot arise.[112] The rationale of the Sirena/Eda-case entails that its findings are equally applicable to users of a trademark obtained by a derivative title, being confronted with imports originating from the original owner himself.

There are, however, equally a number of cases in which the original trademark-owner himself may not exercise his right against parallel branded imports from other member States bearing his mark. Assuming the reverse situation of the one entailing from the Sirena/Eda-case, it is logical that an original trademark-owner will also be denied the right to prevent parallel imports of goods originating from his assignees or licensees abroad, the exercise of his original right resulting indirectly from the agreements the trademark-owner has concluded with his partners abroad. It is otherwise submitted that domestic trademark law itself already will often not permit a trademark-owner to exercise his right against imports originating from his licensee abroad, whenever the law does not allow the trademark-owner to prevent the imports of his own original goods.

In the second place the Grundig-Consten judgement has taught that the original trademark-owner cannot use his right against parallel imports, when a trademark right, although being originally established, was acquired by way of an agreement since the one who had effected international registration of a trademark had undertaken not to exercise his right resulting therefrom in one member State, thus allowing his contracting partner to obtain a national title to that right. The establishment of such a right is original but not autonomous.

In the third place, autonomous and original owners of trademarks in various member States can conclude among them restrictive agreements or perform concerted practices falling under Article 85 and involving as their object, means or the effect of the exercise of a trademark.

In the fourth place situations may arise in which the exercise of a trademark by an autonomous and original owner would constitute an abusive use of a dominant economic position.

Where the autonomous and original owner himself–without the presence of any agreement or dominant economic position–would try to prevent the parallel imports of goods he himself had brought into circulation abroad he will discover that domestic trademark law will not allow such action.[113]

112. Dash-case, President Court, Breda, April 1, 1969, BIE 1970, No. 57; NJ 1969, No. 409.

113. Germany: Maja-case, BGH January 22, 1964, GRUR Int. 1964, 202; Italy: Palmolive/Burlando-case, Corte di Cassazione, October 20, 1956, No. 3781, Foro Italiano 1957, Parte I, col. 1021; Belgium: Email-Diamant-case, Cour de Cassation, May 23, 1945, Pasicrisie 1945, Part I, 168, Netherlands: Grundig I-case, HR December 14, 1956, NJ 1962, No. 242; France: Radio Télé Hall/Simplex Electronique-case (Körting), Cour de Cassation, April 17, 1969, RIPIA, March 1970, No. 79, 5-13 (according to the Advocate General in the Sirena-case, but to others doubtful).

The Sirena/Eda-case pointed to the fact that a major anomally existed in EEC competition law anyway before February 1973. As it is, one can conclude from the Court's judgement that an assignment or licensing agreement lacking any restrictive clause, if held to be prohibited, gives rise to the prevention of the exercise of a trademark-right for the past. On the other hand any agreement involving the imposition of restrictions on the exercise of the rights of any person acquiring or using industrial property rights, was held to be fully valid by the Court in the Bilger/Jehle-case,[114] until its nullity had been declared, while this nullity could not be imposed with a retroactive effect, anyway by the national judiciary. On the strength of this judgement a national judge could not deny to an owner of a trademark the exercise of his right against parallel imports for the past if the assignment agreement contained some restrictive clause, e.g. a re-assignment obligation. Hence such agreements embodying restrictive clauses were better off than agreements without any restriction at all.

After the Haecht II-case the situation has completely changed. No more the agreements complying with the conditions set out in Article 4(2)(2b) of Regulation No. 17/62 are in a better position vis à vis their legal validity than those that must be notified. However the discrepancy remains in that the authorization for "clean" assignment- and licensing-agreements can date back only to the day on which they have been notified while the assignment- and licensing-agreements carrying restrictive clauses can be declared valid right from the very date of their conclusion, according to the provisions of Article 6 par. 1 & 2 of Regulation No. 17/62.

One may wonder whether the Court's judgement is equally applicable to patents. Although the Court inserted in its opinion a phrase to the effect that a parallel between a trademark and a patent should not be drawn too easily, this contention should, however, not be construed in that such possibility can be absolutely excluded beforehand. It may be of importance to note that the Advocate General asserted in his submissions to the Court that trademarks and patents should be treated on a par in this respect. For that reason as well, it seems not too bold to suggest that situations may arise in which the exercise of patent-rights being the object, the means or the result of an agreement cannot be invoked against parallel imports of goods protected by parallel patents abroad belonging either to the original owner himself or to someone who in some direct or indirect way is connected through an agreement to the one having recourse to his exclusive right, if the exercise of such a right affects interstate trade and restricts competition in a perceptible way.

114. Judgment of March 18, 1970, case No. 43-69, *Recueil* XVI, 138; see in this respect the explication given in this paper to Article 4(2)(2b) of Council Regulation No. 17/62, *supra*, 163, 164.

Because of its far-reaching implications this judgement can be held to constitute a leading case on the relationship between industrial property and EEC-competition law.

4. *The DGG/Metro-case*

The case under review will certainly go down in history as a landmark because here the exercise of intellectual and industrial property rights was held to be prohibited not because of the impact of the EEC-rules of competition but on account of the principles underlying the provisions of the Treaty dealing with the free movement of goods within the Community.

In point of fact, the Deutsche Grammophon Gesellschaft (DGG) exercised here its so-called "neighbouring right" to a copyright, i.e. a right on the reproduction and marketing of recordings which is recognised by the German Copyright and Related Rights Act of 1965 as a specific exclusive and absolute right, against its own grammophone records imported and offered at a cheaper price by a parallel importer, known by the name of Metro. The facts underlying the situation were rather complex. On the one hand DGG practices a resale-price maintenance system in Germany. All German dealers have to sign a written undertaking to observe the fixed sales prices. When DGG discovered that the firm Metro did not adhere to the regulated prices and refused to sign a written undertaking that it would respect these prices in future, DGG discontinued its deliveries to Metro. On the other hand DGG distributes its records in France by way of its practically 100% subsidiary Polydor S.A. which had the exclusive right to supply the French market, but that market only, by way of selling along the customary trade channels i.e. the retail trade. Through some irregularities committed by one of Polydor's employees, as DGG would assert later on,[115] a number of records supplied by DGG to Polydor found their way to a Swiss wholesaler. Through this channel Metro managed to obtain supplies of DGG-records and sold them in Germany in total disregard of the regulated prices. DGG considered the sales of its records as a violation of its neighbouring right and obtained a temporary injunction from the Hamburg lower court. When Metro appealed against this judgement the Hamburg Court of Appeal addressed two questions to the Court of Justice of the European Communities for a preliminary decision. These questions were in substance to the effect of whether it would be contrary to the provisions of the Treaty if the German Copyright and Related Rights Act were construed in such a way that DGG could in reliance on its absolute right effectively oppose these imports of its own records and secondly whether the exercise of this neighbouring right implied some abusive

115. Polydor II, Court of Appeal Hamburg of October 28, 1971, GRUR Int. 1972, 95-97; AWD 1971, 591-592; [1972] CMLR, 107 *et seq.*

use of an economic dominant position in view of the higher regulated sales-price of the records in comparison with the price of the reimported original ones.

The Court in its opinion[116] made it clear that to its mind the provisions of the Articles 85 and 86 were not applicable. It could find no agreement or concerted practices since DGG exercised its own originally and autonomously established neighbouring right against the imports. As long as no capability existed to hamper effective competition no dominant position could be found either, while as long as the price-differential could be justified no abusive use was held to exist. In this respect the Parke Davis and Sirena/Eda holdings were duly repeated. But thereafter some surprise was in store. By breaking new ground in its judgement the Court held that it constituted a violation of the rules concerning the free movement of goods within the Common Market if a manufacturer of grammophone records exercises his exclusive right under the legislation of a member State to market the protected products, in order to prohibit the distribution in that member State of products having been sold, either by himself or with his consent, in an other member State, solely on the ground that such marketing did not take place on the territory of the former member State. How did the Court come to this conclusion? After having dismissed the possibility of the applicability of the provisions on competition, the Court wondered whether the exercise of said exclusive right was compatible with other provisions of the Treaty, especially with those relating to the free movement of goods. Since these provisions address themselves to member States only, they cannot spell out obligations for nationals. Realizing this position the Court therefore held that not the provisions themselves, but the principles underlying these provisions outline the rules that would define the obligations to be observed by nationals. In search of the treaty-provisions that could provide for those principles it came across Article 36. This provision embodies an exemption from the member States' obligations to abolish on interstate trade all quantitative restrictions and measures having equivalent effects, in that it allows restrictions of importation which are justified for the protection of industrial and commercial property. However, the member States are not allowed to use this power as a means of arbitrary discrimination or disguised restriction on interstate trade. From this provision addressed to the member States the Court made the inference for the rules directed to nationals which it actually formulated as follows:

First, that Article 36 shows that the Treaty does not interfere with the essence of the rights on industrial and commercial property conferred by the

116. Judgment of June 8, 1971, case No. 78-70 (DGG v. Metro), *Recueil* XVII, 487-514, [1971] CMLR, 631 *et seq.* Commentary by Alexander, op. cit., note 111, 48-51.

domestic legislation of a member State, but that the exercise of these rights may fall under the prohibitions of the Treaty. Hence—as in the Sirena/Eda-case—the same principles were retained from Article 36 as the Court inferred in the Grundig-Consten-case from Article 222. According to the opinion of the Court in the latter case only the abuse of a right was condemned;

Second, that since Article 36 permits restrictions on the free movement of goods which are justified for the protection of industrial and commercial property, such justification is only warranted if the restrictions serve for the preservation of rights constituting the specific subject-matter of such property. Here the Court spelled out more in detail what is understood by the term "essence of the right" it had always used before.

As to the general principles set out in the part of the Treaty devoted to the free circulation of goods the Court held that the use of a neighbouring right to prohibit the distribution within one member State of goods which have been marketed by the owner of the right, or with his consent, on the territory of an other member State, solely on the ground that such marketing had not taken place within the territory of the former State, was in clear conflict with the fundamental objective of the Treaty, viz. the amalgamation of the national markets into one single market. This objective could not be reached if private individuals were capable, on the basis of the different legal systems of the member States, to divide up the market and to bring about an arbitrary discrimination or a disguised restriction of interstate trade within the Common Market. If a manufacturer of records were to exercise his exclusive right in such a way adducing as the sole argument that the marketing had not taken place on the territory of the member State where the right is invoked, such conduct would therefore constitute a violation of the rules concerning the free movement of goods in the Common Market. Thus the Court made inequivocally clear to the German judge which principles he had to observe when interpreting the German Copyright law. These suggestions were duly understood.[117]

This was the first time the Court invoked principles underlying the basic provisions of the Treaty to direct how domestic law should be interpreted. On the other hand it had often applied this method of interpretation before when it wanted to indicate how other treaty-provisions should be construed. In point of fact, it had literally held in the Sirena/Eda-case, that was concerned with the interpretation and application of the EEC-rules of competition, as follows:

> "Although Article 36 forms part of the chapter concerning quantitative restrictions in trade between the member States it stems from a principle that may well apply in competition law . . . ".[118]

---

117. Judgment of the Court of Appeal of Hamburg cited in note 115.
118. *Recueil* XVII, 81; [1971] CMLR, 273.

The Court has now extended this practice to the domain of domestic law.

Although Polydor S.A. was a nearly 100% subsidiary of DGG the Court did not expand on this situation, but merely held that the marketing of the goods in question had been effected within the territory of another member State by the owner of the right, or with his consent. This seems to indicate that even if the marketing had been done by an independent enterprise but with the consent of the owner of the right, the opinion of the Court would have been equally applicable.

It is a striking feature of the judgement that the Court laid much emphasis on the fact that it would not accept the sole argument that marketing had not taken place on the territory of the member State where the owner was exercising his right. One may wonder what additional argument the Court would have deemed as warranted. Maybe the plea that the goods had been marketed abroad under a compulsory licence would have been accepted. With the Scott Paper announcement [119] in mind, equally the argument may be upheld that the imports were effected directly by the licensee-manufacturer abroad belonging to the same group of companies as the owner of the exclusive right that was exercised.

But would the defence have been accepted as relevant that the owner of the right had no parallel exclusive right abroad and hence could not have had the opportunity to reap a proper reward for his achievement? In the present case such an argument could have been validly put forward since French law does not protect a neighbouring right as an absolute and exclusive right. However, the argument was not advanced for reasons unknown. In point of fact it is questionable whether this plea would have been of much avail. The assertion that an exclusive right in itself would be conducive for the owner to receive a special reward for his effort is not compatible with the economic evaluation of the facts practiced by the Court in this domain. It may be recalled that the Court repeatedly has held that the existence of an exclusive right by itself does not warrant the conclusion that its owner holds a dominant position. Since special rewards can only be reaped in monopoloid situations, it should be shown that the owner of an exclusive right is not exposed to effective competition on the market place, before it can be asserted that he has received a benefit for his achievement resulting from this exclusive parallel right. Whether such proof can be furnished depends on an appreciation of the economic value of the exclusive right at issue. It is therefore submitted that—in the light of the DGG/Metro-judgement—it hardly seems relevant whether parallel exclusive rights are held or not, when the goods are brought on the market abroad either by the owner of the exclusive

119. *Supra*, 195.

right or with his consent. Anyway, what additional argument the Court would accept as warranted for an exclusive right to be exercised against parallel imports, is still an open question.

The Commission drew two conclusions of crucial importance from this judgment. First of all it held that to its mind the judgment applied integrally to all exclusive rights in the domain of industrial and commercial property, patents included.[120] Whether this view can be endorsed depends on the way the judgment of the Court should be construed. When the Court intended to say that in the present case the exercise of the neighbouring right was not justified, in that it did not serve for the preservation of rights constituting the specific subject-matter of such property, the criteria decisive for the admissibility of such exercise depend on the characteristics of the exclusive right in question. In that case it seems warranted to distinguish between the various exclusive rights. Even though it is conceded that a patent has more features in common with a neighbouring right than e.g. with a trademark, marked differences remain. One of them is the fact that the patent has a more territorially tied nature while the copyright, because of its cultural connotation, is more universal in character. Therefore it can be assumed that a work of art, once being brought on the market, is free to circulate all over the world. In point of fact the Bern Convention for the Protection of Works of Literature and Art, lastly revised in 1948, proceeds on this principle. The International Convention for the Protection of Performers, Producers of Phonograms and Broadcasting Organisations of 1961 is based on the same principle. Whatever the outcome of the comparison may be, it is submitted that, seen from this angle, it does not seem warranted to draw an overall conclusion from the DGG/Metro judgment in this respect.

The judgment can, however, also be construed in another way. It might be that the Court wanted to indicate that if under these conditions exclusive rights are exercised to prevent imports, this conduct by itself is to be assimilated to an arbitrary discrimination or a disguised restriction of interstate trade, irrespective of the exclusive rights used for that purpose. Since in that context the decisive standards to be applied are no more governed by the characteristics of a specific exclusive right it is logical when a general conclusion is drawn from the Court's judgment in that it spells out principles of law that should equally be applicable to patents. Because the Commission in its declaration of March 15, 1971[121] had qualified such behaviour as a disguised restriction of interstate trade in the sense of Article 36(2) it is explicable that it construed the Court's judgment that way. The Hamburg Court of Appeal shared the Commission's view.[122] However it does not seem

120. First Report on Competition Policy, (Brussels 1972), point 67.
121. Bulletin of the European Communities 1971, no. 5, 41-42 and 1972, no. 2, 58.
122. See note 115; GRUR Int., 96; AWD, 591.

crystal-clear which side the Court itself has taken. Even if one's preference would go out to the first alternative so that the present judgment does not constitute a precedent for patents, this does not take away that the Court at one time may rule that the exercise of a patent right to prevent imports cannot be held to be justified under Article 36(1).

The second conclusion the Commission drew from this judgment was of a even more fundamental nature. It held that the provisions of Article 36 lay down limits on the exercise of industrial and commercial property rights nationals can invoke before the national judiciary.[123] In other words the Commission held that Article 36 carries a direct effect. Can this view be supported? Two critical remarks should be made. First of all, Article 36 addresses member States only, so that it cannot impose obligations on nationals. Whether Article 36 by itself produces a direct effect or not is immaterial in this context, because the limits on the exercise of industrial and commercial property by nationals–the owners of such property rights– are involved. The Commission should therefore rather have adopted the phrasing of the Court that spoke of principles underlying Article 36 and the rules ensuing therefrom. While this lapse may be due to some lack of careful formulation on the part of the Commission, the second issue viz. whether the rules embodied in the principles underlying Article 36 are of such a character that they create rights for nationals–the parallel importers–the national judiciary has to uphold, is fundamental for the relationship between Community Law and domestic law in the field of industrial and commercial property. It would mean that the rules adressing nationals–the owners of the exclusive rights–and deriving from the principles underlying Article 36–and those underlying the Articles 30-34 on which Article 36 constitutes an exception–should, in view of the primacy of Community Law, prevail over domestic law insofar as the explicit provisions in its statutes and established case law are conflicting. Hence, in that respect domestic law is to be set aside without interference of any national legislative or other regulatory authority. Whether such sweepings inferences can be drawn from this judgment is highly questionable.

To reduce the problem to its proper proportions it should be recalled what the real issue was. The Court of Appeal of Hamburg was confronted with the question whether the Copyright Act of 1965 could be construed in such a way that the owner of a neighbouring right to a copyright could with his exclusive right effectively impede the imports of goods marketed abroad by

123. Answer of the Commission to written question No. 344/71 of Mr. Vredeling, O.J. 1972, C 53/1. The footnote to this publication, in that a preliminary answer had already been given, is not correct. Reference is there made to an answer to the question No. 344/70 put by Mr. Romeo (O.J. 1971, C 115/1).

himself or with his consent. The Hamburg Court of Appeal[124] although inclined to decide in favour of the owner of the exclusive right realised that such a judgment might not be in conformity with the spirit of the EEC-Treaty and asked for a preliminary decision of the Court of Justice of the European Communities as to how the German law should be interpreted in conformity with the EEC-Treaty. In doing so, the Court of Appeal implicitely conceded that the Copyright Act left some discretionary power to the judge as to the interpretation in this respect. The German Government in its submissions to the Court of Justice said explicitly that the way of interpretation of the Copyright Act was not settled. In point of fact, in his annotation to the Court of Appeal's order for a preliminary decision Ulmer contended that in view of its history the Act did not allow a copyright to be used to prevent the imports of goods marketed abroad. The Court of Justice held that it was not its duty to direct how domestic law should be interpreted and therefore enumerated a couple of rules that should serve for the national judge as guidelines when interpreting his domestic law. Should these guidelines be construed as rules of a directly effective nature? Anyway, the Court itself has said nothing to that effect. This is significant because hitherto it always explicitly had done so, if it wanted to be known that some rule produced a direct effect. The rather peremptory way the Court expressed itself about the contents of the rules should not be mistaken for an opinion on the legal character therof.

Moreover, the Advocate General in his submissions to the Court also has touched on this issue. He contended, that in view of the vagueness and the lack of clarity of the German Copyright Act and because of the fact that the law was enacted after the EEC-Treaty took effect, the national court was obviously anxious to adopt an interpretation of the national statute which is in harmony with the Community system. For that reason it suffices to analyse the treaty-principles governing the matter in question. Under those conditions it is clear that there is no need to consider whether certain treaty-provisions produce a direct effect, i.e. rules of law nationals can invoke against domestic law, since it must also be assumed that the national legislator has had no wish to disregard the treaty-principles. Hence, according to the Advocate General as well, the issue of the direct effect of the treaty rules was not raised. Therefore, it seems premature to draw firm conclusions to that effect from the Court's judgment.

As to the substantive question whether actually directly effective rules were involved it should be emphasized that not the treaty-provisions directed to member States, but the principles underlying those provisions addressing

124. Court of Appeal Hamburg of October 8, 1970 (DGG v. Metro), GRUR Int. 1970, 377 (with annotation of Ulmer); Rev. Trim. du Droit Européen 1971, 200-208; [1971] CMLR, 631 *et seq.*

nationals are at issue. For treaty-rules to have a direct effect the Court has repeatedly held that the obligations they contain should be precisely laid down ("*doit être precise*") and unconditional.[125] Since principles of law are by their very nature not so clearly outlined and rather spell out broad guidelines, while moreover the term "justified" in Article 36(1) leaves a good measure of discretionary power to the judge for claiming the exemption provided for in that treaty-provision, it cannot be asserted that by implication these rules underlying Article 36 have a direct effect.

It is therefore submitted that the conclusions to be drawn from the DGG/Metro judgment are, although far-reaching, less sweeping than suggested by the Commission. Their real meaning is that, insofar as the national legal order opens up the possibility for the implementation of principles deriving from Community Law when interpreting domestic law, these principles as defined by the Court should be adopted by the national judiciary. But the issue whether the national legal order allows such implementation–insofar as non-directly effective Community Law is concerned–is a question that is entirely governed by domestic law itself. Therefore, if domestic law is such, that for its interpretation it does not permit community-principles to be implemented the question of their applicability does not arise and with it the issue of their supremacy over domestic law. As it is, the problem of the primacy of Community Law should not be confused with the issue of its direct effect.[126]

This all boils down to the following practical conclusion. As far as domestic law contains precise provisions or is determined by established case law so that no leeway exists for the implementation of community principles of law–as may be the case with national patent law–the judiciary can stick to its national rules without infringing Community Law even if domestic law is conflicting with the spirit of the EEC-Treaty. In how far the member States have complied with or have infringed treaty-obligations should be established by virtue of the application of the Articles 169 and 170 of the Treaty. This does not affect the legal position of nationals. Anyway, as a rule, the harmonisation of domestic law should be effected through the machinery of the Articles 100-102.

125. Judgment of June 16, 1966, case No. 57-65 (Lütticke II), *Recueil* XII, 302; [1971] CMLR, 684. Judgment of April 3, 1968, case No. 28-67 (Molkerei Zentrale), *Recueil* XIV, 226; [1966] CMLR, 217.

126. For the relationship between Community and domestic Law: Bebr, "Law of the European Communities and municipal law", 34 The Modern Law Review 1971, 481-500. Mitchell, "*Community Legislation*" in Bathurst *et al.* "*Legal Problems of an enlarged European Community*" (1972), 87-103.

The foregoing arguments prompt to the conclusion that for two reasons it is questionable whether the DGG/Metro judgment by itself is applicable to patents.

First, because of the specific characteristics of the patent, the question is left open whether under Article 36(1) it would be held "justified" for the protection of the patent if it were exercised in order to impede imports under the conditions as spelled out in the DGG/Metro-case. It is, therefore, doubtful whether the judgment laid down principles of Community Law that are equally applicable to patents.

Second, because national patent-law may be found to be guided by domestic principles of law only, no Community Law is being held applicable. Hence, even if the DGG/Metro-case should set out principles of Community Law applicable to patents, such judgment would then turn out to be immaterial in those cases.

V. *Conclusions*

In the preceding chapters the relationship between Community Law and industrial property based on domestic law was explored in a rather complete way. The analysis shows that the whole issue can be divided into two main categories.

The first one deals with the fundamental question in how far the national character of the protection of industrial and commercial property as well as the discrepancies between the various domestic legislations warrant the splitting up of the Common Market into national segments and the restriction of competition. This issue can have an impact on the legal position of third parties effecting unauthorized imports into the territory of the member State where the products in question are protected by an industrial and commercial property right. Thanks to the various judgments of the Court of Justice of the European Communities quite a few problems have been solved in this domain.

Yet a number of questions are left in abeyance even assuming one would accept the Commission's view that the DGG/Metro judgment is applicable to patents as well as entails a direct effect on the domestic legal order. In particular no exhaustive answer has as yet been given to the question under which conditions a restriction on the free circulation of goods is accepted as justified because it is serving for the preservation of rights constituting the specific subject-matter of a specific industrial and commercial property i.e. a patent. This question is relevant not only for the application of the Articles 85 and 86–since the Sirena/Eda judgment held that the interpretation of these provisions should be in conformity with the principles underlying Article 36–but also where the application of the treaty-principles

embodied in the provisions dealing with the free movement of goods is involved, as was contended in the DGG/Metro-case.

Moreover, what kind of additional argument would be accepted as warranted so that the exercise of an exclusive right against parallel imports would not be assimilated to an arbitrary discrimination or a disguised restriction of interstate trade? Which importance should be attributed to situations where parallel exclusive rights in the Common Market come into play? Does it make a difference that no parallel exclusive rights are held abroad either because foreign domestic legislation denies such protection, or because, though such protection exists, it was not applied for or has lapsed for some reason, when the holder of an exclusive right himself had brought the product on to the market in that other member State or had given his consent thereto?

When does the exercise of an exclusive industrial and commercial property right constitutes a conduct reprehended by Article 86? In other words under what conditions is the owner of such a right in a position to hamper the maintenance of effective competition on a significant part of the relevant product market within a substantial part of the Common Market, and what objective grounds can justify that a higher price level of a product is not held to reveal the existence of improper practices of a dominant position? Thus, still a number of important issues in this field are not yet solved by the authorities of the Communities.

The issue of the national character of the protection of industrial and commercial property may also affect the legal position of the contracting partners themselves. Here the licensing agreements with implied territorial restrictions within the Common Market are involved. Those agreements do not carry any restrictive clause to that effect but the licensor owning parallel patents in the various member States achieves this result for instance by dividing his licences among various licensees in the respective member States; the so-called multiple parallel licensing. Through this practice a licensee would not be in a position to export to another member State because lacking the relevant licence he is violating the parallel patent of his licensor abroad. Whether such implied territorial limitation imposed on the licensee is admissible under the competition rules of the Treaty is a burning issue for the Commission. [127]

Up till now it has shown no objection against the grant of licences for a certain territory within the Common Market insofar as manufacturing is concerned. [128] This is comprehensible since manufacturing does not consti-

127. Schlieder, *op.cit.*, 40 Antitrust Law Journal, 1972, 946.

128. Davidson-decision of June 9, 1972, O.J. 1972, L 143/31; [1972] CMLR, D 52 *et seq.*; Burroughs decisions of December 22, 1971, O.J. 1972, L 13/50 and L 13/53; [1972] CMLR, D 67 *et seq.* and D 72 *et seq.*

tute a market-conduct. Hence a restriction in this field does not in itself entail a restriction of competition. But where the grant of licences entails implied territorial restrictions on sales the Commission seems more hesitant. When this issue cropped up in the Scott Paper-case [129] the Commission announced it would take a benevolent attitude towards two intra-group trademark-licensing agreements after having extracted assurances from both licensees to the effect that the trademark would not be used against parallel imports originating from the other licensee "at the trading level". However, they remained free to oppose direct exports effected by the other licensee-manufacturer. Thus the Commission allowed territorial sales-restriction to be imposed on the licensees in this case. It is surmised that the fact, that both licensees belonged to the same group of companies, was not completely foreign to the Commission's position. Anyway it should be recalled that this announcement of the Commission's intentions was published in 1968 and that up till now it has not been followed up by a decision.

In the Burroughs-case the question could not crop up because sales-licences were granted for all countries in the Common Market. In the Davidson-case the Commission dodged the issue by insisting on the insertion of a new clause into the various exclusive licensing agreements to the effect that no stipulation of the contracts should be construed so as to hamper the sale of products under contract from one member State to the other. In doing so the Commission introduced explicitly the possibility for all the licensees to export freely all over the Common Market. The preceding incident demonstrates that the Commission is not very favourably inclined towards the grant of sales-licences confined to one member State only if parallel patents exist. But hitherto no frontal attack against it has been launched.

The second category of issues regarding the inter-relationship between industrial property and competition law concerns the admissibility of clauses inserted in patent-licensing agreements and in agreements on the transfer of know-how. In its Notice on patent-licensing agreements of December 24, 1962 [130] the Commission spelled out a number of clauses it regarded as falling outside the scope of Article 85(1) since they are considered to constitute the object of the exercise of industrial property itself. By and large the Commission still seems to stick today to its views expressed at that time especially where territorial restrictions (within the territory for which the patent is valid), time limits (within the period of validity of the patent) and quantity restrictions are concerned. [131] It should, however, not be overlooked that in some other respects the Commission has made significant de-

129. *Supra*, 195.
130. *Supra*, 166-168.
131. First Report on Competition Policy, (Brussels 1972), point 69.

partures from its Notice in the past. As to clauses in agreements on the transfer of know-how the secrecy clause as well as the clause on stopping the application of know-how after termination of the agreement may seem to be the only ones qualifying for escaping Article 85(1) altogether.[132]

Where the clauses in licensing contracts are concerned that could be exempted by virtue of Article 85(3) where one is confronted with a domain that hardly has been broached. Hence quite some spadework in this field still lies ahead.

In view of the approximately 1,300 notifications of licensing agreements that are still awaiting examination by the Commission, as well as the large number of notifications to be anticipated because of the extension of the European Community with Great Britain, Ireland and Denmark there is an urgent need for category-exemptions in this field since individual treatment will be unfeasible. The Commission has already the necessary tools at its disposal to cope with the situation since Council Regulation No. 19/65[133] empowers it to issue a regulation on category-exemptions for licensing agreements, while Council Regulation No. 2821/71[134] authorises the Commission to issue a regulation on category-exemptions for research and development agreements and for the exploitation of the results thereof. Nevertheless it seems hardly conceivable that these regulations will be issued at rather short notice. The number of decisions taken on individual cases in this domain is as yet too small for an established practice to develop. For the Commission to acquire enough experience a fairly large number of test-cases will have to be examined and decided upon before it can venture in the field of category-exemptions.

It can be taken for granted that the phenomenon of multiple parallel licensing for sales is a recurrent feature confronting the Commission in the approximately 1,300 notifications of licensing agreements still awaiting examination. Since the Commission could not yet make up its mind as to what stand to take on this issue this situation may be one of the reasons why no category-exemption had been promulgated hitherto. The Commission could find no support in the Sirena/Eda-case, where equally the parallel assignment to different users of an industrial property right was involved, since the Court's judgment dealt with imports performed "at the trading level" only, while moreover trademarks were involved. The test to be applied seems to be whether the exercise of the domestic patent against imports

132. Schlieder in "Panel discussion on the dissemination of technology", 40 Antitrust Law Journal 1972, 956.

133. *Supra*, 168, 169.

134. *Supra*, 174, 175.

performed by the licensee under a parallel patent abroad, is justified for the preservation of rights constituting the specific subject-matter of the domestic patent.

From the synopsis of the questions still pending the conclusions can be drawn that although up to some extent clarity has been reached in a number of issues, it is undeniable that still more complexities lie ahead for further exploration.

Chapter 9

DIFFERENTIATION AND DISCRIMINATION IN COMMUNITY ANTI-TRUST LAW[1]

by *Mr. B.H. ter Kuile*

1. *Introduction*

The Commission's first report on its policy in the field of competition[2] discusses the application of Article 60 of the ECSC-Treaty regarding price discrimination,[3] but does not remark on the Commission's policy in respect to Article 85, section 1, sub d and Article 86, sub c of the EEC-Treaty, the special anti-trust provisions concerning discrimination. Probably there is nothing accidental in this. Neither the public authorities and business nor the courts and science are particularly interested in these special EEC-provisions. In a sense this is surprising since the prohibition of applying unequal conditions in respect of equivalent supplies contained in Articles 85 and 86, not only relates to price discrimination but could, in view of its broad wording, also apply to a wide variety of business transactions daily concluded within the Common Market. In practice, however, but little is heard of problems of anti-trust law arising from Article 85, section 1, sub d or 86, sub c. Apparently, an undertaker does not readily feel that he is the victim of discriminatory practices on the part of his customers, principals, suppliers or competitors. In his view, unequal conditions in respect of equivalent supplies are most likely to result from commercial motives justifying the discrepan-

1. No doubt, the practical problems dealt with hereunder do not spring from the mind of the author but have arisen many times in the United States and perhaps even in the European Coal and Steel Community (cf Art. 4, 60 ff). However, because of the nature of the Articles 85 and 86 of the EEC-Treaty a comparative study of workable solutions of these problems in the United States and in the ECSC is left undone. A decision which possibly might solve discrimination questions resulting from the Articles 85 and 86 EEC has to be based on the spirit, the economy and the terms of these provisions as well as on the system and the aims of the EEC-Treaty. Therefore, any comparison of solutions reached in other systems of law in the United States or elsewhere will not be relevant for problems originating from the EEC-Treaty (cf. Court of Justice of the European Communities in "Continental Can" (case 6/72), 21st February, 1973, par. 22).

2. Commission of the European Communities, "First Report on the Competition Policy", April 1972, herinafter to be referred to as FRC.

3. FRC, First Part, Ch. I, para 6.

cies. In that case we may be dealing with lawful differentiation as opposed to illegal discrimination.

Even though the above special provisions of the EEC-Treaty may not cause burning problems in need of immediate discussion, some questions do arise in this connexion which are worthy of consideration. In the first place e.g. to what extent, if any, application of Article 85, section 1, sub d and of Article 86, sub c differ, provisions which are couched in almost identical wording. Furthermore whether the EEC-Treaty distinguishes between lawful differentiation and illegal discrimination, and if so, where the dividing line between these two concepts must be drawn.

2. *Article 85, section 1, sub d*

It has been said[4] that Article 85, section 1, sub d refers to agreements, whether legally binding or not, decisions or concerted practices to the effect that the parties concerned undertake to stipulate unequal conditions in respect of equivalent supplies in their future contracts with their customers in the trade (third parties). That Article 85, section 1, sub d only relates to "trusts" is in the opinion of various writers so self-evident that but few arguments have been urged in justification of this thesis. It is apparently economically and commercially unacceptable that this treaty provision should also apply to two or more agreements in which in relation to customers in the trade unequal conditions in respect of equivalent supplies have been stipulated.

If Article 85, section 1, sub d only refers to an underlying "trust agreement" or "trust decision" rather than to two contracts stipulating in effect unequal conditions, in respect of equivalent supplies an enterprise may in principle legally apply, in relation to its customers in the trade, unequal conditions in respect of equivalent supplies, at least so long as the undertaking concerned does not have a dominant position within the meaning of Article 86 EEC.

A case in point are the standard contracts of sale in which the supplier always stipulates delivery ex factory. If the unequal conditions merely and exclusively refers to a difference in price, Article 85, section 1, sub d probably does not apply since the supplier is neither de facto nor de iure bound under a "trust agreement" with third enterprises to stipulate such differences in price in his contracts with his customers and therefore the relevant requirement laid down in Article 85, section 1, sub d has not been satisfied.

4. Cf. e.g. Wohlfahrt-Everling-Glaesner-Sprung, "Die Europäische Wirtschaftsgemeinschaft. Kommentar zum Vertrag" (Berlin, Frankfurt 1960), 245; Deringer, "Das Wettbewerbsrecht der Europäische Wirtschaftsgemeinschaft." Kommentar Art. 85, Anmerkung 59, 60; Franchescelli-Plaisant-Lassier, "Droit Européen de la Concurrence" (Paris 1966), 49; Gleiss-Hirsch, "E.W.G. Kartellrecht" (Heidelberg 1965), 152.

Probably this should be taken to mean that in such circumstances the relevant agreement, decision or practice does not conform to the definition given in the preamble to Article 85, section 1, i.e. the object or effect of which is to prevent, restrict or distort competition within the Common Market. It is doubtful that generally speaking this interpretation of Article 85, section 1, sub d is correct.

It may be true that it is not the object of a variable price stipulation in standard contracts for the supply of certain goods to restrict or distort competition within the Common Market, but all other terms of delivery being equal it cannot be denied that this may be precisely its effect. When it comes to selling, the buyer at a relatively high price will be at a competitive disadvantage compared with his competitor who obtained the product from their common supplier at a lower price. The same can be said of varying terms in standard exclusive agency contracts granting one distributor the right to sell substitute products of the supplier's competitor while denying this right to another.

Such differences in price, exclusive rights etc. are generally the result of differences in selling power, bargaining power of the customers at the time of the conclusion of their individual contracts with their common supplier (manufacturer). Such differences in selling and bargaining power may be the immediate result of greater business acumen and success in the competitive struggle among the supplier's customers. Although in view of the above circumstances application of Article 85, section 1, sub d in the case of disparate prices, all other conditions in respect of equivalent transactions being equal, does not appear to recommend itself, there is insufficient justification for the assumption that for this reason alone the above treaty provision only refers to underlying "trust agreements" and "trust decisions" to the exclusion of the very contracts which stipulate unequal conditions in respect of equivalent supplies. In the above cases exemption by virtue of Article 85 section 3 should be granted. However, the logical though in practice unattractive consequence of this line of thinking is that (price) differentiation, which is a common and natural commercial practice, constitutes an illegal discrimination until exemption pursuant to Article 85, section 3 has been granted. In practice this would only be possible by way of a category-exemption. Until that time the conception that Article 85, section 1, sub d only refers to underlying "trust agreements" admittedly makes sense in practice, but it cannot be readily justified in theory.

Perhaps the theoritical foundation of this practical interpretation of Article 85, section 1, sub d may be re-enforced by the following.

If this treaty provision applies not only to "trust agreements" but also to two or more contracts containing unequal conditions in respect of equivalent supplies, it may be asked which of such contracts is illegal and therefore null and void. If there are two such contracts are both illegal and therefore null and

void pursuant to Article 85, section 2? Is the earlier contract null and void as of the day the subsequent agreement is concluded? Is it possible for a contract which is illegal pursuant to Article 85, section 2 to be dissolved and to expire? Did the subsequent agreement ever exist and if not, can it being null and void affect the legality of the first contract?

For discrimination to exist at least two different provisions in two separate contracts are required which need not necessarily have been concluded simultaneously. This fact hampers simple application of Article 85, section 1, sub d to discriminatory contracts. Problems of this kind do not arise in relation to trust agreements which bind the parties de iure or de facto to discriminate *vis à vis* third parties.

3. *Article 86, sub c*

Should it therefore be inferred that only the prohibition contained in Article 86, sub c extends to discriminatory contracts? Only the improper exploitation of a dominant position within the Common Market is illegal but perhaps exploitation may be said to exist if an enterprise has the power to discriminatory practices on the market. A distinction should be made here between transparent and non-transparent markets.

On transparent markets, the conditions on which certain goods are sold and services are sufficiently known so as to prevent discrimination in general while no single enterprise is able to impose unequal conditions on his customers in the trade. If, however, an enterprise does possess such power, discriminatory practices and hence abuse of a dominant position becomes possible.

On non-transparent markets matters are different since customers in the trade are not sufficiently, if at all, familiar with the conditions granted to their competitors in respect of equal transactions and performances. Especially on a non-transparent market, the enterprises are not familiar with the precise conditions secured by their competitors in respect of transactions which are in themselves equal.

In view of this unfamiliarity it is relatively simple to impose unequal conditions in respect of equivalent transactions, thus placing some enterprises at a competitive disadvantage.

The enterprise which on a non-transparent market makes use of this unfamiliarity on the part of its customers in the trade for the purposes of discriminatory practices, does not always have a dominant position within the Common Market or within a substantial part thereof. Therefore Article 86 sub c cannot entirely prevent discriminatory conditions in respect of equivalent transactions on non-transparent markets within the European Economic Community.

Matters will only be otherwise if the concept of a dominant position

envisaged in Article 86 is defined according to the measure of transparency of the relevant market. The extent of the control required for a dominant position could for instance be proportionate to the extent of the transparency of the relevant market. However, so to link the concept of a dominant position within the meaning of Article 86 to the degree of transparency on the relevant market appears to be an impractical and for the purposes of a policy in the field of competition an unmanageable device, with the additional drawback of leaving the undertakers entirely in the dark. The fact that on a non-transparent market terms of contract and other trade conditions may differ in respect of equivalent transactions may be said to be the very result of competition, of a difference in business acumen and bargaining power on the part of the customers operating on this market.

If Article 85, section 1, sub d only refers to trusts and Article 86, sub c only applies in cases of the improper exploitation of a dominant position, many discriminatory agreements within the meaning of these treaty provisions may be perfectly legal. If there is no discriminatory trust agreement and no improper exploitation of a dominant position, discrimination arising from unequal conditions in respect of equivalent transactions are not illegal, even if customers in the trade are thereby placed at a competitive disadvantage within the Common Market.

Until any and all unequal contracts or other trade conditions are considered illegal discriminatory practices, this conclusion may be accepted. It is a matter of distinguishing between legal differentiation and illegal discrimination. Probable, however, not all unequal conditions in respect of equivalent transactions not coming under either Article 85, section 1, sub d or Article 86, sub c may be taken to constitute legal differentiations. In some circumstances one might feel the need for the prohibition contained in the two treaty provisions while being unable to enforce it. To stop this gap could require an interpretation of Article 85, section 1, sub d in the sence that this rule of Community law also applies to discriminatory agreements even if there is no underlying trust agreement or trust decision.

4. *Illegality per se?*

Is it true that Article 85, section 1, sub d and 86, sub c do not apply if a disparity of the conditions in respect of equivalent transactions can be justified on commercial and economic grounds? Such grounds can be found in a difference in cost to the enterprise stipulating the unequal conditions on the one hand, or in a difference in selling or bargaining power on the part of its customers in the trade on the other hand.

The answer to this question need not be identical for both articles. If the requirements for the application of Article 85, section 1 have been met, the ban contained in this section can be lifted only by means of an exemption

granted pursuant to Article 85, section 3. If it is true that Article 85, section 1, sub d may also apply to discriminatory agreements, decisions and practices not resulting from and underlying trust agreement or trust decision, a ground in justification as meant above will not simply entail inapplicability of Article 85, section 1. In this interpretation any disparity of trading conditions and terms of contract in respect of equivalent transactions is illegal, until pursuant to Article 85, section 3 exemption has been granted on a valid ground in justification, thus changing illegal discrimination into lawful differentiation. Transmutation from discrimination into differentiation is thus determined by the criteria laid down in Article 85, section 1.

In practice this consequence of the above interpretation of Article 85, section 1, sub d raises some difficulties. Many examples can be given in which competition between customers in the trade and other commercial and economic grounds mentioned above produce differentiation as to trading conditions and terms of contract. In order to avoid the cumbersome procedure of Article 85, section 3 in numerous daily transactions between enterprises within the Common Market, Article 85, section 1 should not in general apply to such differentiations or there should at least exist an easily practicable category-exemption as envisaged in Regulation 19/65.

The wording of Article 86 seems to point in the same direction. Improper exploitation of a dominant position may specifically consist in the application of unequal conditions in respect of equivalent transactions. In that case such exploitation can be said to exist, even though grounds justifying disparity of the trading conditions and terms of contract could be adduced. As mentioned above, such an interpretation of Article 86 is better suited to a transparent market than to a non-transparent market. In the case of non-transparent markets a prohibition per se regarding discrimination appears hard to enforce in practice.

On a non-transparent market as on other markets the first result of a prohibition per se will be a non-stipulated automatic "most favoured treatment clause" which will operate imperfectly. Customers in the trade do not possess adequate information about the trading conditions and terms of contract which their competitors have been able to secure or have been forced to accept from their common supplier in respect of equivalent transactions. It is unsuitable for customers in the trade to be able to claim damages from the other party to their contracts years or months after the expiry of the contract, on the ground of discriminatory contracts which did not come to their knowledge until much later. On a non-transparent market, prohibition per se will result in the application of a most favoured treatment clause granting rights which can only be enforced imperfectly if at all. This is less true, if at all, for a transparent market.

In the second place, according to current commercial notions, improper exploitation of a dominant position is commonly said to exist only if unequal

conditions in respect of equivalent transactions cannot be justified on standard grounds. Aren't we overshooting the mark, particularly in the case of a non-transparent market, if we interpret Article 86 as prohibiting per se all discrimination precisely because exemption cannot be obtained?

In spite of the wording of Article 86 which appears to point in an opposite direction, it must be inferred that improper exploitation of a dominant position may be said to exist only if the unequal conditions in respect of equivalent transactions cannot be justified on generally accepted commercial and economic grounds, such as disparate cost for the enterprise imposing the conditions, and a disparate competitive position and selling power on the part of the customers in the trade concerned.

This means that, contrary to Article 86, sub c, Article 85, section 1, sub d declares discrimination illegal per se, collective and individual exemptions being possible, however. In other words, unequal trading conditions or terms of contract in respect of equivalent transactions which place customers in the trade at a competitive disadvantage are generally illegal, if such agreements affect trade between Member-States and their object or effect is to restrict, prevent or distort competition within the Common Market. All this if this treaty provision can be taken to apply to discriminatory contracts as such rather than only to agreements, decisions and practices for the purposes of discrimination.

5. *Unequal conditions in respect of equivalent transactions.*

Articles 85, section 1, sub c and 86, sub c do not indicate further what is meant by unequal conditions in respect of equivalent transactions. Is the issue equivalence from the point of view of the enterprise which practices discrimination or from the point of view of the victim? Do they exclusively refer to terms of contract and transaction concluded by contract? Is there a distinction between equal and equivalent transactions and is there also a margin between equal and equivalent conditions when comparing the relevant conditions? May Articles 85 and 86 be interpreted in practice as if they read "non-equivalent conditions in respect of equal transactions"? If the Treaty is interpreted in this way, differentiation would be legal in many more cases than is the case in a narrower interpretation.

This kind of question is less abstract if discussed in the light of a simple example.

A buys from supplier Y one hundred identical chairs, ex stock, ex factory at a price of Fl. 30.– each. B simultaneously purchases from the same supplier fifty of the same chairs, also ex stock, ex factory, at a price of Fl. 33.– each. Buyers and supplier have their head office in different member-States and the buyers intend to sell the chairs elsewhere and on this market A and B are competitors.

Does Article 85, section 1, sub d c.q. Article 86, sub c apply?

What are the equivalent transactions in this example? There seems to be little doubt that Y's supplies to A and B should be considered as the relevant transactions. Since in our example all of Y's other performances are equal, it must be decided whether the discrepancy as to quantity can be said to preclude equivalence. If the term "equivalent" is interpreted broadly, the answer to this question will be more likely to be negative than if the term is interpreted so narrowly that equivalent becomes "equal".

If in spite of the discrepancy as to quantity Y's performances are regarded as "equivalent", we have further to examine whether Y's conditions of delivery and sale in respect of A and B are equal. Well then, these conditions are entirely identical save for a difference as to price: Fl. 30.– and Fl. 33.– each. Since in a purchase the purchase price is of paramount importance, it looks as if a difference in price of 10% in equivalent transactions is tantamount to unequal conditions. If a narrow interpretation of the word "unequal conditions" is adopted, the question is more likely to be answered in the negative than in the case of a broad interpretation in which unequal is equated with "non-equivalent".

In our example we assumed that the transactions had been concluded by contract stipulating certain conditions. Whether transactions are considered equivalent or conditions unequal depends on whether possible differences in price in daily practice in respect of such transactions are considered desirable or not. If so, transactions will be less readily considered to be equivalent and conditions unequal than in the reverse case.

All this again depends on the problem we mentioned above, i.e. whether justification of disparate conditions in respect of comparable transactions are allowable. Such justification may be based upon disparate cost on the part of the allegedly discriminatory party as well as on a difference in selling and bargaining power of the customers in the trade, including the potential victim of the discrimination. Above we have already seen that as parameter the degree of transparency of the relevant market may be of importance.

The supplier may conceivably have sound commercial grounds for granting his customer A (customer in the trade) a discount for quantity of 10% on an order for 100 units (chairs) in view of reduced operating costs (low price for raw materials because the supplier also received a discount for quantity, plant working at full capacity for a considerable time, etc.).

It is also possible that a greater bargaining power enabled A to secure better conditions than B being less familiar with marketing possibilities and not having investigated them so thoroughly. A is a big customer with an expanding trade, B is a small enterprise which is of ever less importance on the market.

From the economic point of view it is, in view of the above, proper to give due regard to such grounds when considering the desirability of permitting unequal conditions in respect of equivalent transactions and performances. For reasons of expediency it is advisable to allow (price) differentiation rather than to agree too quickly that such (price) differentiation is prohibited pursuant to Article 85, section 1, sub d and 86, sub c.

This probably means that, stretching the wording a little, these treaty provisions must be interpreted as if they read "non-equivalent conditions in respect of equal transactions". For in frequent cases, as illustrated above, Article 85 and 86 would not apply since the transactions concerned would not be "equal", or at least the difference in purchase price would not be tantamount to non-equivalent conditions. It is for the European Court to decide whether such pragmatic interpretation of Article 85, section 1, sub d and Article 86, sub c can be allowed.

However this may be, the words transactions and conditions cannot refer exclusively to "transactions concluded by contract" and "conditions stipulated in contracts" since else a narrow interpretation would preclude any considerations of grounds of justification and this would mean illegality per se. On the other hand, many questions arise as to what is to be done if in a lawsuit the plaintiff relies on Articles 85 and 86 and the defendant who allegedly practiced discrimination pleads in justification the selling power of his customers in the trade and his cost accounting in respect of the various "transactions". What macro-economic norms or norms of business economics should the competent authority apply? And the burden of proving on which of the parties is it cast?

6. *Competitive disadvantage*

Articles 85 and 86 only apply if the customer(s) in the trade is/are placed at a competitive disadvantage.

Who are A's and B's competitors and which is the relevant market?

To stick to our example: do the two treaty provisions refer to competition between A and B as customers of Y or rather to the competition the traders A and B will meet on their respective markets? In their latter capacity A and B may find themselves competing on the same market, but the treaty provisions do not explicitly require this. It appears to be sufficient that customer B is placed at a competitive disadvantage as a result of the unequal conditions in respect of equivalent transactions imposed by Y, regardless of whether Y's other customers also operate on B's market.

In this interpretation of the treaty provisions the norm of what constitutes discrimination is probably stretched too far since fairly to compare the conditions imposed by Y on his customers in the trade is difficult, or at least

it is hard to measure the adverse effect on the competitive position of the victim of Y's discriminatory practices. Although this cannot be inferred from the text, we shall assume in the following that the competitive disadvantage mentioned in Articles 85 and 86 refers to the interrelationship of the customers of the party practicing discrimination. They may be competitors both as customers of the discriminatory supplier Y and as sellers of Y's product.

If a customer has to pay a high purchase price as compared with other customers, the former is placed at a competitive disadvantage when selling. The effect of a high purchase price may be a relatively high cost price and hence the seller may be placed at a competitive disadvantage. The competitive position of a buyer will strongly affect his position as a seller.

If the treaty provisions envisage equalisation on the respective purchase prices paid by A and B by obliging supplier Y to charge equal prices regardless of quantity and of the selling power of his customers, an important driving force of the competition between A and B as buyers is eliminated and this may tend to dull competition between A and B as sellers at the expense of the user/consumer. A litteral interpretation of Article 85, section 1, sub d and 86, sub c may thus affect the interpenetration of the national markets and consequently the realisation of the Common Market.

Here, too, the parameter is the transparency of the relevant market. In this connection, a distinction should be made between the relevant market of the discriminatory supplier as a basis for the consideration of the merits of his performance and conditions of sale and the relevant market of his customers in the trade, including the victim of the discriminatory practices as a basis for measuring the competitive disadvantage.[5]

The market on which Y's customers sell may have a greater degree of transparency than the market on which they buy. A case in point is the tobacco market: by reason of the tobacco excise consumer prices are often fixed so that a brand will fetch the same price in the entire territory in which the excise is levied. Therefore consumer prices are not subject to competition and hence a competitive disasvantage within the meaning of Articles 85 and 86 cannot occur.

In what way could a customer in the trade then be placed at a competitive disadvantage? When products sell for fixed consumer prices strong competi-

5. For the purposes of Art. 85 s. 1 sub d there may yet be another market, i.e. the market divided between e.g. the manufacturers who have agreed among themselves to sell their products to wholesalers or retailers upon discriminatory conditions. The market upon which manufacturers thus restrict competition as a result of a trust agreement need not be the same market on which the manufacturer-supplier transacts his business and stipulates unequal conditions in his transactions with his customers-wholesaler or customers-retailers, still leed the market on which these customers offer the products concerned to the following link in the distributive chain or to the user/consumer.

tion to widen the marge of profit is generally bound to occur. Thus customers in the trade compete to secure the best possible discount arrangements from their suppliers. This market need not by any means be transparent so that a supplier may very well grant different terms (of delivery) in respect of equivalent transactions to his various customers.

This example shows that probably the words "placed at a competitive disadvantage" as used in Article 85, section 1, sub d and Article 86, sub c need not always be taken to mean so placed on the relevant market, i.e. the market on which the competitors concerned operate as sellers. In the case of fixed vertical prices for the products concerned and their substitutes, the competitive disadvantage will often refer to the competitive position of the customers in the trade as buyers. To this extent not only the transparency of the relevant market but also the vertical price-fixing will serve as a parameter for the purposes of Article 85, section 1, sub d and 86, sub c.

Whoever relies on the prohibition of discriminatory practices contained in Articles 85 and 86 will have to prove that he is indeed placed at a competitive disadvantage. Will he also have to show that such disadvantage could reasonably be foreseen by the discriminatory party who after all may not be familiar with the market on which his customer is placed at a competitive disadvantage? For often this market is not the market on which the latter either buys or sells.

Here, too, a common interpretation of the operative words is impossible. It is often important to a manufacturer that the product bearing his trademark is correctly offered to the customer. Even though this last market in the process of distribution is not the market on which the manufacturer practices discrimination, he is often familiar with the entire distributive pattern which his branded product follows.

Therefore he is able to appreciate whether one or more of his customers are placed at a competitive disadvantage on the market on which they operate as sellers. In these circumstances the supplier will be able to foresee that the discriminatory practices will place his customers in the trade at a competitive disadvantage, thus satisfying a possible requirement to this effect. Even so, this is not always the case.

Two suppliers offer identical goods for shipment to a carrier who conveys them at a different rate from the same place of shipment to the same destination and delivers them to the respective buyers. Carrier's discriminatory practice vis à vis his principals, places one of his principals at a competitive disadvantage. However, since the carrier not being a seller is not personally interested in knowing the peculiarities of the relevant market, he is not familiar with the relevant market and thus can hardly if at all foresee the disadvantage.

Therefore the requirement of a foreseeable disadvantage has not been

satisfied in respect of this discriminatory practice. It is however uncertain whether this fact is of importance for the purposes of Articles 85 and 86. Perhaps a distinction should be made between the extent of the disadvantage and the disadvantage itself. A carrier may possibly foresee that this principal will be placed at a competitive disadvantage as a result of his discrimination, but not to what extent.

7. *Alignment*

A rigid interpretation of Articles 85, section 1, sub d and 86, sub c would entail that it is illegal for a supplier to adjust his sales price to the price of his competitors. The problem arises when a supplier operates on several segment markets and the competition between suppliers result in disparate prices. Such segment markets do exist in practice, sometimes coinciding with the national frontiers of the member-States. Although national segment markets may be generally detrimental to the realisation of the Common Market, there may be determinants which promote this phenomenon while preservation by artificial means of such segment markets cannot be laid at the door of the suppliers. Such determinants may differ in kind such as for instance special national requirements in respect of packaging, technical service and such, special rights granted by the national authorities to distributors in the utility sector and such. In that case, a segment market is simply a hard fact both to the supplier and the buyer.

The intensity of competition may differ on segment markets. Supplier Y may be compelled to grant special price concessions in respect of his transactions on segment market p in view of the competition of his rivals offering identical or similar products, whereas such price concessions are not necessary on segment market q because competition is less keen.

Different price levels on the various segment markets are thus caused by price alignment on some of them. Since price alignment is the result of competition between suppliers, in general Articles 85, section 1, sub d and 86, sub c ought not to apply, saving special circumstances, lest EEC anti-trust law overshoots its mark by prohibiting price differences which are the result of competition.

Articles 85 and 86 would not apply in cases of price alignment if in such cases the transactions concerned would not be considered "equivalent" or if a competitive disadvantage (on segment markets) on the part of the customers would not be thought to exist. In the latter case, this would imply that for the purposes of these treaty provisions the competition which each of the customers in the trade meets as a seller on his own segment market would be relevant, even if on such markets no other customer of his supplier operates so that the customers in the trade of the same supplier cannot be said to be competing sellers on the same market.

Chapter 10

A CASE INVOLVING ARTICLE 90 OF THE EEC-TREATY

by *Prof. Mr. P. VerLoren van Themaat*

The public sector of economy is sometimes used as an instrument of general economic policy. Cases in point are Italy and, to a less degree, France and the United Kingdom. To use public undertakings or public participations in economy for purposes of industrial policy, regional policy, income policy and other parts of economic policy may cause distortions of competition. In the case of State trading monopolies such distortions are prevented by means of Article 37 of the EEC-Treaty. With regard to the public sector of economy in general, Article 90 of this Treaty applies. On July 14, 1971 the Court of Justice handed down its first judgment concerning this important article. In the following, this judgment is summarised and annotated. Neither this judgment nor the extensive literature concerning Article 90 published so far have as yet fully dealt with the issue of the public sector of economy. It is the purpose of this essay to provide some starting-points for a further discussion of the legal aspects. For the economic aspects the reader is referred to a study undertaken by Professor Zijlstra upon the request of the EEC-Commission and published in 1966.[1]

Case 10-71. Public Prosecutor of Luxemburg v. Madeleine Muller, widow of the late J.P. Hein, and others (application for a preliminary ruling made by the Tribunal d'Arrondissement de Luxembourg). "Port de Mertert".[2]

Article 90 of the EEC-Treaty.

Judgment

Without prejudice to the exercise by the Commission of the powers provided for in Section 3 of Article 90 of the EEC-Treaty, Section 2 of this article cannot, at the present stage, create individual rights which the national courts must uphold.

1. Zijlstra, La politique économique et la problematique de la concurrence dans la CEE et les Etats membres, (Série Concurrence no. 2, Brussels 1966).

2. Judgment of July 14, 1971, *Recueil* XVII, 713 *et seq.*

Facts

The material facts underlying this important judgment concerning Article 90 EEC are as follows: By law of July 22, 1963 on the construction and management of a Moselle port at Mertert, the construction and management of this port had been entrusted to a mixed enterprise, later named "Société du port fluvial de Mertert". According to Article 12 of the above law, construction, establishment or management of any (other) harbour and wharf on the river Moselle required a permit from the Government, to be granted after consultation with the mixed company. In 1968, this article was amended and strengthened by means of a penalty provision. After the canalisation, the Hein company which from of old had engaged in dredging on the Moselle, had to terminate this activity. Thereupon the company applied *inter alia* for a permit to use its wharf for port operations, but they were only granted a permit for minutely defined operations for their own account in connection with sand grit, shingle, gravel and stones originating from sand pits or stone quarries. In 1968 it was clear that the Hein company had used its harbour facilities for the unloading of coal products and criminal proceedings were instituted. The competent Luxemburg court considered that the facts with which the defendants were charged, had been proved and had been declared illegal by the above law of July 22, 1963, as amended in 1968; however, in the opinion of the court, there were grounds for postponing the decision as to the guilt of the defendants and the penalty to be imposed until the Court of Justice of the European Communities had given a preliminary ruling on the following questions:

a. are the relevant rules of Community law in general self-executing *vis-à-vis* private persons as subjects of national law and is this specifically the case in regard to the subject matter of the Luxemburg law of July 22, 1963 on the construction and management of a Moselle port as amended by the law of July 26, 1968?

b. If so, are the provisions of the above laws incompatible with the letter and spirit of the Rome Treaty or with regulations or otherwise binding measures of the organs set up by this Treaty, and if so, to what extent?

From among the *Considerations* I quote:

4. Considering that, in spite of the imprecise wording of the questions, the purpose of the application is made perfectly clear by the grounds given in the judgment;

5. that the national court specifically states that, in view of the facilities and privileges which have been granted by law to Société du port de Mertert which has been entrusted with the construction and management of the port concerned, and in view of the resulting unfavourable competitive situation in which other enterprises engaged in port operations on the Moselle find themselves, the court is in some doubt as to the compatibility of these laws with

the rules of competition of the Community;

6. that, before applying to private persons the punitive provisions of Article 2 of the law of June 26, 1968 in regard to infringement of the provisions restricting port operations of third parties, the national court considered it necessary to apply to the Court of Justice for a preliminary ruling as to whether subsequent national rules of law are compatible with the Community rules of competition;

7. that within the scope of Article 177, the Court is not competent to rule upon the compatibility of a national provision and the Community rules of law, that however from the wording of the questions put by the national court—and considering the information provided by the latter—the Court may infer those elements which properly come within letter a), the interpretation of this Treaty, of said article;

8. Considering that, as is apparent from the information provided by the national court, the subject matter of the questions comes within the field of application of Article 90 of the Treaty;

9. that according to Section I of this article, it is in general unlawful, in the case of public undertakings and enterprises to which member States grant special or exclusive rights, for member States to enact or to maintain in force any measure contrary to the rules contained in the Treaty, in particular to those rules provided for in Article 7, and 85 to 94 inclusive;

10. that, however, Section 2 of this article provides that enterprises entrusted with the supply of services of general economic interest, shall be subject to these rules, in particular to the rules of competition so far as giving effect to such rules does not obstruct the achievement in law or in fact of the particular task assigned to them, provided the development of trade is not affected to such an extent as would be contrary to the interests of the Community;

11. that the latter provision may apply to an enterprise which handles the greater part of the river-borne trade of the State concerned while enjoying certain privileges for the achievement of the task with which it is entrusted by law and while maintaining close contact with the authorities for this purpose;

12. that to answer the questions therefore requires an inquiry as to whether Article 90, Section 2 is self-executing *vis-à-vis* private persons whose rights must be upheld by the national courts;

13. Considering that Section 2 of this article does not give an unconditional rule;

14. that indeed application of this provision entails an appreciation of the requirements which are inherent in the achievement of the particular tasks entrusted to the enterprises concerned, on the one hand in the protection of the interests of the Community, on the other hand;

15. that such appreciation is part and parcel of the purposes of the general

economic policy which member States pursue under the supervision of the Commission;

16. that consequently, without prejudice to the exercise by the Commission of the powers provided for in Section 3 of Article 90, Section 2 of this article cannot, in the present stage, create individual rights which must be upheld by the national courts.

Note

1. *The questions*

The Commission, and still more emphatically the Luxemburg Government, had denied that the questions as worded could be submitted to the Court of Justice. Therefore, they had concluded that the application would be set aside. However, upon a proposal of the Advocate General, the Court supplied a new remarkable instance of its willingness and capacity to restate inadmissible questions so as to make them allowable under Article 177, as witness considerations 4 to 8 of its judgment.

We are indebted to this restatement for an important contribution to the interpretation of one of the most obscure articles of the EEC-Treaty, which in view of the importance of the subject regulated therein, *i.e.* the "public sector" of economy, has already given rise to an extensive literature.

In practically all its important elements Article 90 is indeed obscure, but its lack of clearness is also due to some inconsistencies in logic. For instance, Section 1 of Article 90 provides that it is *inter alia* illegal for member States to take measures which are contrary to the rules of Articles 85 and 86, whereas these articles only impose obligations upon enterprises so that in the nature of things it is hard to see how member States can act in contravention of these rules. Conversely, Section 2 of Article 90 *inter alia* declares treaty rules, which only apply to member States, equally applicable to the enterprises in question and this appears logically to be impossible. As to the literature on this article, the reader is referred to point 10 of this note.

2. *The lack of clearness of Article 90*

According to the writers, the main point on which Article 90 lacks clarity concerns its nature. Does it add rules of substantive law to what follows from the other provisions of the Treaty in connection with the public sector of economy or does it rather contain only supplementary safeguards for the enforcement of those other treaty provisions? Whether the public sector is to function in conformity with the market rather than remain (France and Italy) or become (Benelux, Germany) an instrument of socio-economic policy the use of which is to be coordinated on Community level or not, hinges on the

answer to this question. History and place of Article 90 indicate that this article is first and foremost intended to provide a *supplementary* safeguard against the public sector causing distortion of competition, *in addition to* the general rules of competition which also apply to this sector. On the one hand, such supplementary safeguard lies in the additional obligations which Section 1 of Article 90 imposes upon member States in addition to the obligations which already arise out of Articles 7, 85 and 86 for the public undertakings themselves. On the other hand, such safeguard is found in the special powers which Section 3 of Article 90 gives to the Commission in connection with the public sector when used as such an instrument by member States, again quite apart from the obligations arising out of Articles 7, 85 and 86 for the enterprises themselves. However, the *wording* of Article 90 admittedly offers room for both this view and its opposite which holds that the rules of competition of the Treaty should impede as little as possible the proper functioning of the public sector as an instrument of socio-economic policy and that specifically Section 2 of Article 90 is first and foremost to be considered as a safeguard on behalf of the public sector. As will appear, the present judgment seems to leave it primarily for the Commission to answer this question of interpretation. However, this note will show in the following that the point of view of the Court necessarily requires further elucidation.

3. *Applicability of other articles*

Understandably, the Advocate General regretted that the first question of the Luxemburg national court had not been a little clearer as to the provisions of the Rome Treaty and of the rules of Community law based thereon which it had in mind when the court applied for an interpretation. In view of the arguments of the partners of Muller-Hein, the Luxemburg Government and the Commission, the Advocate General concludes that above all Article 90 was contemplated. However, he then proceeds to examine and repudiate the applicability of Article 37. In addition, the partners of Muller-Hein had also considered Article 86. Evidently, however, neither of the latter articles applies in this case. Clearly, Article 37 does not apply because it refers to State trading monopolies, whereas the port of Mertert has certainly not been set up for purposes of inter-state commerce, but at best has a monopoly for port operations, that is for (a small sector of) services within the meaning of Article 60. Article 86 does not apply because this article refers to enterprises and to regard the prosecution of the Hein company as improper practices of a dominant position by Société du port de Mertert, on the ground that this mixed company, as the Hein company pointed out, has a legal say in the licensing policy is stretching this article too far.

Neither can the Hein company rely on other self-executing provisions of

the EEC-Treaty, such as *e.g.* Articles 7, 53 and 62, since these articles refer to discrimination on the ground of nationality and there is no such discrimination in this case. True, the Luxemburg port law of 1963 also restricts the supply of port services in behalf of charterers and ship-owners from other member States, but identical restrictions apply to such services in behalf of Luxemburg nationals. Since Article 59 EEC is usually interpreted as prohibiting discrimination, the standstill provision of Article 62 EEC cannot help the Hein company either. Apart from Article 90, the only provisions which conceivably might apply, are Articles 92 and 93 EEC which are moreover part of the rules of competition to which the preamble of the Luxemburg national court explicitly referred, for the full summary of the facts makes it clear that the law of 1963 had granted Mertert Port various aids within the meaning of Article 92. However, reliance on this article and on Article 93 EEC would presumably not have helped the Hein company either, since Article 92 is certainly not self-executing[3] and Article 93 at best can only result in an immediately effective prohibition in relation to aids which have not been notified or which have been suspended or declared illegal by the Commission. It is nevertheless remarkable that in the course of the proceedings nobody referred to these articles. The explanation might be that the aids concerned had been notified and were thus eligible for a declaration of compatibility under Article 92 Section 3 c), so that nullity of the port law on this ground had been ruled out in any case.

4. *The importance of the present judgment for the public sector of economy*

It was on purpose that I duscussed at some length the applicability of self-executing treaty provisions *vis-à-vis* enterprises entrusted with services of general economic interest. The problems arising from Article 90, Section 2 follow precisely from the very existence of such self-executing provisions, in connection with the assignment to supply such services, or the discriminating implementation by the Government of its assignment or the performance of the enterprise itself. In theory, the Luxemburg authorities could infringe Article 62 EEC by attaching to the assignment or the permits conditions which discriminate against ship-owners or charterers form other member States in favour of the national ship-owners or charterers. Mertert port could on its own initiative proceed to such discrimination and in that case Article 7 or Article 86 would apply. Now, if in stead of with Mertert we were dealing with a bank of one of the member States which, being entrusted with granting credits in the general economic interest, practices discrimination, it is clearly of great practical importance whether Article 90, Section 2 is self-

3. This is decided in a preliminary decision of the Court of Justice of June 9, 1973, case No. 77-72 (Campolongo-Maya), not yet published.

executing or not. An example from the field of goods traffic would be if public utilities were instructed to place contracts for new installations exclusively with national producers. As is apparent from the judgment, the Commission was of the opinion that both Article 90, Section 1 and Article 90, Section 2 are self-executing, Section 2 at any rate insofar as it regulates the conduct of the enterprises. The Commission regarded Article 90, Section 3 (supervision by the Commission with decision-making powers) as an additional safeguard which cannot affect the self-executing character of the first two sections of Article 90. The Court did not give its opinion as to Article 90, Section 1, but it did deny that Section 2 is self-executing on the ground that it does not give an unconditional rule.

According to the Court, application of this provision implies an appreciation of the requirements which are inherent in the performance of the particular tasks of the enterprises concerned, on the one hand and in the protection of the interests of the Community, on the other hand. This appreciation, the Court continues, is part and parcel of the purposes of the general economic policy which member States pursue under supervision of the Commission. Contrary to the Commission's conception, the Court thus puts the ultimate responsibility for the supervision of the application of Article 90, Section 2 squarely on the Commission which may address appropriate directives or decisions to member States. *The first practical conclusion to be drawn from this is that the Commission must now abandon its relatively passive attitude of wait-and-see vis-à-vis public undertakings.*

5. *Some still open questions*

Not all questions regarding the practical importance of the judgment have as yet been answered, however. Specifically, this judgment does not, to my view, warrant the conclusion, in spite of the semblance of the opposite view, that Article 90, Section 1 contains no elements whatever which the national courts must enforce. Take the hypothetical case that Société du Port de Mertert concludes a tariff agreement with German and French port enterprises which restricts competition. One of the customers refuses to pay the tariffs on the ground that the agreement is null under Article 85. In its action Société du Port de Mertert relies on Article 90, Section 2 as interpreted in the present judgment. *At the very least, the court will then have to entertain Article 90, Section 2 in the sense of not applying Article 85 or suspending the proceedings while awaiting a decision by the Commission pursuant to Article 90, Section 3.* Furthermore, if in a dispute regarding an agreement concerning the rate of interest, a bank relies in its action on Article 90, Section 2, should not the court at least also examine whether the bank concerned is indeed entrusted with services of general economic interest? And then, can it be said to be entirely satisfactory that according to Considera-

tion 15 the member State concerned is to judge in the first instance whether application of Article 85 would in fact or in law prevent the achievement of the particular task entrusted to the harbour enterprise or the bank of our examples? Similar questions may arise when an injured third party relies on Articles 7 and 86. And is Article 90, Section 3 the sole remaining safeguard for interested parties if the authorities, when entrusting the supply of services of general economic interest to an enterprise, accompanies the assignment with regulations which infringe Articles 7, 12, 30, 53, 62, 92,or 95? In view of the wording of Article 90, Section 2, it may certainly be inferred that the term "rules contained in this Treaty" refers to any and all rules of the EEC-Treaty rather than to the rules of competition only.[4] If so, the Court's present judgment would, in view of the enormous importance of the public sector of economy, have made a big breach in the legal protection of the individual which it has built up so carefully in a long series of decisions. In any case, the present judgment leaves a great many questions unanswered which, it is hoped, will be answered satisfactorily in further preliminary proceedings.

6. *Criticism and personal view*

The way in which the Luxemburg national court framed the questions is undoubtedly the main reason why the judgment is unsatisfactory. If the latter had asked what is meant by an enterprise entrusted with services of general economic interest, whether specifically the kind of rules given in the law concerned are adequate so as to permit acceptance of such an assignment and whether Article 90, Section 2 bars application of Article 86 to such enterprises as are envisaged in Section 2 of Article 90, a more satisfactory answer might have been obtained. If in the present case the national court had asked, in addition, whether Article 86 may also be applied in relation to criminal proceedings which indirectly protect a particular enterprise, the Court of Justice might not even have considered Article 90 at all.

It will be clear that I personally would have preferred it if, like the Commission, the Court had considered Article 90, Section 2 to be self-executing at least insofar as the conduct of the enterprises is directly regulated by it. Specifically in connection with the first sentence of Section 2 I hold that all conditions as enumerated again in the Advocate General's conclusion, had been satisfied. In my opinion, the national courts are fully competent to decide whether an enterprise has been *entrusted* with the tasks mentioned in the first sentence of Section 2 as well as whether the task so entrusted

4. In this sense Wohlfahrt and others, *Die Europäische Wirtschaftsgemeinschaft Kommentar zum Vertrag*. (Berlin, Frankfurt, 1960), 265 and Colliard, *Le regime des entreprises publiques*, in Ganshof van der Meersch ed. *Droit des Communautés Européennes* (Brussels, 1969) No. 2166.

prevents in fact or in law compliance with *the material obligations as laid down by the national court under Articles 85 and 86* or any other self-executing provisions. In my opinion, the obligation of observing Articles 85 and 86 with the restrictions as indicated, in particular, is certainly clearly specified. In fact, the Court's judgment denies not only that Article 90, Section 2 is self-executing, but also that Articles 85 and 86 are self-executing—as far as public undertakings are concerned. I, too, think it self-evident that subject to the reservation set out below under nr. 7, Article 90, Section 2 cannot be enforced by national courts. Only the Commission is competent to determine the interests of the Community, but the Commission's task would be considerably lightened if the national court has already established that the exception contained in Article 90, Section 2 applies. Even so, the privileges granted to public undertakings with particular tasks and their function as an instrument for the purposes of general economic policy which sometimes verges on infringement of treaty provisions, still constitute a problem within the Community which competing private enterprises and those Governments which do not so use public undertakings rightly view with some concern. The irony of the matter is that according to the literature, precisely such concern on the part of the Governments of the Benelux countries gave birth to Article 90!

For the important problems of general economic policy and competition in connection with public undertakings, the reader is referred to Professor Zijlstra's illuminating study Economic Policy and Problems of Competition in the Common Market and Member States.[5] A maximum protection by the courts, as advocated here, could undoubtedly greatly relieve the far from simple supervisory task of the Commission in this field.

7. *Applicability of Articles 7, 85 and 86 to enterprises as envisaged in Article 90*

It is a remarkable fact that, unlike the Advocate General, the Court of Justice did not, in support of its argument that Article 90 Section 2 is not self-executing, turn to the thesis that implementation of the obligation contained therein requires further action by the Commission. The reason may be that precisely Articles 85 and 86 and the requirement as further defined in Article 90, Section 2 that public undertakings comply with the rules contained in these Articles, cannot be enforced on the strength of Article 90, Section 3. Such enforcement must be based upon Articles 85 and 86 and the implementing regulations, since Article 90, Section 3 only empowers the Commission to issue directives or decisions to member States, not to the enterprises concerned also. Only in the improbable and unusual case that a

5. *Op. cit.*, note 1, 28-30, 47-50 and 65-68.

member State has instructed its public undertaking to resort to practices which distort competition and thus, in principle, constitute an infringement of Articles 7, 85 and 86 will it be possible for the Commission to issue decisions to member States.

In view of the Court's present judgment, the Commission will, I think, have to contemplate the issuance of a general directive making such instructions illegal insofar as they have not been notified to the Commission within a period to be fixed in the directive.

In my opinion, the notification procedure provided for in Regulation No. 17[6] remains applicable if no instructions to resort to such practices have been given. As observed above, however, the Commission will now also have to consider the most efficient way in which to perform the general task of supervising the application of Article 90, Section 2 which has now been left to its sole care. As to Article 90, Section 1, here the judgment still leaves room for the hope that the Court, like the Commission, will regard this rule as self-executing, at least in respect of measures which are contrary to equally self-executing treaty provisions. In any case, no public undertaking which does not also come under Article 90, Section 2, may invoke Article 90, Section 1 so as to escape application of Articles 7, 85 and 86. For applicability of these articles to public undertakings and to enterprises which have been granted particular or exclusive rights by a member State (though neither entrusted with the supply of services of general economic interest nor having the character of a fiscal monopoly), does not spring from Article 90 but rather from Articles 7, 85 and 86. According to its wording which in this respect is entirely clear, Article 90, Section 1 contains only an additional obligation for member States; it is not an exemption nor does it contain any other provision in regard to certain enterprises.

8. *Application of other treaty provisions*

If the instructions given by a member State to the enterprises in question constitute as such an infringement of an immediately enforceable treaty obligation *vis-à-vis* member States, I think that such obligation remains fully and immediately enforceable. Consider for instance an instruction to buy only national products; this would undoubtedly constitute an illegal measure since its effect would be similar to the effect of a quantitative import restriction. Article 90, Section 2 is not a permit enabling member States to escape their obligations by using enterprises as instruments of general economic policy. Furthermore, Article 90 remains, in my opinion, equally applicable to aids granted to such enterprises and to aids granted by the enterprises concerned though financed by the State. They must be notified to the Com-

6. O.J. p. 204/62.

mission in pursuance of Article 93, Section 1. In that respect therefore the inroad made by the Court's judgment in the system of legal protection of private persons still appears to be limited.

9. *Procedural aspects*

The present judgment demonstrates once again that the Court's zeal to restate inadmissible questions from national courts so that they can be allowed, has drawbacks as well as undeniable advantages. In this case a drawback looms as large as life in that the parties and the Commission in such cases do not provide the Court of Justice with sufficient information about the fundamental issue, if they themselves regard the questions inadmissible.

Only in the oral proceedings, and according to the summary in the judgment even then only casually, did the Commission say something about it. This objection could be largely eliminated if the Commission when discussing preliminary questions, would never take it for granted that they should be dismissed. It is not the first time that the Commission underrated the Court's willingness to restate questions. The Commission could make useful suggestions also with a view to a possible restatement of questions submitted to the Court of Justice.

10. *Literature*

A summary of the most important specialised literature on Article 90 published before 1968 can be found in the beginning of Colliard's contribution mentioned above to "Les Nouvelles", Droit des Communautés Européennes.[7]

Important essays on this subject which have been published since, may be found in L'Enterprise publique et la concurrence, Semaine de Bruges 1968,[8] as well as in V. Emmerich, Das Wirtschaftsrecht der öffentlichen Unternehmen,[9] with a very extensive bibliography. It is a remarkable fact that neither the extensive specialised literature on Article 90 nor the general commentaries on the EEC-Treaty have been much concerned with exactly defining the problems attached to the application of treaty provisions other than rules of competition, in connection with the public sector of economy, although the unanimous opinion seems to be that the term "rules contained in this Treaty" as used in Article 90, Section 1 and 2 must be taken to mean all the rules of the EEC-Treaty. In this respect the Luxemburg national court hit the nail on the head when it couched its questions in very general terms!

In the above I have tried to illustrate the practical importance of the

7. *Op. cit.*, note 4, Nos. 2149-2170.
8. (Brugge, 1969), 21-140 and 277-452.
9. (Berlin-Zürich, 1969), 365-472.

matter on which so far the writers have been silent. Only a monograph, however, could do full justice to the problems arising from Article 90.

Final remarks

1. Having concluded this essay I happened to read Emmerich's note on this judgment in Europarecht.[10] Also citing other writers, Emmerich defends in this note the thesis that the Luxemburg port law is contrary to the self-executing Article 90, Section 1, because this law enables or permits the port enterprise to take improper advantage of a dominant position or because its effect is otherwise incompatible with the rules of competition (distortion of competition, VvT). Emmerich has his eye on Article 86 in particular. To my view, the very wording of Article 90, Section 1 precludes that granting a quasi-monopoly to enterprises as contemplated here should be considered as such to be contrary to this section on the ground that its effect will be a restriction of competition.

2. Emmerich's criticism in his above-mentioned annotation on the Court's interpretation of Article 90, Section 2 runs in part parallel to my criticism. It culminates in the following conclusion: Thus the Court's interpretation implies that the enterprises which are to provide services, are in general not bound by the Treaty and that they are to observe its rules and above all the rules of competition only in exceptional cases, when the Commission has previously taken the necessary measures in pursuance of Article 90, Section 3. However, the purpose of Article 90 is exactly the opposite, namely to make the Treaty binding also upon such enterprises and only in certain exceptional cases to allow them to act in contravention to its rules. In connection with a possible action by the Commission, Emmerich then hopefully draws attention to the dictum's statement that Article 90, Section 2 is not immediately enforceable in the present stage (only). An analogous conclusion was implicitly reached in my note.

10. EuR 1972, 37-47.

Register I

DECISIONS OF THE COMMISSION OF THE EUROPEAN COMMUNITIES applicating Articles 85 and 86 and the EEC Treaty

Date	parties	sources	
		O.J.	CMLR
March 11, 1964	Grosfillex – Fillistorf	p. 915/64	[1964] p. 237
June 1, 1964	Bendix – Mertens en Straet	p. 1426/64	[1964] p. 416
July 30, 1964	Nicolas Frères – Vitapro	p. 2287/64	[1964] p. 505
September 23, 1964	Grundig – Consten	p. 2545/64	[1964] p. 489
October 22, 1964	Dutch Engineers and Contractors Associations	p. 2761/64	[1965] p. 50
July 8, 1965	DRU – Blondel	p. 2194/65	[1965] p. 180
September 17, 1965	Hummel – Isbecque	p. 2581/65	[1965] p. 242
December 17, 1965	Jallatte – Voss and Jallatte – Vandeputte	p. 37/66	[1967] D 1
June 27, 1967	Transocean Marine Paint Association	1967 p. 163/10	[1967] D 9
February 26, 1968	Eurogypsum	1968 L 57/9	[1968] D 1
July 17, 1968	Alliance de constructeurs français de machines – outils	1968 L 201/1	[1968] D 23
July 17, 1968	Socemas	1968 L 201/4	[1968] D 28
July 17, 1968	ACEC – Berliet	1968 L 201/7	[1968] D 35
November 6, 1968	Cobelaz – Usines de synthèse	1968 L 276/13	[1968] D 45
November 6, 1968	Cobelaz – Cokeries	1968 L 276/19	[1968] D 68
November 6, 1968	C.F.A.	1968 L 276/29	[1968] D 57
November 6, 1968	Rieckermann – AEG Elotherm	1968 L 276/25	[1968] D 78
March 13, 1969	Exposition européenne de la machine – outil	1969 L 69/13	[1969] D 1
May 5, 1969	Convention Chaufourniers	1969 L 122/8	[1969] D 15
June 18, 1969	Christiani and Nielsen	1969 L 165/12	[1969] D 36
June 25, 1969	VVVF	1969 L 168/22	[1970] D 1

Date	parties	sources	
		O.J.	CMLR
June 30, 1969	SEIFA	1969 L173/8	
July 16, 1969	Entente internationale de la quinine	1969 L 192/5	[1969] D 41
July 22, 1969	Clima – Chappée – Buderus	1969 L 195/1	[1970] D 7
July 22, 1969	Jaz – Peter	1969 L 195/5	[1970] p. 129
July 24, 1969	Matières colorantes	1969 L 195/11	[1969] D 23
December 5, 1969	Pirelli S.p.A. – Société Dunlop	1969 L 323/21	
June 30, 1970	Kodak	1970 L 147/24	[1970] D 19
June 30, 1970	ASPA	1970 L 148/9	[1970] D 25
June 29, 1970	ASBL pour la promotion du tube d'acier soudé électriquement	1970 L 153/14	[1970] D 31
October 28, 1970	Julien – van Katwijk	1970 L 242/18	[1970] D 43
October 28, 1970	OMEGA	1970 L 242/22	[1970] D 49
December 23, 1970	Supexie	1971 L 10/12	[1971] D 1
December 29, 1970	Carreaux céramiques	1971 L 10/15	[1971] D 6
February 1, 1971	CICG – ZVEI/ZPU	1971 L 34/13	[1971] D 23
May 28, 1971	FN – CF	1971 L 134/6	
June 2, 1971	GEMA	1971 L 134/15	[1971] D 35
July 28, 1971	S.A. Raffinerie tirlemontoise	not published	
June 18, 1971	Enquête dans le secteur de la bière	1971 L 161/2 1971 L 161/6 1971 L 161/10	
July 2, 1971	Asphaltoïd – Keller S.A.	1971 L 161/32	
September 24, 1971	CEMATEX	1971 L 227/26	
November 9, 1971	S.I.A.E.	1971 L 254/15	[1972] D 112
November 25, 1971	Boehringer	1971 L 282/46	[1972] D 121
December 9, 1971	Continental Can	1972 L 7/25	[1972] D 11
December 16, 1971	V.C.H.	1972 L 13/34	[1973] D 16

Date	parties	sources	
		O.J.	CMLR
December 16, 1971	Safco	1972 L 13/44	[1972] D 83
December 20, 1971	Sopelem – Langen	1972 L 13/47	[1972] D 77
December 22, 1971	Burroughs – Delplanque	1972 L 13/50	[1972] D 67
December 22, 1971	Burroughs – Geha	1972 L 13/53	[1972] D 72
December 23, 1971	Henkel – Colgate	1972 L 14/14	
December 23, 1971	N.C.H.	1972 L 22/16	
January 17, 1972	MAN – SAVIEM	1972 L 31/29	
February 23, 1972	Wild – Leitz	1972 L 61/27	[1972] D 36
June 9, 1972	Davidson Rubber Co	1972 L 143/31	[1972] D 52
June 9, 1972	Raymond – Nagoya	1972 L 143/39	[1972] D 45
July 24, 1972	GEMA II	1972 L 166/22	[1972] D 115
July 26, 1972	Papeteries Bollové	1972 L 182/24	[1972] D 94
October 20, 1972	Chauffage central	1972 L 264/22	[1972] D 130
September 28, 1972	Rodenstock *et al.*	1972 L 267/17	[1973] D 40
September 28, 1972	Misal *et al.*	1972 L 267/20	[1973] D 37
November 23, 1972	Pittsburgh Corning Europe	1972 L 272/35	[1973] D 2
December 14, 1972	Zoja – CSC/ICI	1972 L 299/51	[1973] D 50
December 18, 1972	Cementregeling voor Nederland	1972 L 303/7	
December 22, 1972	Cimbel	1972 L 303/24	
December 22, 1972	GISA	1972 L 303/45	[1973] D 125
December 22, 1972	W.E.A. Filipacchi Music S.A.	1972 L 303/52	[1973] D 43
January 2, 1973	European Sugar Industry	1973 L 140/17	[1973] D 65

JUDGMENTS OF THE COURT OF JUSTICE OF THE EUROPEAN COMMUNITIES
concerning the rules of competition of the EEC Treaty

date	case No.	parties	sources	
			Recueil	CMLR
April 6, 1962	13-61	De Geus v. Bosch and van Rijn	VIII, p. 89	[1962] p. 1
June 30, 1966	56-65	Société Technique Minière "STM" v. Maschinenbau Ulm "MBU"	XII, p. 337	[1966] p. 357
July 13, 1966	56 and 58-64	Grundig – Consten v. Commission	XII, p. 429	[1966] p. 418
July 13, 1966	32-65	Government of the Italian Republic v. Council and Commission	XII, p. 563	[1966] p. 39
March 15, 1967	8-11/66	Noordwijkse Cement Akkoord v. Commission	XIII, p. 93	[1967] p. 77
December 12, 1967	23-67	Brasserie de Haecht v. Wilkin and Janssen	XIII, p. 525	[1968] p. 26
February 29, 1968	24-67	Parke Davis v. Beintema – Interpharm and Centrapharm	XIV, p. 81	[1968] p. 47
February 13, 1969	14-68	Walt Wilhelm *et al.* v. Bundes-kartellamt	XV, p. 1	[1968] p. 100
July 9, 1969	5-69	Völk v. Vervaecke	XV, p. 295	[1969] p. 273
July 9, 1969	10-69	Portelange v. Smith Corona Marchant International	XV, p. 309	
March 18, 1970	43-69	Bilger Söhne v. Heinrich and Maria Jehle	XVI, p. 127	
June 30, 1970	1-70	Parfums Marcel Rochas v. Helmut Bitsch	XVI, p. 515	[1971] p. 104
July 15, 1970	41-69	ACF Chemiefarma v. Commission	XVI, p. 661	

date	case No.	parties	sources	
			Recueil	CMLR
July 15, 1970	44-69	Buchler and Co. v. Commission	XVI, p. 733	
July 15, 1970	45-69	Boehringer Mannheim v. Commission	XVI, p. 769	
February 18, 1971	40-70	Sirena v. Eda	XVII, p. 69	[1971] p. 260
May 6, 1971	1-71	Cadillon v. Höss Maschinenbau K.G.	XVII, p.351	[1971] p. 420
June 8, 1971	78-70	Deutsche Grammaphon v. Metro-Sb-Grossmärkte	XVII, p. 487	[1971] p. 631
July 13, 1971	8-71	Deutscher Komponistenverband v. Commission	XVII, p. 705	
November 25, 1971	22-71	Béguelin v. Import Export and Marbach	XVII, p. 949	[1972] p. 81
July 14, 1972	48-69	I.C.I. v. Commission	XVIII, p. 619	[1972] p. 617
July 14, 1972	49-69	B.A.S.F. v. Commission	XVIII, p. 713	[1972] p. 630
July 14, 1972	51-69	Bayer v. Commission	XVIII, p. 745	[1972] p. 634
July 14, 1972	52-69	Ciba-Geigy v. Commission	XVIII, p. 787	[1972] p. 637
July 14, 1972	53-69	Sandoz v. Commission	XVIII, p. 845	[1972] p. 637
July 14, 1972	54-69	Francolor v. Commission	XVIII, p. 851	[1972] p. 641
July 14, 1972	55-69	Cassella v. Commission	XVIII, p. 887	[1972] p. 644
July 14, 1972	56-69	Hoechst v. Commission	XVIII, p. 927	[1972] p. 644
July 14, 1972	57-69	A.C.N.A. v. Commission	XVIII, p. 933	[1972] p. 647
October 17, 1972	8-72	Vereniging van Cementhandelaren v. Commission	XVIII, p. 977	[1973] p. 7
December 14, 1972	7-72	Boehringer Mannheim v. Commission	XVIII,	
February 6, 1973	48-72	Brasserie de Haecht v. Wilkin-Janssen	XIX,	[1973] p. 287
February 21, 1973	6-72	Continental Can v. Commission	XIX,	[1973] p. 199

SELECTIVE BIBLIOGRAPHY, CONCERNING COMPETITION LAW

W. Adams (Ed.), The structure of American industry, 1971

W. Alexander, "The domestic courts and article 85 of the Rome Treaty", 1 C.M.L.Rev., 1963/64, 431-455.

W. Alexander, "Article 85 of the EEC-Treaty and the exclusive licence to sell patented products", 5 C.M.L.Rev. 1967-8, 465-475

W. Alexander, "L'établissement du Marché Commun et le problème des brevets parallèles", 4 Rev. trim. dr. europ. 1968, 513-537

W. Alexander, "Industrial property rights and the establishment of the EEC", 9 C.M.L.Rev. 1972, 35-52

G.C. Allen, Monopoly and restrictive practices (London 1968)

A. André, "Evidence before the European Court of Justice, with special reference to the Grundig/Consten Decision", 5 C.M.L.Rev., 1967/68, 35-49

Pl. Arceda, Antitrust analysis, Little, Brown and Company (Boston/Toronto 1967)

J. Backman, "Joint ventures and the antitrust laws", 40 New York University Law Review 1965, 651 *et seq.*

J.S. Bain, Barriers to new competition, 1956

Bebr, "Law of the European Communities and municipal law", 34 The Modern Law Review 1971, 481-500

N. Bernaud, Le règlement no. 17 et la politique commune du transport. La décision dans les Communautés européennes (Brussel 1969), 343-365.

G. Bernini and G.W. Tookey, "Patents and anti-trust laws" in "Comparative aspects of anti-trust law in the United States, the United Kingdom and the European Economic Community", International and Comparative Law Quarterly Supplementary Publication 1963 nr. 6

J.F. Beseler, "EEC protection against dumping and subsidies from third countries", 6 C.M.L.Rev., 1968/69, 327-352

W.A.G. Blonk, Regulation (EEC) no. 1017/68 of the Council applying rules of competition to transport by rail, road and waterway, 6 C.M.L.Rev. 1968/69, 451-465

S.E. Boyle, "The joint subsidiary: an economic appraisal", VI The Antitrust Bulletin 1960, p. 303 *et seq.*

K. Brewster, Antitrust and American business abroad, (New York, 1958)

D.P. O'Brien and D. Swann, Information agreements. Competition and Efficiency (London 1968).

P.C. Canellos-H.S. Silbert, "Concentration in the Common Market", 7 C.M.L.Rev., 1970, 5-35 and 138-166

N. Catalano, "La jurisprudence de la Cour de Justice à l'égard des contracts dits de l'exclusivité", Cahiers de droit européen, 1967, 20-48

B. Cawthra, "Restrictive Agreements in the EEC. The Need to Notify", (London, 1972).

E. Cerexhe, "L'interprétation de l'article 86 du Traité de Rome et les premières décisions de la Commission", 8 Cah. dr. européen 1972, 272-298.

E.H. Chamberlin, The theory of monopolistic competition (Cambridge/Mass. 1947).

Champaud, "The group exemptions of EEC Regulation 67/67", 5 C.M.L.Rev., 1967/68, 23-34

S. Chesterfield Oppenheim, Federal antitrust laws (1959)

Colliard, Le régime des entreprises publiques in: Ganshof van der Meersch ed., Droit des Communautés Européennes, (Brussels 1969), Nos. 2149-2170

EEC-Commission memorandum to the member states on concentration of enterprises in the Common Market (Studies on competition, No. 3, Brussels 1965), CCH Comm. Mat. L. Rep. No. 26, 1 (separate print)

A. Dashwood, Joint Sales Agencies and Article 85 of the EEC-Treaty, 9 C.M.L.Rev., (1972), 466-477.

Arved Deringer, "The distribution of powers in the enforcement of the rules of competition under the Rome Treaty", 1 C.M.L.Rev., 1963, 30-40

Arved Deringer, "The interpretation of Art. 90 (2) of the EEC-Treaty", 2 C.M.L.Rev., 1964, 129-138

P. Dixon, "Joint ventures: what is their impact on competition?", VII The Antitrust Bulletin, 1962, p. 398 *et seq.*

H. Drion, "Restraint of buyer's freedom under Art. 85", 1 C.M.L.Rev., 1963/64, 148-155

P. Düesberg, Unternehmenskonzentration und Kooperation im Lichte des europäischen Wettbewerbs", 22 WuW. 1972, 695-705

Ebb, "Patent and trademark licence agreements in the Common Market and antitrust law" in Rahl ed., Common Market and American antitrust Overlap and Conflict (New York, 1970), 244-311

V. Emmerich, "Die Auslegung von Art. 85 Abs. 1 EWG-Vertrag durch die bisherige Praxis der Kommission", 6 Europarecht 1971, 295-335

W. Fellner, Competition among the few (1949).

W. Fikentscher, Kooperation und Gemeinschaftsunternehmen im Lichte der Art. 85 und 86 EWG-Vertrag. Postdoctorale leergang 1967/68 Europees kartelrecht, 177-212 (Leuven 1969)

L. Focscaneanu, "Les prix imposés dans la CEE-droits nationaux et droit communautaire", Rev. trim. dr. europ. 1967, 173-223

S. Gabriël, "Aufeinander abgestimmte Verhaltensweisen unter wettbewerbspolitischen Aspekt", WuW 1961, 802-812

W. van Gerven en F.H. Luhoff, Commercial agency and distributor agreements and related problems of licencing in the law of the EEC-countries and the European Communities. Report of the seminar organized by the Institute of Commercial Law of the University of Louvain 19-22 maart 1969 (Leuven 1970)

A. Gleiss, "Der Begriff der aufeinander abgestimmten Verhaltensweisen in Art. 85 EWG-Vertrag", WuW 1964, 485-493

Alfred Gleiss, "Zum Begriff "abgestimmtes Verhalten" im EWG-Vertrag". Aktuelle Probleme des EWG-Kartelrechts (Kartellrundschau, Heft 8, Köln 1965), 163-175

Goldman, "Les effets juridiques extra-territoriaux de la politique de la concurrence", (1972) Rev. Marché Commun, no. 157, 612-623.

R. Graupner, The rules of competition in the European Economic Community (The Hague 1965)

R. Graupner, "Alleinvertriebsverträge im englischen Recht und rechtsvergleichende Probleme", 16 AWD 1970, 49-55

M. Grünning, "Die Anwendbarkeit der Wettbewerbsregeln des EGKS-Vertrages in der erweiterten Europäischen Gemeinschaft und den Ländern der Freihandelszone", 23 WuW. 1973, 173-179.

Guide to legislation on restrictive business practice (OECD 1971)

W. Hadding, "Die zivilrechtliche Wirksamkeit angemeldeter Vereinbarungen oder Beschlüsse im Sinne des Art. 85 EWG-V", WuW 1965, 371-383

G.E. Hale, "Joint ventures: collaborative subsidiaries and the antitrust laws", 42 Virginia Law Review 1956, p. 937 *et seq.*

M. Handler, Antitrust in perspective (1957)

M. Handler, "Recent antitrust developments", 63 Michigan Law Review 1964, p. 85 *et seq.*

M. Handler, "Emerging antitrust issues: Reciprocity, diversification and joint ventures", 49 Virginia Law Review 1967, p. 433 *et seq.*

W. Harms, "Intra-concern conspiracy? Ein rechtsvergleichender Beitrag zur Auslegung der Art. 85 EWG-Vertrag und Art. 65 EGKS-Vertrag", Europarecht 1966, 230-272

G. van Hecke, "Government enterprises and national monopolies under the EEC-Treaty", 3 C.M.L.Rev., 1965/66, 450-461

Helmut Heinrichs, "Die "conscious parallelism" Doktrin des US Antitrustrechts und der Begriff "aufeinander abgestimmte Verhaltensweisen" in Art. 85 EWG-Vertrag, WuW 1965, 95-105

E. Hennipman, "De taak van de mededingingspolitiek", De Economist 1966, 379-418

F. Hepp, "Les conventions de licences exclusives au regard des règles de concurrence de la CEE", S.E.W. 1964, 85-94

E. Heuss, Algemeine Markttheorie, 1965

H.W. van den Heuvel, "Some unsolved problems in Community Law concerning restrictive trade practices", 4 C.M.L.Rev., 1966/67, 180-196

Huber, "Konzerninterne Vereinbarungen im EWG-Kartellrecht nach der Kommissionsentscheidung im Fall Christiani und Nielsen", 15 AWD 1969, 429-433

A. Hunter, Competition and the law (London 1966)

U. Immenga, "Die extraterritoriale Anwendung des E.W.G.-Kartellrechts nach dem Farbstoff-Urteil des Europäischen Gerichtshofes", 91 Zeitschrift für Schweizerisches Recht 1972, 417-432

A.P. Jacquemin, "The criterion of economic performance in the antitrust policies of the United States and the European Economic Community", 7 C.M.L.Rev., 1970, 205-225

R. Jaume, "Accords de Licences et Règles de Concurrence", (1972) Rev. Marché Commun No. 158, 674-690.

Jeantet: "Le principe de la territorialité du droit des marques dans le Marché Commun après l'arrêt Grundig" in "Brevets et marques au regard du droit de la concurrence en Europe et aux Etats-Unis" (Brussels 1968)

R. Joliet, The rule of reason in antitrust law (The Hague 1967)

R. Joliet, "La coopération entre entreprises selon la jurisprudence de la Commission des Communautés Européennes", Cahiers de droit européen 1969, 127-180

R. Joliet, "Prix imposés et droit européen de la concurrence", Cahiers de droit européen 1971, 16-53

H.W. de Jong, "Concentration in the Common Market", 4 C.M.L.Rev., 1966/67, 166-179

H.W. de Jong, "The position of the dominant firm in a changing economy", 6 C.M.L.Rev., 1968/69, 371-374

H.W. de Jong, "Aspects économiques du comportement parallèle sur le Marché", Cahiers de droit européen 1971, 550-561

C. Kaysen and D.F. Turner, "Antitrust policy", (Cambridge (Mass.), 1965)

L.J. de Keyser, "Territorial restrictions and export prohibitions under the United States and the Common Market antitrust laws", 2 C.M.L.Rev., 1964/65, 271-299

V. Korah. Monopolies and restrictive practices (1968)

R. Kruithof, "The application of the Common Market antitrust provisions to international restraints of trade", 2 C.M.L.Rev., 1964/65, 69-94

H.C. Leo, "Konzerninterne Marktregelungen im Lichte des EWG-Kartellrechts". Aktuelle Probleme des Kartellrechts (Kartellrundschau, Heft 8, Köln 1966), 11-43

I.A. Macdonald, "The restrictive practices court. A lawyer's view", 17 Oxford Economic Papers 1965, 354-376

F. Machlup, The economics of seller's competition (Baltimore 1956)

C.S. Maddock, "Know-how licensing under the antitrust laws of the United States and the Rome Treaty", 2 C.M.L.Rev., 1964/65, 36-68

Mailänder, "Restrictive patterns by multiple agreements", 6 C.M.L.Rev., 1968/69, 353-367

F.A. Mann, The English approach to the extraterritorial effect of foreign antitrust legislation (with special reference to the EEC). Droit communautaire et droit national. Cahiers de Bruges (Brugge 1965), 381-388

F.A. Mann, "The Dyestuffs Case in the Court of Justice of the European Communities", 22 Int. Comp. L. Qu. 1973, 35-50.

K. Markert, "Vorläufige Gültigkeit und Verfahrensaussetzung im EWG-Kartellrecht", 12 AWD 1966, 41-47

K. Markert, "Neue Entwicklungen im englischen Kartell- und Monopolrecht", 14 AWD 1968, 178-183

J.W. Markham, "The nature and significance of price leadership", Readings in Industrial organisation and public policy (American Economic Association, 1958).

H. Matthies, "Gemeinschaftsunternehmen in der Montanunion- in Wirtschaftsordnung und Rechtsordnung", Festschrift zum 70. Geburtstag von Franz Böhm (Karlsruhe, 1965), 319-343

Mergers, a guide to Board of Trade practice (HMSO 1969)

J. Megret, "L'aménagement des monopoles français en exécution de l'article 37 du traité instituant la CEE", 8 Rev. trim. dr. europ. 1972, 558-577.

Megret, Louis, Vignes, Waelbroeck, Le droit de la Communauté européenne, Tome IV (Concurrence) (Brussels 1972)

E.J. Mestmäcker, "Concentration and Competition in the EEC: Part II", 6 J.W.T.L. 1972, 615-647 and 7 J.W.T.L. 1973, 36-63.

Mitchell, "Community legislation" in Bathurst *et al.* Legal problems of an enlarged European Community (1972), 87-103

Mok, "The procedure of the EEC-Commission in antitrust cases", 1 C.M.L.Rev., 1963/64, 327-338

Mok, "The cartel policy of EEC-Commission 1962/1967", 6 C.M.L.Rev.,1968/69, 67-103

P. van Ommeslaghe, "Die Anwendung der Art. 85 und 86 des Rom-Vertrages auf Fusionen, Gesellschaftszusammenschlüsse und Gemeinschaftsunternehmen" in Beiträge zum EWG-Kartellrecht (Köln 1966), 41-109.

P. van Ommeslaghe, "L'application des articles 85 et 86 du Traité de Rome aux fusions, aux groupes de sociétés et aux entreprises communes", Rev. trim. dr. europ. 1967, 457-506

R. Pitofsky, "Joint ventures under the antitrust laws", some reflections on the significance of Penn-Olin, 82 Harvard Law Review 1967, p. 1007 *et seq.*

J.A. Rahl, "The nature and extent of conflict between American antitrust law and laws in the Common Market" in: J.A. Rahl (editor), Common Market and antitrust (New York, 1970) p. 181 *et seq.*

J.A. Rahl, "Competition and antitrust in American economic policy: Are there useful lessons for Europe?", 8 C.M.L.Rev., 1971, 284-312

H. Rasch, "Kartellvertrag oder Gemeinschaftsunternehmen", WuW 1961, 79-88

H. Rasch, "Die Interessengemeinschaft in Kartellrechtlichen Sicht", WuW 1962, 233-240

D. Reiner, "Preis- und Vertriebsbindungen im gemeinsamen Markt", GRUR 1966, 509-522, 566-572

Report of the Attorney General's National Committee (1955)

P. Rew, "Actions for damages by third parties under English law for breach of Art. 85 of the EEC-Treaty", 8 C.M.L.Rev., 1971, 462-474

C.K. Rowley, "The British Monopolies Commission" (London 1966)

R. Saint-Esteben, "Une concentration internationale d'entreprises dans la CEE" (l'affaire Continental Can), 99 Journal du Droit International 1972, 249-266.

I. Samkalden and I.E. Druker, "Legal problems relating to Art. 86 of the Rome Treaty", 3 C.M.L.Rev., 1965/66, 158-183

G.L. Samwer, "Auswirkungen der Territorialität des Patentrechts in EEG-Bereich", GRUR 1969, 1-14

O. Sandrock, "Probleme der Gemeinschaftsunternehmen nach europäischen Kartellrecht", 16 AWD 1970, 337-344

U. Schatz, "Ausübungszwang und Zwanglizenzen im gemeinsamen Markt", GRUR 1968, 278-280

F.M. Scherer, Industrial market structure and economic performance (Chicago 1971).

Schlieder in "Panel discussion on the dissemination of technology" Annual Meeting of the American Bar Association, July 1971, 40 Antitrust Law Journal 1972 no. 4

P. Schindler, "Public enterprises and the EEC-Treaty", 7 C.M.L.Rev., 1970, 57-71

W.R. Schluep, Der Alleinvertriebsvertrag, Markstein der EWG-Kartellpolitik (Bern 1966)

Schmitt, "Coopération et dimension en matière de recherche et de développement au regard de la législation européenne". Contribution to the International Colloquium on "R. and D. and competition in the European Communities" organised by the University of Grenoble in April 1970

H. Schwaiger, "Die Unternehmenskonzentration im Recht gegen Wettbewerbsbeschränkungen innerhalb der Europäischen Gemeinschaften" 18 AWD. 1972, 49-58.

G. Schwartz, Ausschliesslichkeitsverträge und Vertriebsbindungen nach EWG-Kartellrecht in: Aktuelle Probleme des EWG-Kartellrechts, (Köln 1966), 197-214

L.B. Schwartz, Parallel action in oligopoly markets (economic and legal problems). Kartelle und Monopole im modernen Recht, (Frankfurt/Karlsruhe 1961), 433-449

W.G. Sheperd, Market power and economic welfare (New York 1970).

K. Spormann, "Förderung europäischer Spezialisierungskartelle", 23 WuW. 1973, 165-173.

Steindorff, Volle Wirksamkeit angemelderter Wettbewerbsbeschränkungen in der Europäischen Wirtschaftsgemeinschaft, Der Betriebsberater 1969, 980-982

H. Stumpf, Der Lizenzvertrag (Frankfurt 1964)

L.P. Suetens, "Belgian antitrust law in action", 2 C.M.L.Rev., 1964, 325-339

A. Sutherland, "Economics in the Restrictive Practices Court", 17 Oxford Economic Papers 1965, 385-426

Tessin, "Anmerkung zur Kommissionsentscheidung im Fall Christiani und Nielsen", Die Aktiengesellschaft 1969, 294

P. Tractenberg, "Joint ventures on the domestic front: A study in uncertainty", VIII Antitrust Bulletin, 1960, p. 797 *et seq.*

J. Treeck, "Konzerninterne Vereinbarungen im EWG-Kartellrecht", 15 AWD 1969, 367-368

J. Treeck, Joint research ventures and antitrust law in the US, Germany and the EEC, 3 New York University Journal of International Law 1970, 18-55

E. Ulmer, "Wettbewerbbeschränkende Absprachen im Rahmen von Unternehmenszusammenschlüssen". WuW 1960, 163

E. Ulmer, Das Recht des unlauteren Wettbewerbs in den Mitgliedstaaten der EWG (Köln 1965)

E. Ulmer, "Europäisches Kartellrecht auf neuen Wegen?", AWD 1970, 193-198

Ulrich, "Anmerkung zum Urteil des Gerichtshofs der Europäischen Gemeinschaften von 18 März 1970 (Rechtssache 43/69), GRUR Int. 1970, 382

G. Vandersanden, "La validité provisoire des ententes (Smith Corona-Portelange)", Revue du Marché Commun 1969, 473-483

W.M. Vaughn, "Transnational Policy Programme Networks in the European Community: The Example of European Competition Policy", 11 J. Common Mkt. Stud. 1972, 36-60

P. Verloren van Themaat, "The antitrust policy of the European Economic Community" in "Comparative aspects of antitrust law in the United States, the United Kingdom and the European Economic Community", International and Comparative Law Quarterly Supplementary Publication 1963, nr. 6.

P. Verloren van Themaat, "Article 36 in relation to Article 85 and patent licensing agreements", 1 C.M.L.Rev., 1963/64, 428-430

P. Verloren van Themaat, "Competition and planning in the EEC and the member States", 7 C.M.L.Rev., 1970, 311-322

M. Waelbroeck, La validité provisoire des ententes notifiées et des ententes non sujettes à notification. Europees Kartelrecht-Postdoctorale leergang 1967/68 (Leuven 1969), 121-137

R. Wägenbaur, "Wettbewerbsregeln für das Verkehr in der EWG", 15 AWD 1968, 415-424

R. Wägenbaur, "Les règles de concurrence applicables aux transports", Cahiers de droit européen 1970, 645-663

D. Walker-Smith and L. Gombos, "Restrictive practices and monopolies; a comparison of British and Common Market law", III Virginia Journal of International Law 1963, no. 1

G.J. Werner, "Gemeinschaftsunternehmen in der EWG", WuW 1963, 285-307

H.W. Wertheimer, "National trademark law and the Common Market rules of competition", 4 C.M.L.Rev., 1966/67, 308-325 and 399-418

H.W. Wertheimer, "Droit des marques et concurrence", Cahiers de droit européen 1970, 451-472

H.W. Wertheimer, Licensing agreements under EEC-antitrust law. Commercial agency distribution agreement and related problems of licensing in the law of the EEC-countries and of the European Communities, 114-139. Report of the seminar organized by the Institute of Commercial Law of the University of Louvain edited by W. van Gerven and F.L. Luhoff (Leuven 1970)

H. Wiebringhaus, "Le droit des ententes dans le cadre de la CEE et de l'EFTA", Revue du Marché Commun 1966, 755-764

H. Wiebringhaus, Market power and the law. A study of the restrictive business practice laws of OECD member countries and of the EEC and ECSC dealing with market power. Report of the Committee of experts on restrictive business practices (Paris 1970)

Wohlfahrt and others, Die Europäische Wirtschaftsgemeinschaft. Kommentar zum Vertrag. (Berlin-Frankfurt 1960)

J. Zijlstra, La politique économique et la problematique de la concurrence dans la CEE et les Etats-membres. (Serie Concurrence No. 2, Brussels 1966)

INDEX